If you're a productivity novice or an expert, check out this book — you'll find something to streamline your life. The three simple tools approach feels very achievable, and the included action plan is essential.

— PAULA RIZZO, media consultant, author, speaker

In an era where the way we approach and think about work is going through drastic changes, this book provides a practical guide for successfully navigating your relationship with work and life.

— BILL BECKER, associate professor, Virginia Tech

This extremely practical and compelling book is written by a true expert on productivity, setting (and sticking to) priorities, and time management. I wish it existed 20 years ago — particularly when our children were young and we were doing it all on very little sleep. Ann's approach is simple, solution-oriented, and very achievable. Her tried and tested approach is backed by data and examples we can all relate to. Keep it close at hand for continual reference. We can all become Workday Warriors!

— VAL SORBIE, partner and managing director, Gibraltar & Company

If you have a zillion things to do and you're feeling frustrated with lack of control of your time, this book will help you. While you can't find time or make time, you CAN *protect* time. The secret is to narrow your priorities, reduce your flexibility (counterintuitive, I know!), and limit your complications. Let Ann Gomez help you become a Workday Warrior.

— DAPHNE GRAY-GRANT, publication coach

I was so busy, yet at a standstill in my business until I read *Workday Warrior*. These tools solved my dilemma and have allowed me to take my business to the next level!

— ALYSON SCHAFER, parenting expert, TV personality, and author

Ann Gomez provides the core strategies that professionals need to align their efforts and optimize their performance. This book is a wonderful companion, guide, and cheerleader for anyone who wants to level up their productivity, efficacy, and confidence.

— MARISA MURRAY, author, TEDx speaker, and
chief executive coach at Leaderley International Inc.

Ann Gomez is a true expert in time management. The three simple tools she shares in *Workday Warrior* makes it easy for anyone to successfully manage their time. You will be surprised at how much time you will save each week if you follow the strategies in Ann's book. Ann taught me these valuable skills when I first started my business. Twelve years later, I am still using these principles to simplify my life.

— LAURA BERG, professor, author, and president of My Smart Hands Inc.

Ann Gomez understands that if you need to get something done you give it to a busy person. This book is a must-read for anyone who has too much to do and not enough time, as it gives you the strategies and tools to become much more productive, even when you consider yourself already productive. Ann Gomez and her team at Clear Concept understand these challenges better than anyone, and this book illustrates this!

— MARTY PARKER, president and CEO, Waterstone Human Capital

Ann has written an engaging and compelling book about our most valuable resource: our time. I've always considered myself to be productive, and yet I still learned several strategies that would have saved me countless hours over the years. This book is a must-read for anyone who feels stretched too thin.

— BRUCE BOWSER, chair, AMJ Campbell

Time is a great equalizer. We are all given the same twenty-four hours a day. It's what we do with them that matters most. In *Workday Warrior*, Ann Gomez lays out easy-to-action steps to truly seize each day.

— STEPHEN "SHED" SHEDLETZKY, speaker and author of *Speak Up Culture*

Ann has a special talent for motivating and inspiring others. In a culture where being busy is tied to our identity, this book helps us to step back and become more productive.

— MARTY BRITTON, president and CEO, Britton Management Profiles Inc.

WORKDAY WARRIOR

ANN GOMEZ

WORKDAY Warrior

A Proven Path to Reclaiming Your Time

DUNDURN
PRESS

Publisher: Kwame Scott Fraser | Acquiring editor: Kathryn Lane | Editor: Dominic Farrell
Cover and interior designer: Laura Boyle
Cover image: istock.com/ Guzaliia Filimonova

Library and Archives Canada Cataloguing in Publication

Title: Workday warrior: a proven path to reclaiming your time / Ann Gomez.
Names: Gomez, Ann, author.
Description: Includes bibliographical references.
Identifiers: Canadiana (print) 20220412227 | Canadiana (ebook) 20220412251 | ISBN
  9781459749597 (softcover) | ISBN 9781459749603 (PDF) | ISBN 9781459749610 (EPUB)
Subjects: LCSH: Time management. | LCSH: Work-life balance.
Classification: LCC HD69.T54 G66 2022 | DDC 650.1/1—dc23

We acknowledge the support of the Canada Council for the Arts and the Ontario Arts Council for our publishing program. We also acknowledge the financial support of the Government of Ontario, through the Ontario Book Publishing Tax Credit and Ontario Creates, and the Government of Canada.

Dundurn Press
1382 Queen Street East
Toronto, Ontario, Canada M4L 1C9
dundurn.com, @dundurnpress 𝕏 f ◎

To my husband, Enrique, and our four incredible children: Christopher, Taylor, Michael, and Daniel. Together, you are the reason why I'm inspired to make the most of our time.

Contents

Part 3: Simplify

Introduction

The greatest victory is that which requires no battle.
— Sun Tzu

I'VE BEEN INTRIGUED BY PRODUCTIVITY STRATEGIES SINCE MY days in university. At first I was only mildly interested. Two decades ago, though, there was a tipping point, and I became determined to tackle this subject. It was 2002 — the peak of my time crisis and a year before my first baby was born.

For as far back as I could remember, I had kept a hectic schedule, jumping from one activity to the next. I had been following the recommended path to success: work hard — *really hard* — in school and then get a good job. Then go back to school for a master's degree and become a management consultant. Then work, work, work some more. Sure, I felt time was scarce throughout all those years, but I had been able to fit in *most* of what I wanted to do. Plus, I still had time to exercise, sleep, and socialize.

But eventually, this so-called strategy stopped working. No matter how I organized my schedule, I simply didn't feel in control of my ever-expanding to-do list. As a consultant, I was flying all over North America, regularly working from 8:00 a.m. until well past midnight, and eating meals in front of my computer. To make matters worse, I consistently worked on my weekends. It seemed to me that most of my peers were running at the same pace, so I assumed I didn't have another option.

But a voice in my head kept telling me I had to find a better way, especially if I wanted to keep advancing in my career. The clock on the boardroom wall wasn't alone in advancing far too fast. My internal clock was also racing, and my husband and I were keen to have children. But I couldn't see how I could possibly fit anything else into my overloaded days.

Fast forward a year. I was strolling through a beautiful park with my baby. It was spring and the cherry trees were in full bloom. Little Christopher was sleeping soundly in his stroller. On that day, a few months into my maternity leave, and for the first time in years, I felt like I had time to think. I had time to reflect. And one thought kept coming to mind: *I need to make a shift.*

After a year I was ready to board the paid-work train again. But by then I had gained a fresh perspective. My precious infant needed more of my time — time I wanted to give. I couldn't continue pouring endless hours into my career as if I was drawing water from a bottomless well. I was no longer willing to let work fill every waking moment (or dip into sleep time either). They say necessity is the mother of invention. Well, this mother needed to get better at managing her time.

So began my quest to conquer productivity. I started to notice that a select few of my peers were winning the battle against overwhelm, while many others, like me, were struggling. Someone needed to show us a better way. I wanted to be that person, and pursuing that goal eventually led me to where I am today — helping hard-working, talented people just like you become Workday Warriors.

ARE YOU TOO BUSY TO READ THIS BOOK?

Do you feel you're too busy to read this book? If so, the irony is not lost on me. Although if that's true, may I suggest you need this book more than ever? I acknowledge your time is stretched thin right now, but please indulge me and let me review some simple math to illustrate how reading this book will pay off.

The average adult reads about three hundred words a minute. I know you're anything but average, but let's play this out. This book is approximately eighty thousand words, which means it will likely take you a little more than four hours to read it from cover to cover. This equals approximately 17 percent of one day. Yet the strategies outlined here can help you reclaim this amount of time, or more, each day for the rest of your career. You can't save time, as we'll discuss later, but you can redirect your time and achieve a bigger payoff.

> This book will take you approximately four hours to read, which you can do over a few weeks. In return, you will reclaim exponentially more time.

Your career is an endurance event, a marathon. While you may feel like you are always sprinting, you want to consider the long game; you want to set yourself up so that you can excel over the course of a long journey. Ultra-marathoners plan to stop in rest stations, despite competing in events where every minute counts. Similarly, race-car drivers pause for pit stops in the middle of lightning-fast races so they can refuel and re-tire. Expert chefs take the time to sharpen their tools before a big culinary event. Professionals in every industry invest in their continuing education throughout their career. As all of these examples show, elite performers value the power of continuing to invest in themselves.

Think of this book as your re-tooling. You are about to discover strategies that will help you spend more time on what you love — in every aspect of your life. These tools will help you feel less stretched, more accomplished, and even happier. This book will help you become a Workday Warrior.

WHAT IS A WORKDAY WARRIOR?

What exactly is a Workday Warrior? The term likely conjures up an image of someone involved in an intense battle to get through yet another gruelling day. You can probably relate to this. You may feel like it takes all your blood, sweat, and tears to survive the barrage of work that's regularly fired at you.

But I see things differently. True warriors excel in challenging careers in a manner that could be considered almost superhuman. At the same time, they balance rich and dynamic personal lives. Yes, they work hard. But they also leverage tools and strategies to make results come *easier*. Indeed, they seem to be relaxed and even enjoying the thrill of meeting the challenges they face. Watching them in action is captivating.

> A Workday Warrior excels in a challenging career while balancing a dynamic personal life.

Workday Warriors have the same demands placed on them as everyone else. Yet they manage them with much more finesse. They run their days instead of letting their days run them. They work smarter, not harder. This doesn't mean they skimp on quality. On the contrary, they are the ones scaling the biggest hurdles and making the most impressive impact. They are the ones getting promoted and enjoying the financial rewards and personal satisfaction.

Workday Warriors aren't fictional characters. They are walking among us, in our midst. You likely work with a handful of Workday Warriors. I do, and many of those I met earlier in my career served as my inspiration to become a Workday Warrior myself.

The ways of a Workday Warrior don't need to be kept secret, known only to an elite few. Rather, they are extremely learnable and well within your reach. You can be a Workday Warrior too. You, too, can adopt their winning strategies and radically transform your work *and your life* for the better. This book will show you how.

IS IT REALLY POSSIBLE TO MAKE WORK EASIER?

Many people (and this may include you) have searched for a streamlined approach to how they work, which isn't necessarily easy to find. But I assure you, an easier way does exist. We *can* level up. We *can* win the battle against time. We *can* overcome overwhelm and all the stress associated with too much work. We *can* change how we work and get more done without working more. In fact, we can often work less.

But no one can simply cross their fingers and hope they'll stumble upon a way to better manage their time. Believe me, I've tried. Early in my career, I found myself running faster and faster on the proverbial hamster wheel. I kept throwing time at my growing list. In turn, I regularly neglected sleep, exercise, friends, and more. But doing so only provided short-term fixes. I was still struggling with the underlying problem: my work habits hadn't scaled with my career. Despite my efforts, I couldn't find enough time. Little did I know I could use a better, and easier, approach.

IS IT REALLY POSSIBLE TO *MAKE* TIME?

I often hear people say they have to find time for this, or make time for that. I've said the same thing many times over. It really is an enticing concept. But is it really possible to make time? Or to find time?

The simple answer is no. It's not possible to make or alter time. As of when this book went to press, time machines still didn't exist. We can't create, save, or borrow time. We have the same twenty-four hours a day that everyone else has. More specifically, we all have a finite 1,440 minutes a day and 168 hours a week, or, roughly, four thousand weeks in the life of the average person living today, as highlighted by Oliver Burkeman, bestselling author of *Four Thousand Weeks*.[1]

> We can't find time.
> We can't make time.
> We can *protect* time.

So, we can't find time. We also can't make time. But we can *protect* time. And once we do, our calendar opens up in ways you may never have imagined. I'm excited to show you how to make this happen.

But before we get there, we need to address the top three underlying barriers that sabotage our time.

Top three time barriers

After almost two decades working with busy people, I've discovered that they share three common time challenges. I'd like to share these now and ask you if you can relate to them.

- **Time-limiting barrier #1 — Too many priorities**: When we try to do too much at once, we spread ourselves thin, which often leads to longer work hours and marginal results.
- **Time-limiting barrier #2 — Too much flexibility**: When we don't protect time and establish necessary boundaries, we are forced to adopt a reactive mode — we always feel pulled and always feel "on."
- **Time-limiting barrier #3 — Too much complication**: It doesn't matter how productive we are, many days can still feel too complicated, leaving us with no breathing space for the inevitable unknowns that land on our desk and set us even further behind. If we want to continue growing, we need to find opportunities to simplify.

Overcoming these barriers doesn't require more willpower, more discipline, more stamina, or new magical powers that allow us to fabricate more time. Nor do we need to push harder and make more sacrifices. The ironic truth is that at a certain point working harder and longer rarely leads to better long-term results. Short-term sprints can help us meet a pressing deadline. But if we're *always* racing, burnout ensues and our pace inevitably slows. The quality of our work drops, we struggle to meet deadlines, and we feel frustrated.

You may have been searching for more time for years. Or perhaps you know you could be making better use of your time. Or maybe you're tired of constantly pushing yourself well past your limits. If you are busy — *too busy* — you are due for a fresh, practical approach to overcome modern-day time scarcity. It's time for you to become a Workday Warrior.

HOW TO BE A WORKDAY WARRIOR

Not surprisingly, Workday Warriors work a little differently than most others. You may find your current schedule feels like a dam ready to burst. But I'm about to introduce you to the Workday Warrior approach — a simple three-step strategy, complete with three supporting tools. This strategy will help you to *clarify*, *fortify*, and *simplify*. Once you apply this strategy, your days will be centred around what you value most. You'll be less distracted by interruptions and other tempting pursuits. Finally, you will learn how to simplify your work so you can create some much-needed room for *thinking* and *being*.

These three crucial steps can be seamlessly integrated into your busy life, helping you shift from the edge of being overwhelmed into a transformed way of living.

⌛

This book is divided into three parts, each with a supporting tool and the power to help you better manage your time:

- **Part 1: Clarify.** This first section is designed to help you clarify your core priorities and effectively manage all the other demands on your time. You will learn about a key tool, your **Main Action Plan**, which will empower you to do this in the most effective way.
- **Part 2: Fortify.** This second section will help you protect time for what's most essential at work and in life. You will learn about another key tool, your **Proactive Routine**, which will help you create boundaries and balance in both your professional and personal life.

- **Part 3: Simplify.** This final section will help you scale up. You will learn about the third key tool leveraged by all Workday Warriors, the **Simplify Filter**. This tool will help you scale back, streamline, and seek help, so you can skillfully navigate unexpected time constraints and carve out necessary space in your day.

Together, these three proven tools will help you to weave the best time-management approaches into your daily work schedule. Using them won't require an extra dose of discipline. As I'll show later, quite the opposite is true; these tools will help you to streamline your efforts and concentrate your time according to how you want to work and live.

> Time management doesn't need to be complicated.

Time management doesn't need to be complicated. Think of these tools as an upgraded operating system running quietly in the background and expertly orchestrating the myriad details of your schedule. Sure, it might take some time to learn how to use these tools, just like it takes a bit of time to learn any new computer application. But once you adopt the Workday Warrior strategy, you'll wonder how you ever lived without it. I have witnessed this over and over: once people become Workday Warriors, they don't look back.

DO YOU NEED ANOTHER BOOK ABOUT TIME MANAGEMENT?

Does the world really need another book on time management? In many ways, no. As everyone knows, there is a wealth of helpful advice available online, a few keystrokes away. I myself regularly learn from other time-management experts.

Yet far too many people continue to struggle. If the time-management puzzle has been solved, why are so many people still so time-stressed? Why are they working so hard and yet feeling as though they are underperforming?

Why are they racing from one urgent deadline to the next, with days full of meetings and little time to breathe? Why do their backlogs grow bigger each day, despite all their efforts to keep up?

I have been teaching productivity skills for almost two decades. So it pains me to report that I see the time-scarcity problem continuing to grow. This is likely no surprise to you; the number of people looking for strategies to help them reclaim their time continues to increase.

So yes, I do believe the world needs another productivity book. But what makes this one different? *Workday Warrior* focuses on three practical steps to help you reclaim your time and overcome the three most pressing time challenges. This is a simple approach, supported by three powerful tools that seamlessly integrate into your life. Yet this is also a comprehensive approach. And most importantly, it is a proven approach, having helped thousands of other busy people just like you.

If you are half as excited about reclaiming your time as I am about helping you to do that, we're going to have fun. Thank you for reading my book. But more importantly, thank you for joining the battle against overwhelm. I know you'll love being a Workday Warrior.

HOW TO READ THIS BOOK

I read a lot of books. I typically have several books on the go, working through each one at a different pace. Sometimes I gobble up a book in a week. Other times it takes me a year to get through a book. I keep a large pile of books on my nightstand and others in my office. I keep a book in my purse, another in my family room, and several on my Kindle app. I've also been a long-time subscriber to Audible so I can listen to books while on the go. Basically, I'm always trying to make the most of my book time. But unlike my varied approach to reading, I suggest you consume this book in a more structured way.

I'd like you to make the most of this book, and I'd like to give you a strategy to do so. I have no false pretenses that you picked up this book to escape into other characters or a fantasy world, like we often do with fiction.

I'm aware that you chose this book with the promise that it will lead to better days ahead. Regardless, my intention is for you to be engaged by the relatable stories and practical solutions.

I designed this book with you, a busy professional, in mind. I know your time is precious, so I set out to make this book engaging and easy to read. But that doesn't mean I suggest you read it non-stop. I believe the best way to consume this book is to read it over three weeks. Spend the first week reading and adopting the principles in part 1. Then do the same over the next two weeks for part 2 and part 3. These weeks don't even need to be consecutive. But I don't suggest spreading them out too much, or you'll risk losing momentum.

Workday Warrior Action:
Block one hour a week over the next three weeks to read parts 1, 2, and 3. Even better, meet with an accountability partner to help one another apply these strategies.

Usually, reading is a solo activity, but I suggest that you work through this book with an accountability partner. Plan to meet briefly, once during each of the three weeks, to share how you have applied the concepts you're about to learn in this book. As I like to say, nothing drives productivity like a deadline. And external deadlines, the kind when we are accountable to others, are the best kind. But don't let a lack of a buddy stop you from turning to the next page. Let's dive into the first of three time barriers, which will equip you to circle back and recruit a productivity partner.

PART 1

Clarify

1

Time Barrier #1:
Too Many Priorities

One who chases two rabbits catches neither.
— Confucius

AS A WEALTH MANAGEMENT DIRECTOR FOR AN INTERNATIONAL bank, Ahmet was certainly busy. He regularly met with many of the bank's top clients. He also led a team of eight senior managers who each had their own teams and often invited Ahmet to join their meetings. As well, he championed two large bank initiatives: a new client portal and a new service extension pilot project. Not surprisingly, his days were filled with meetings — usually consuming more than six hours a day. His inbox was flooded with over two hundred emails every day, and he was often fielding direct calls from his team and clients. Plus, there were other partners across the bank he regularly connected with. Finally, he was juggling a few of his own projects — the ones that kept him working around the clock.

Ahmet struggled with a common time barrier: he was juggling too many priorities at the same time. He spent hours reviewing work long after others had shut down for the day. He prepared his executive reports late in the evening after his young children were asleep. He updated his weekly reports on Sunday mornings. And throughout the week, he combatted the onslaught of email during practically every other waking moment. His long workdays consistently bled into his evenings and weekends. He hated the pattern he had slipped into — working during the time that should have been protected for his family. He was constantly responding to messages on his phone, whether he was at his daughter's volleyball game or during family movie night. It didn't matter how many extra hours he worked — it wasn't enough to keep up. He was constantly running, constantly fielding follow-up messages from others seeking his overdue replies, and constantly feeling behind.

For years Ahmet had been keen to get promoted to the position of vice-president. He liked his work and was a good leader. He loved the banking industry, got a thrill out of solving complex client needs, and generally liked the company where he had spent the last sixteen years of his career. But he was beginning to have doubts about his future at the bank. Frankly, he didn't know how he could manage any more work. He was also starting to think his leaders were doubting his potential as well.

Should he resign himself to living a life of non-stop running, frustration, and personal sacrifice? Was it time to switch to a less demanding role? A recruiter had called Ahmet the week before with an enticing offer: a comparable role at another bank with the promise of a better work/life balance. Yes, this would require a small pay cut, but Ahmet was starting to think this would be worth the gain of interruption-free family time and vacations without his laptop. Was it time to walk away from his colleagues, many of whom he considered friends, and the company where he had spent most of his career? Or was it possible to rework *how* he worked? These were the questions he was struggling with when I first met him.

IS PRIORITIZATION THE ANSWER?

Ahmet was grasping for a fix. He kept telling himself he needed to prioritize. This *seemed* like the right solution. Like Ahmet and so many others, you may turn to prioritization to combat overwhelm.

The word *prioritization* is tossed around the workplace as freely as a kid tosses water balloons at a summer party. But if everyone agrees that prioritization is what's needed for effective time management, why isn't it working the way it's supposed to work?

In theory, prioritization is brilliant. It promises you supercharged days filled with progress and that oh-so-satisfying feeling of being in control. It conjures the dream of having big blocks of time to focus on your most essential work. It paints a compelling vision of the wonderful ways in which your life will be changed: *Yes, you'll work hard, but not all the time, and you'll achieve so much more.* Prioritization also renews your confidence in your big goals. *Land a new client. Build a new program. Learn to speak a new language. Finally figure out how to solve a Rubik's cube.*

But sadly, most people never see these prioritization promises fulfilled. I often hear it said that prioritization is broken. But the problem isn't with prioritization.

> Prioritization is the solution. But few people have learned how to prioritize effectively.

Prioritization *is* the solution. But few people have learned how to prioritize effectively. They know *what* to do. They just don't know *how* to do it. We all want to make the most of our time. But the secret to doing so has remained elusive for too long. It is my mission to change that.

After decades of coaching busy people like you, I assure you that crossing this chasm may be easier than you think. But just as you would when preparing for any journey, you'll need some tools and strategies to ensure you reach your goal. I can't wait to share a truly effective approach to prioritization — an approach embraced by Workday Warriors. But before we go there, we must establish why diluting our efforts is such a flawed way of working.

MORE IS NOT MORE

My husband and I decided we wanted to make some changes in our garden. I handed our detailed wish list to our landscaper. I told her we wanted some rare specimen plants and intricate stonework. I also requested the work be done before our big family summer party. Then I added an appeal for her best price.

She looked me in the eye and said, "Ann, I can make this really good. I can deliver it fast. And I can give you a low price. But you can only get two of your three wishes."

With landscaping, as with any other project at work and in our personal lives, we are always dealing with these resource constraints: time, cost, and scope. Project managers refer to these as the triple constraints (see figure 1).

These project constraints are linked to each other, like the three sides of a triangle. Any changes made to one affect the others. If we take on more work (increase scope), the other constraints must also change to maintain quality. Either our timeline grows longer, or our costs increase; for example, we may pay for additional support. Sometimes it's necessary to adjust both

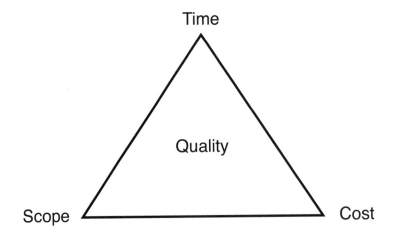

Figure 1. Triple constraints

our timelines and costs. If this isn't done, the quality of our work (scope) inevitably declines.

We navigate these triple constraints every day at work. And it is easy to *talk* about increasing scope — overzealous leaders, individuals, and committees are often keen to pursue good ideas. But the luxury of extending timelines and adding more people to get the job done isn't always possible. More often, those tasked to work on a project must spend extra time working to meet their deadlines. Can you relate to this?

It's clear we can't change one side of the triangle without impacting the others. Yet we live in a world of *more*. So, we spread ourselves thin and prolong the time it takes to complete our work. If your inbox is overflowing, if you're scrambling to meet deadlines, if you're constantly playing catch-up and feel like you're not making enough progress, if you're neglecting sleep, exercise, key relationships, and self-care, you are likely trying to do too much and are diluting your efforts.

WHAT'S WRONG WITH TOO MANY PRIORITIES?

I used to play Whac-A-Mole with my tasks. All my tasks felt urgent and important. I was constantly tackling one pressing task after another.

Like many people, I used to juggle maybe twelve, or possibly fifteen, projects at the same time. I'm not exactly sure what the number was — I never had time to count. I was trying to do it all. But as I now know, I didn't have clear priorities, so none of these projects got the attention they needed; I may have called them priorities, but I didn't treat them like priorities. As Karen Martin, author of *Clarity First* and *The Outstanding Organization* wisely said, "When everything is a priority, nothing is a priority."[1]

Too many priorities = Slower progress

We know the shortest distance between any two points is a straight line. The more detours we take, the longer the trip. This is great if you're keen to explore an area. But when you're trying to get somewhere in the most efficient way, you want to take the straightest path.

The same is true with work. Overcommitment and lack of progress move in sync with each other, like a couple dancing a tango. Overburdened workers start with project A and then switch to B. Then they head into a meeting for project C. Then they're pulled into project D — *Just this one time, to help a colleague.* They blink, and before they know it, two weeks have flown by with practically no time spent on project A — their so-called top priority. While spinning in circles can be fun when dancing, doing the same at work is just plain dizzying.

Conflicting priorities are like eager schoolchildren vying for your attention. *Pick me! Pick me!* Every project comes with its own set of meetings, emails, impromptu calls, deadlines, colleagues to support, and risks that need to be managed. We tell ourselves it is just an hour here. And then another. And then another. But the time you pour into one project takes away time from other projects. There are only so many ways you can divide your time. Progress is difficult to make because every project requires justifiable detours and involves unforeseen tasks.

> The more we try to do, the less we accomplish.

When we constantly shift our focus from one project to another, we drastically hamper our progress. Projects languish, piles accumulate, chaos ensues. No project gets the love it needs. We may burst out of the starting gate, excited to launch a new project, but almost inevitably, we end up struggling to make it around the track. It can feel like we are Alice in Wonderland, running as fast as we can but not moving ahead.

Those with too many priorities make less progress, since an excess of their time is squandered in recovery mode: *Where was I? Where did I leave off? What was that brilliant thought I had?* They are also more likely to procrastinate, telling themselves they need big chunks of time to jump back in, which isn't true — more on this in chapter 14, where we talk about the power of tiny steps.

The more goals we chase, the less time we have to spend on any one of them. The cruel irony is that the more we try to do, the less we accomplish. When we have too many so-called priorities, we don't make reasonable progress on *any* of them. Juggling umpteen priorities leads to lower quality work. When we try to do too much at once, we can't do anything well.

Too many priorities = Always reacting

The more work we have, the more time we spend reacting and the less time we have available to be proactive. Pausing occasionally to reflect on the big picture is absolutely necessary if we want to perform at our best. But *thinking* time is impossible to cram into our schedule between non-stop meetings, emails, and quick *Do you have a minute?* chats.

The more priorities we have, the more we race to keep up. There are always pressing deadlines and urgent situations to navigate. Before we know it, all our planning time is overtaken by commitments. When we're always reacting, it's difficult to make real progress.

Too many priorities = More stress and frustration

Being too busy is an experience shared by most. If you ask practically anyone how they are, they are apt to say, "Busy." People are

Planning for too many priorities is like planning to fail. Too many priorities lead to slower progress, always reacting, more stress and frustration, personal sacrifices, and higher costs.

plagued with time scarcity everywhere. And while this isn't the worst problem someone can face, it isn't a very satisfying situation.

Numerous studies confirm that work is the biggest source of stress among North American adults. The majority of this job-related stress, 66 percent, is driven by workload and the struggle to balance our work and personal lives. The stress experienced by those who perceive that they have little control of their time and workload, yet have a great many demands placed on them, is associated with increased risk of heart attacks, hypertension, and other disorders.[2]

As well, many people agree this busyness hinders their potential. They feel this way despite having so much going for them: talent, meaningful goals, a strong work ethic, and more. The longer this slow progress persists, the more likely they are to lose confidence in themselves and doubt their potential. They dampen their dreams and put limits on their goals. They may want a promotion, but they can't imagine taking on any more responsibility.

Above all else, trying to do too much only leads to one result: struggle.

Too many priorities = Personal sacrifices

Long before the pandemic hit, people were making personal sacrifices to address overwhelm. They were working through lunch, staying late at the office, taking calls at the gym, and fielding email on vacation (or sometimes skipping vacations altogether).

During the pandemic, these personal sacrifices became even more prevalent. For many, they weren't simply working in their homes. Rather, they felt as though they were living at work. Hybrid work arrangements continue to blur the line between work and personal time, with work time often winning the battle.

It's no surprise that overload cuts into personal time. But it isn't the work alone that's fully responsible for the related stress we feel. It's the *anticipation* of having to respond to work emails at home that causes stress. This was a finding based on a study that was aptly called "Killing Me Softly."[3]

As William Becker, co-author of the study and associate professor at Virginia Tech Pamplin College of Business, said, "Every time you check your email or glance at your phone to see if you have an email or other communication, your brain shifts back to work mode. And so, what can happen is you can get stuck in work mode all the time." Plus, one glance at your email tells you others are working at 10:00 p.m. on Wednesday and 7:00 a.m. on Sunday, which naturally prompts you to consider whether you should be working too.

Perhaps even more alarmingly, this strain is extended to family members. "We surveyed employees and we found that frequent monitoring or higher expectations to monitor caused stress in the form of anxiety and that the anxiety contributed to poor sleep quality and lower reports of well-being and health. And we also saw that the *spouse* reported lower sleep quality and lower health and well-being."

The drain that employees feel as a result of always being on has prompted many progressive companies to introduce policies that limit work emails during evenings and weekends. Many countries have introduced laws to limit employers from contacting employees outside of their working hours, such as the *Working for Workers Act* passed in 2021 in Ontario, Canada, where I live. This legislation modified the *Employment Standards Act* to require employers to adopt disconnect from work policies.

For this reason, my team has agreed to try to avoid sending emails after 6:00 p.m. As someone who shifted some of her work to evenings in the past, I thought I might struggle to abide by this rule. But setting a delivery delay for any emails I craft during the evening makes this much easier than I thought. At first, I was surprised at how many communications could wait until business hours resumed. And I continue to be amazed at the difference it has made to my personal life; it is so liberating to *not* have new emails and new work continuing to arrive throughout the evening.

Too many priorities = Higher costs

The more projects we have, the more resources we need, from bringing on extra team members to hiring external consultants. We often need extra tools, such as equipment, software, or apps to support these projects. Plus, we also tend to pay premiums for products we didn't have time to order in advance, extra fees for rush jobs, and penalties for late payments. Each new project comes with a cost. Yet budgets are not always as flexible. Something has to give. Cuts need to be made somewhere. Without the latitude to spend more money, existing team members end up covering the gap by spending extra time working.

> Having too many priorities is worse than having no priorities at all.

It's clear that more is not more. From making slower progress to always reacting to facing more stress and frustration to succumbing to personal sacrifices to absorbing higher costs, we pay a steep price when we take on too much work at the same time. Simply put, having too many priorities is worse than having no priorities at all. If we want to get prioritization right, we need to scale back. We need to concentrate our efforts because the solution is clear: *less is more.*

WHY IS CONCENTRATED WORK BETTER WORK?

After many years studying, teaching, and playing with productivity, I can confidently point to the best way to improve productivity and reduce stress.

It is simply to do less.

There are oodles of recommendations about how to work productively. But the more we embrace this one core strategy, the more effective we become. Our biggest results come when we concentrate our efforts. With this approach, it's so much easier to execute a short list exceptionally well.

We've already discussed the drawbacks of spreading ourselves too thin. I've been there and I'm guessing you have too. In contrast, a concentrated approach allows us to dedicate sustained blocks of time to a few select priorities.

If you need more convincing, let me share three compelling reasons why a concentrated approach leads to optimal results.

Concentrated focus = Faster progress

As each date grew closer for each of my university exams, my pace of studying escalated. Earlier in the term, I worked but I didn't work *hard*. Sure, I kept up with assignments and otherwise let what I was being taught trickle into my brain. But I didn't study until the exam crunch time came. Then I really hit the books. The result: a waterfall of knowledge flooded my brain. Unlike before, I didn't go to the campus bar; I didn't prolong meals with classmates; I didn't watch television. I dove in and learned the entire content of my courses in a matter of a few short days.

> Our progress is inversely related to our number of priorities.

It is incredible what we can accomplish in a short amount of time when we are focused. We're more efficient. We don't dawdle. We don't spend precious time following tangents. We spend less time *Where was I?*-ing. We don't squander time in choppy ramp-up mode. We *are* ramped up.

Our progress is inversely related to our number of priorities. The more priorities we have, the slower our progress. Consider the chart in figure 2. If

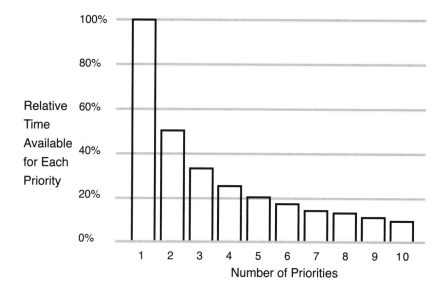

Figure 2. Priorities vs. time available

we spend an equal amount of time on each of our priorities, the time available for each priority drops off with the addition of every new pursuit. It's hard to imagine we can make meaningful progress when we don't dedicate enough time to any of our priorities.

Conversely, when we concentrate on a select few core priorities, we pour more time into the precious few, and this focus leads to much more rapid progress. Progress also gives us an incredible injection of confidence. Big projects don't feel so daunting. So, we are more likely to attempt grander and more meaningful pursuits. When we concentrate our efforts, we can afford to go bigger. We are more likely to play at the level of our potential.

Concentrated focus = Better results

Any kid who has played around with a magnifying glass can tell you that concentrated focus generates better results. A concentrated beam of sunlight shining through a magnifying glass can spark a fire. But too many adults fail to apply this knowledge to their work. I'll admit that I didn't appreciate the importance of this early in my career. I'm glad I was able to reclaim my childhood wisdom and concentrate my focus on a much shorter list of priorities.

Productivity is directly correlated with what we choose to focus on every single day. The more time and energy we shine on a small number of areas, the better our results. This is why the world's most prolific producers bring the concentration principle to everything they do, leaders like Sandy Hudson, co-founder of Black Lives Matter Canada, Patricia Gauthier, general manager of Moderna Canada, and Gary Keller, real estate entrepreneur and bestselling author. These incredibly successful people maintain a narrow focus and hone in on specific goals, which they are incredibly passionate about. The result is that what they do, they do very, very well. Keller, who co-authored *The One Thing*,[4] emphasizes the need for ultimate focus on your single most important goal. As Keller says, "Extraordinary results are directly determined by how narrow you can make your focus ... when you spread yourself out, you end up spread thin."

> Workday Warriors concentrate on no more than three core priorities.

Concentrated focus = More satisfaction

The benefits of a concentrated approach extend far beyond productivity. You will feel a tremendous improvement in your mental health as well. Kevin Kruse, multi-bestselling author and the CEO of Leadx, conducted research in 2015 on more than four thousand professionals. Kruse found that those who stuck to their most important task each day experienced higher levels of happiness and energy.[5]

Not surprisingly, concentrated focus leads to more progress. But we are beginning to learn how empowering progress can be. Progress is a powerful yet underestimated source of motivation. Progress on meaningful work is found to be the most powerful source of momentum, according to groundbreaking work led by Teresa Amabile and Stephen Kramer, authors of *The Progress Principle*.[6] They rigorously analyzed twelve thousand diary entries based on a multi-year study that prompted workers across a number of industries to report on their daily experiences. They found that small wins had a remarkably positive effect on productivity. As Amabile and Kramer note, "Of all the things that can boost emotions, motivation, and perceptions during a workday, the single most important is making progress in meaningful work."

Progress also helps us feel less stressed. Progress mitigates the nagging feeling that there isn't enough time. Progress makes us feel less scattered. We swiftly work through challenging situations instead of suffering through them for extended periods. We even sleep more soundly — with less ruminating over myriad incomplete tasks and competing priorities.

This upward wave of momentum gives us even more energy to direct to our ideal pursuits, leading to an even greater boost in progress and quality. It's a cascade of positive emotions, one that is exhilarating to ride.

LESS IS MORE

The message of this chapter can be summed up in one simple sentence: *Less is more.*

If you want to achieve big goals, if you want to feel less overwhelmed, if you want to take control of your time, you need to *concentrate* your efforts. Yes, you likely need fewer priorities. Saying no to great opportunities will likely feel uncomfortable. But when we choose to say yes to fewer initiatives, it doesn't mean we do less. It means we do *more* of what matters most.

As Sean Covey, co-author of *The 4 Disciplines of Execution*,[7] said, "Focusing on the wildly important requires you to go against your basic wiring as a leader to do more, and instead, focus on less so that your team can achieve more."

Exactly what is the right number of initiatives you should focus on? And how do you handle all the other tasks? Well, I'm glad you asked. The next chapter will answer these questions and more.

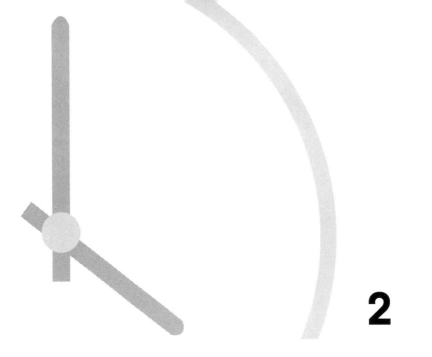

2

The Power of Three

The successful warrior is the average [person],
with laser-like focus.
— Bruce Lee

LET'S DIVE NOW INTO THE FIRST OF THREE PIVOTAL CONCEPTS in this book — the one that will help you cut through distractions, concentrate your effort, and make real progress with your most important goals. In this chapter, I will tell you why focusing on three core priorities (and no more) is your winning strategy. First, I'll share why three is the magic number when it comes to your core priorities. Then I'll guide you to answer the most important question in this book: What are your three core priorities?

WHAT IS A CORE PRIORITY?

Your core priorities are your three most important goals *at this time*. Your top projects. Your brightest stars. If you were to reach three milestones this year, what would you want them to be? These are your core priorities.

There are two types of core priorities: ongoing work and discrete projects. Most roles have evergreen work — the type of work that keeps renewing — that serves as a core priority. If you are a sales professional, one of your core priorities is likely to *grow existing accounts*; another might be to *acquire new clients*. If you are a lawyer, one of your core priorities is likely to *advise your clients*. If you are a facilities manager, one of your core priorities may be to *manage your tenants*. And if you are a leader, you will likely identify *leading your team* as one of your core priorities. In all of these examples, one would continue to focus on these core priorities. You'll reach certain goals and then set new ones. These examples of ongoing work tend to remain your core priorities for as long as you're in that role.

> Your core priorities are your three most important goals *at this time.*

But a core priority can also have a clear finish line. A core priority can be a project that creates something *new,* such as a new product, a new deal, such as a merger, or a new performance-management system. Yes, these are mammoth projects, but eventually you will cross over to the other side. Once you have launched the product, finalized the merger, or integrated the new system, you won't need to spend as much time on the project. Ongoing tasks may be absorbed into your daily routine or delegated to someone else. You'll still need to give it some attention from time to time, but this project no longer requires your concentrated focus.

If any of your core priorities are projects like these examples, they have a definite end point. Once you achieve your end goal, you no longer need to give this project the concentrated attention of a core priority. You can focus on a new core priority.

I've shared examples of both ongoing and discrete core priorities. You may have one or more of each kind. Regardless, your three core priorities are unique to your role and what you are trying to achieve.

WHAT ABOUT YOUR OTHER TASKS?

I recognize you perform many other tasks unrelated to your core priorities. It would be entirely naive to suggest that you can only focus on three things, even if they are all big projects. You also spend a great deal of time on supporting tasks, such as attending team meetings, supporting colleagues in other departments, revising contracts, preparing updates for your leader, processing expenses, or investing in your own professional development, like you're doing right now. But as important as these activities are, they are likely not your core priorities — they are likely your supporting tasks. (Of course, there may be some exceptions, depending on your role — if you work in the Accounts Payable department, processing expenses may be one of your core priorities.)

I think we can agree some parts of your work are more important than others. And clearly, your core priorities are more important than your supporting tasks. As a Workday Warrior, you want to pay extra attention to your core priorities. The supporting tasks still need to get done, but you don't want them to overtake your core priorities. We'll come back to your supporting tasks in the next chapter, but for now, let's stay focused on your core priorities.

SHOULDN'T WE HAVE JUST ONE PRIORITY?

Okay, you're right. Priority is a singular word. It means "the most important." So it makes sense that we should limit ourselves to only one priority. The most effective way to complete a project might be to sequester yourself in a remote cabin without Wi-Fi and work relentlessly on your goal. Or you could travel to a remote destination and fully immerse yourself in a different culture to learn a new language. But for most people, these are rare luxuries.

Yes, it would be ideal if we could simply focus on one priority at any time, but I don't work in ideal conditions. I'm guessing you don't either. Having only one priority is rarely possible.

Most roles demand more than one priority

Most of our jobs don't allow us to have the luxury of a single focus. You could be a lawyer focused on serving your clients while also pursuing new clients and managing your practice group. You could be an executive leading a large team while also managing a global launch and overseeing local operations. Whatever the case may be, you likely need to manage more than one portfolio of work.

Most roles require us to wear multiple hats. Leaders have both internal and external commitments. Entrepreneurs have customers, products, and colleagues that they must give their attention to. Students study multiple subjects each semester. Stay-at-home parents have childcare, meal prep, and household responsibilities. Most jobs require us to manage multiple goals.

Thankfully, we don't need to limit ourselves to only one priority.

Ideas need time to grow

When we step away from a project — for an hour or a day — our unconscious mind continues to toil. To get that perfect cup of freshly brewed coffee, you have to let it percolate; ideas need time to develop, too. We can generate some of our biggest ideas while walking through the woods, struggling to hold a yoga pose, or sitting on a beach.

We also look at our work with fresh eyes after taking short breaks. We see our flawed logic and incomplete processes. We also catch the tiny changes we can make that will contribute to a quality product.

Plants don't grow any faster when we water them non-stop. On the contrary, too much water drowns them. A better approach is to regularly give them just enough of what they need. The same is true when pouring your time and energy into your priorities.

I'm not suggesting you park a project for extended periods. Don't stuff your most important project in a bottom drawer for three months. Ideas grow stale; momentum gets sluggish; starting again feels too hard.

But short breaks give your work the breathing room it craves. Shifting your focus away from your priority for two hours or an entire afternoon or even a week *can* be exactly what that core priority needs at that time. The systems we're building to in this book will help you strike this ideal balance.

Short breaks refuel our momentum

Distance can make the heart grow fonder. This is true for both people and projects. Stepping away from one priority to attend to another helps us to renew our motivation. When I sit down to my morning writing after not looking at that file for twenty-four hours, I feel the exhilaration of reconnecting with my project. *Hello, dear friend. I've missed you.*

If we don't step away, we don't experience the surge of energy that comes with reconnecting. Yet we don't want to break for too long. Otherwise, we have to work through the awkward phase of catching up and refamiliarizing ourselves again. We end up squandering time as we ramp up again, instead of jumping right back in where we left off as we'd be able to if we take only a short break.

We often need feedback from others

Work, like life, is a team sport. We send our creations to others for their review. Then we wait for their feedback or their additions before we can advance to the next level. At other times, we need to hold back before approval is granted for our next step.

We are not working in isolation and can't always control the timeline. Sometimes, our next step is to wait for others. This doesn't mean we can't influence the process. We can encourage them to give their feedback faster by proposing short-term deadlines. But we still have to account for the time it takes them to do their part.

⧖

For all of these reasons, we *can* have more than one priority. But we can't let the pendulum swing too far in the opposite direction and use these breaks as an excuse for taking on a bunch of other projects. If we have too many priorities, we end up spending too long away from each of them. I'm about to show you why having three priorities allows you to strike the right balance.

THE POWER OF THREE

There is great power in having three core priorities. This is a concept that benefits both individuals and companies.

I believe we can learn a lot about productivity from both busy people and successful companies — and it's hard to find someone with more responsibilities than the late CEO of the biggest company of all time.

Steve Jobs insisted on a concentrated approach while running Apple. During management retreats, he and his top one hundred employees would brainstorm, deciding what the company should focus on during the next fiscal period. After much debate, they would identify a long list of opportunities — a list with an abundance of compelling pursuits. Then they ranked the top ten ideas — ideas that could easily be adopted as priorities. You might think that ten priorities would be a more than reasonable number for a mammoth organization like Apple. Certainly, there are many examples of smaller organizations that strive to pursue more.

But Jobs knew ten priorities was too many and that devoting resources to all of them would only serve to diminish the company's success. So, after these brainstorming sessions, Jobs did something many others would consider ruthless: he crossed off the bottom seven ideas. He declared that no Apple resources — no time and no money — would be dedicated to the bottom seven projects. The *only* opportunities Apple was going to focus on were the top three priorities.[1]

Apple is one of the most innovative companies of all time. It may be the most *focused* company too. Tim Cook, the CEO of Apple, said this in 2008:

> We are the most focused company that I know of, or have read of, or have any knowledge of. We say no to good ideas every day. We say no to great ideas in order to keep the amount of things we focus on very small in number so we

can put enormous energy behind the ones we do choose.
The table each of you are sitting at today, you could probably put every product on it that Apple makes, yet Apple's
revenues last year were $40 billion.[2]

Apple's success speaks for itself. They concentrate their efforts. And what
they do, they do very well.

Unfortunately, Apple's concentrated approach is rare. In every industry
you'll find multiple examples of people (and companies) trying to pay attention to too many so-called priorities at the same time. This misguided
approach can be self-inflicted — individual employees may choose to pursue
multiple projects at once. Or it might be part of their company culture — a
culture that believes in the myth that more is more. Often, it is driven by both.

I know how easy it is to fall into this trap; I did it myself — I juggled
many more projects than I could manage for far too many years. And if I'm
honest, I used to ask my team to do too much at the same time as well. But
now that I know better, I work hard to maintain a concentrated approach —
in my own work and in my team's work. I am still tempted to take on new
projects, but I now know how to navigate this frequent dilemma.

Over the past twenty-five years, I've worked with hundreds of organizations, ranging from the top Fortune 500 companies to small teams with
a handful of employees. Consistently, I see too many organizations, too
many teams, and too many people juggling far too many priorities. They
are pulled in too many directions and so aren't able do any of them as well
as they should be able to.

Research confirms my observations. A global survey of 1,800 executives
found a rare number of companies — just 13 percent, to be precise — had
three or fewer priorities. Some 33 percent of companies had four to ten priorities, and 5 percent had even more. Perhaps even more alarmingly, 49 percent of executives said their company had no list of firm-wide priorities.[3] This
makes me picture all their team members rowing in different directions, pulling against one another and going nowhere fast. In contrast, the most focused
companies translated their strategy into better results. Companies with one
to three priorities were most likely to report above-average revenue growth.

While it's clear that many companies do not have a concise list of priorities, we have some solid role models — organizations that are thriving with a concentrated approach — that can serve as inspirations. Apple's focus on three priorities, as mentioned earlier, is perhaps the most well-known example. Similarly, Amazon, with its vast reach, maintains a relentless commitment to the customer experience. Year-over-year analysis of founder Jeff Bezos's annual letter to shareholders demonstrates this ongoing priority.[4]

This concentrated focus is seen in long-standing industries as well, such as the automotive industry. Ford Motor Company went through a massive restructuring between 2006 and 2011, designed to simplify many of their overly complex operations. They discontinued six of their eight brands, streamlined their auto parts manufacturing, reduced the number of suppliers they worked with, and consolidated their organizational structure. This helped them shift from a company operating in the red in 2007 to earnings of more than $20 billion in 2011.[5]

> Companies with one to three priorities were most likely to report above-average revenue growth.

The authors of the book *The 4 Disciplines of Execution*,[6] who have helped over a thousand companies focus on getting their most important work done, advocate having two to three priorities: "With 2–3 priorities, you'll likely achieve them all with excellence," write Chris McChesney, Sean Covey, and Jim Huling. "[W]ith 4–10 priorities," they go on to say, "you will likely achieve only 1–2 with excellence. With 10 or more priorities, you will be unlikely to achieve any with excellence."

Über-successful investor Warren Buffett also recommends a concentrated approach. He advocates maintaining an "ignore at all costs" list, focusing on five or fewer priorities at any one time.

Admittedly, some of the above examples recommend three to five priorities, objectives, or goals. But this doesn't mean all your goals deserve your attention now. A concentrated focus on three or fewer priorities *at one time* is your surest path to achieve the results you want.

⧗

As we've already established, focusing on just three priorities doesn't mean you accomplish less. Rather, it means you do more of what matters most. This means you'll make faster progress with what you value most, thus leading to making a bigger impact.

Three or fewer

It's clear by now I recommend having no more than three core priorities at any one time. Of course, you could have fewer priorities. You could choose to concentrate on only one or two priorities to meet some key deadlines and reach some big goals. Then you could expand back to three core priorities. But as a Workday Warrior, you'll have at most three core priorities at one time.

I won't claim it will be easy to limit yourself to three core priorities. If it were, everyone would be highly focused and super-productive. You will have to make some gut-wrenching decisions. As I write this book, I am keen to launch a podcast. I won't get into all the reasons why I'm so excited about this. But because it isn't currently one of my core priorities, it hasn't made the cut (yet). Right now, I am committed to spending no time building a podcast. I don't interview other podcasters or take calls from podcast vendors. Even small investments of time in creating a podcast would take time away from the initiatives I have ranked higher — my core priorities. Heck, I feel I shouldn't even be talking about my future podcast here!

Workday Warriors concentrate their focus on three core priorities or fewer.

I can't stress it enough — four priorities are too many. If you have an inner voice trying to convince you that you can juggle four or five priorities, I encourage you to resist it. When you juggle too many projects, balls get dropped. Progress is delayed; quality drops; frustration ensues; stress rises; workdays expand.

At any time Workday Warriors concentrate their focus on three core priorities.

Or fewer.

WHAT ABOUT YOUR PERSONAL PRIORITIES?

We are on the cusp of identifying what your unique core priorities are. But before we do that, I'd like to address a question you're probably asking: *What about my personal priorities?* This book is mostly focused on your work life. But you also have a full life outside of your career. And it is just as easy to spread ourselves thin in our personal life.

We all have distinct personal and professional lives, with goals in each. Yes, our personal and professional lives overlap and influence the other. But our goals tend to be distinct in these two key areas of our lives.

Therefore, it is only fitting that we have separate core priorities, one set for our professional life and one set for our personal life. Your personal core priorities may relate to self-care, family, friends, community, philanthropy, household projects — there are many possibilities.

You can effectively manage up to three core priorities in your professional life and up to three core priorities in your personal life. This total of six would be too much if it were in one aspect of your life. But with a clear division between these two worlds, it works.

If exercise is one of your well-established habits, it is clearly an example of your self-care core priority — one that is supported by your self-care routines. As you'll learn in part 2, routines are another powerful tool used by Workday Warriors. But since exercise is already integrated into your life, it does not require all the fresh start-up energy of a new habit. If, however, you are looking to expand or grow your exercise routines — for example, you want to move from being a casual runner to being a marathoner — this becomes the focus of your self-care core priority.

Other examples of personal core priorities could include the following:

- Self-care: upgrading your morning routine, starting with a minimum of five minutes dedicated to stretching, gratitude journaling, visualization, and meditation
- Family: dedicating the month to enhancing your family harmony with consistent family dinners, a family gratitude practice, and a renewed family value to speak respectfully

- House project: digitizing your family photos in time for Grandma's eightieth birthday

In your personal life, just like in your work life, you juggle many different activities. You likely have many fully established routines, from your morning routine to your bedtime routine and everything in between. These recurring activities are part of your daily routine. Like brushing your teeth or commuting to work, these routines tend to be well established. Routines lead to habits, which require much less energy than brand new activities. Core priorities, on the other hand, help you achieve specific goals (running a marathon) or build new routines (exercising five times a week).

These are only a few examples of personal priorities. As we head into the next section, I encourage you to think about your three core priorities in both your personal and professional life.

MY CORE PRIORITIES

As you reflect on your core priorities, it may be helpful to know what my core priorities are. Of course, your priorities will be different; different roles will have different needs. But examples can be helpful.

In my professional life, my core priorities are client service, content development, and company growth. For each of these core priorities, I have a specific goal with a specific what, why, and when. Each of these core priorities includes multiple tasks and deadlines. And no, your core priorities don't all have to start with the same letter. (There's just something about how my brain works that likes this parallelism.)

In my personal life, my core priorities are self-care, family, and special projects. Admittedly, each of these core priorities include a vast set of micro-goals, and I can't focus on everything at the same time. For self-care, I am focusing on resetting my exercise routine, which got a bit sidetracked during the most recent pandemic shutdown. Once that routine is well established again, I'll be able to shift my focus to another self-care goal.

HOW TO CHOOSE YOUR CORE PRIORITIES

Let's circle back to the question I posed at the beginning of this chapter: *What are your core priorities?* As I said, answering this question is the most important step in this entire book. This is the foundation of your productivity. This is your first step in becoming a Workday Warrior.

On the surface this is a simple question. But most people struggle to answer it. They may initially cite multiple pursuits — all great. But if they try to focus on all of these goals, they dilute their impact and practically invite frazzled days. I'd like to help you answer this question in a decisive way. I'd like to help you definitively cite your core priorities faster than you can say *ABC*.

You may find it helpful to corral all your goals and activities so you can identify what is most important. Often, notes about goals and related tasks are found all over — like unpenned livestock — hiding in many places: handwritten sticky notes, flagged emails, project files, to-do apps, piles, the corners of your memory, and more. Plus, you likely have many core priority–worthy ideas captured in your business plan. Pulling your tasks together and taking stock of the vast array of your work helps you highlight your core priorities among everything else.

The following template (see exercise 1) may help you consider your range of work. If it helps, scan through your sent email, plus your physical and digital files, to identify more items to add to this list. This record will help you identify most of what you do, which is good enough. I don't suggest you spend more than ten minutes on this exercise. You could spend another two weeks carefully tracking all your work, but this level of precision is not necessary at this point. Let's keep this activity simple.

EXERCISE 1. IDENTIFY THE TYPE OF WORK YOU DO

Check all that apply.

- ☐ Client work
- ☐ Business development
- ☐ Team support
- ☐ Partner support
- ☐ Negotiations
- ☐ Presentations
- ☐ Sales
- ☐ Marketing
- ☐ Public relations
- ☐ Event planning
- ☐ Specific projects

- ☐ Product management
- ☐ Research
- ☐ Writing
- ☐ Editing
- ☐ Professional development
- ☐ Strategic planning
- ☐ Financial management
- ☐ Account management

- ☐ Operations
- ☐ Human resources
- ☐ Training
- ☐ Mentoring
- ☐ Contract management
- ☐ Facilities management
- ☐ Reporting
- ☐ Community relations
- ☐ Other

Now that you have a list of your wide range of work, it is easier to identify your three core priorities. You will instinctively consider many factors when choosing your most important work. Which projects are the best of the best? Which ones are most clearly aligned with your vision and bold goals? Which of your activities yield the best results? Which goals are the most meaningful to you? What are you most excited about? What is your boss most excited about? (We can't ignore the power of political capital.) On which outcomes will you be evaluated? At the end of this year, what will you celebrate?

You may be tempted to identify more than three core priorities, because there are so many good opportunities offered to you — a good problem to have. But as we've already established, it is so crucial to pick just three core priorities. But recall that a core priority can be a group of related tasks. Serving your clients could be one of your core priorities, and this would include many discrete tasks related to a range of clients.

YOUR CORE PRIORITIES: A CLEAR WHAT, WHEN, AND WHY

NASA's goal in the 1950s was to lead the world in space exploration. This was a compelling goal. But the truth was NASA's space program was struggling. They were working hard, but their mandate to explore the universe was unfocused and infinitely vast.

Then in 1961 President John F. Kennedy set a clear mandate: "Put a person on the moon by the end of the decade and return that person safely home."[7] This gave NASA a specific goal to focus on.

The entire team pulled together to work toward this exciting stretch goal. And on July 20, 1969, Neil Armstrong took his first step on the moon. With a clear mandate, NASA's performance had skyrocketed.

As with NASA's renewed mandate, a core priority is a meaningful goal with a clear outcome and a specific timeline. You might wish to launch a new product, lead an Instagram campaign, or learn a new language. But without a clear deadline and a measurable result, those wishes are just that — wishes.

> Your core priorities are specific goals, each with a clear what, when, and why.

Your core priorities are specific goals, each with a clear what, when, and why. It's relatively easy to describe a clear outcome for distinct projects like writing a book or launching a podcast. Defining a target for evergreen streams of work, such as serving your clients or leading your team, may be harder, but it's still absolutely essential. Regardless of the nature of your priority, you need a clear goal to work toward.

A clear goal motivates you and keeps you focused. It gives you a clear sense of how far you've come — and how much further you need to travel. This is why marathons have every kilometre or every mile (depending on which country you're racing in) carefully marked.

What are you trying to accomplish?

Your core priorities need an unquestionable finish line. What is the outcome you are aiming for? How will you know when you've reached your goal? Google calls these specific outcomes "key results," and the company stresses the importance of having clear, measurable key results for each of their objectives. Former Google vice-president Marissa Mayer once said, "If it does not have a number, it is not a Key Result."[8] Google relies on this OKR (objectives and key results) system to focus their team's efforts for optimal results.

How can you make the goals of your core priorities objective and quantifiable? If your core priority is to grow revenue, can you cite a dollar figure you are targeting? Can you pinpoint which products and services or which region you expect to grow? What period of time are you measuring? Are you aiming for recurring revenue or new growth?

"Grow our revenue" doesn't have a clear outcome. "Grow our revenue to $10 million" is better. "Grow our revenue to $10 million in our European product extension during Q4" is even more specific, which makes it better still.

If your core priority is to provide excellent customer service — an admirable goal and a common core priority — add the right language to make your goal specific. For example, your goal could be to increase your customer satisfaction ratings to 90+ percent by the second quarter. If your core priority is to grow revenue, your goal could be to earn $5 million from a new service line by the end of this fiscal year. If your core priority is to lead a high-performance team, identify how you will measure the factors proven to foster a high-performance culture, such as trust, engagement, autonomy, and meaning. For every core priority, you want to define a specific outcome.

Once you reach your clear goal, you can set your eyes on a new destination. Many runners, after crossing the finish line for one marathon, immediately set their next goal. (Or they promise to never run a marathon again, but this frees them to take on a new challenge and commit to a new core priority.)

When will you reach this goal?

Each of your core priority goals needs a deadline. Deadlines drive productivity. As Gina Raimondo, United States secretary of commerce, said, "The difference between a dream and a goal is a deadline."[9] On the other hand, the lack of a deadline invites procrastination.

Your deadline can be a self-imposed target. Or you may be accountable to someone else: your customer; your leader; the market; your mother. If no deadline exists, create one yourself. Then invite someone else to help hold you accountable. We'll discuss why this is so valuable in chapter 4.

> Deadlines drive
> productivity.

Why is this priority meaningful to you?

Identify why each of your core priorities is personally meaningful to you. Be specific about why they matter to you and how they make you feel.

When you're deep into the gritty work, or when your motivation inevitably lags, you need a compelling purpose to fuel your efforts. The same is true when you hit an obstacle or setback. This purpose helps you overcome intimidating challenges.

A strong sense of meaning will also help you make better decisions and avoid insignificant tangents. It is easy to meander down loosely connected paths — I am often tempted myself. But if we step back and consider our overriding intention, we'll realize we don't need to follow this tangent. Similarly, our "why" helps us avoid perfectionism. When we consider the big picture, we realize that good enough is more than good enough.

As I write this chapter, this book is the focus of my content development core priority. It is meaningful to me, as I want to help you use your time in the best way possible. This matters to me because I feel I squandered too much time when I unknowingly violated productivity principles early in my career, and I'm passionate about helping you avoid doing the same.

If one of your personal core priorities is to upgrade your morning routine, starting with waking up earlier, you might be tempted to press snooze when the alarm goes off early. But having a compelling reason to get out of bed can help you transition through a potentially painful shift. Let's say you decide to improve your mornings by creating a new meditation habit, which gives you a greater sense of peace and clarity and brings more flow to the rest of your day. You recognize that meditation helps you be more patient and more open to others' views, making you feel more connected. You know meditation helps you be more present and less anxious about stressful possibilities. All of this can serve as your motivation to commit to your upgraded morning routine and resist pressing the snooze button.

IDENTIFYING YOUR CORE PRIORITIES: MORE HELPFUL STRATEGIES

By now, you're probably close to identifying your three core priorities. Here are some more tips to help you finalize this important decision:

Think big

A core priority is often a big project, with several sub-steps. A core priority is bigger than any one discrete task. "Edit that document" is not a core priority. Instead, this is a task aligned to one of your core priorities. Of course, if you are an editor (as my editor wisely pointed out), editing is sure to be one of your core priorities. In this case, there will be several discrete activities associated with this priority, several documents to edit; several deadlines to meet. Any single task is aligned with a core priority; it is not a core priority itself.

For each of your core priorities, I encourage you to set a bold goal that stretches you. We thrive when we step outside of our comfort zone. Frankly, your goals should scare you a little bit. If your goals don't scare you, you probably aren't thinking big enough.

Given the scale of big goals, you may need to work on them for several weeks; you might need months, or even years. Examples might include "Product Extension" or "New Country Expansion." And of course, the bigger the goal, the more activities are aligned to that core priority.

Think small

While I encourage you to set bold goals, I also advocate taking on a high-quality sprint goal if the right opportunity arises. For example, if you are offered the opportunity to plan a strategic planning session for your board of directors, you might jump at the opportunity. Understandably, this new core priority would absorb a lot of your time. Therefore, I encourage you to think about replacing one or more of your existing core priorities with this new one for a few short weeks. Let me be clear: adopting a new, short-term core priority should not result in you having four core priorities. In this case, you need to swap one for another, *for now*. Sometimes these quick wins are irresistible opportunities and can give you the momentum to tackle more unwieldy, yet bigger-impact goals.

Quick wins can be more rewarding than victories won following long, drawn-out battles. But we want to be cautious and avoid overplaying our reliance on smaller, shorter-term goals. Otherwise, we start to play small and never get around to tackling the bigger, longer-term goals we're capable of conquering.

Consider umbrella goals

All goals connect with several outcomes. But some special goals have a bigger positive effect on other goals. I call these *umbrella goals*. Investing in your well-being is an excellent example of an umbrella goal. For example, committing to a regular exercise routine helps you get better quality sleep and often prompts you to make more nutritious food choices. Exercise also gives you more energy to work more productively and helps you manage stress.

You get the most leverage when one of your core priorities complements another one of your core priorities. For example, if one core priority is to provide exceptional client service, another core priority — strengthening your product — supports the first. If one of your core priorities is to grow your followers, another core priority — expanding your online presence — supports the first.

Choose a word or phrase

Identify a word or a short phrase to represent each of your core priorities. You can quickly recite it — to yourself or others. Examples include "clients" or "team" or "business development." Of course, the one or two words you use won't convey a clear outcome to others, but *you* will know the specific goal behind each of these words.

Rank your core priorities

Once you have identified your core priorities, you may naturally want to rank them. I encourage you to do this. Ranking your three core priorities will help you to decide how much time to dedicate to each of them. Obviously, you will want to give more time to your #1 core priority. As you'll learn in part 2, I recommend you dedicate at least 60 percent or more of your work time to your core priorities, which we will come back to in part 2. But that doesn't mean each of your core priorities warrants an equal share of your time. You might choose to allocate this in the following way: 30 percent of your time to core priority #1; 20 percent to core priority #2; 10 percent to core priority #3. The actual split of your time isn't as important as the ranking.

This ranking also helps you make trade-off decisions and manage expectations during crunch periods. For example, my top priority always centres on my current clients. If one of my clients requires more time than I budgeted for, I know I have to scale back on my other two core priorities.

The ranking of your three core priorities can also shift as required. As I mentioned above, my client work is typically in the #1 position. But in the weeks leading up to this book's final deadline, I cleared client commitments from much of my calendar to allow this core priority to step into first place.

Tell others

The more visible our core priorities are, the more accountable we are. Also, we are more likely to set bold and objective goals if encouraged by others. Telling others also helps us rally support. Our champions will often work behind the scenes, with or without our knowing, to send resources, opportunities, and connections our way.

Link priorities

I believe everyone's priorities within an organization should be synchronized. Core priorities should seamlessly cascade down from the organization's overall vision and mission. Every team member should be clear about how their actions contribute to the entire team and greater organization. I can picture this cascade of goals, like a waterfall, in my mind, but I don't often see it in practice when talking to others about their priorities. Make your team the exception. Ensure your core priorities align to your team and overall organization goals.

Workday Warrior

Action: Identify your three core priorities in both your professional and personal life.

WHAT ARE YOUR THREE CORE PRIORITIES?

Use the following templates (see exercise 2 and exercise 3) to capture all of the above advice as you identify both your personal and professional core priorities. These templates are also available at clearconceptinc.ca /WorkdayWarrior.

EXERCISE 2. IDENTIFY YOUR PROFESSIONAL CORE PRIORITIES

	Core priority #1	Core priority #2	Core priority #3
Why is this meaningful to you?			
What is your ideal outcome and one to three related metrics?			
When do you plan to reach your goal?			

EXERCISE 3. IDENTIFY YOUR PERSONAL CORE PRIORITIES

	Core priority #1	Core priority #2	Core priority #3
	_____	_____	_____
Why is this meaningful to you?			
What is your ideal outcome and one to three related metrics?			
When do you plan to reach your goal?			

CORE PRIORITY CHECKLIST

Once you have identified your core priorities, use this checklist to gauge the strength of your top focus areas.

- ☐ Can you clearly name your three core priorities? Do you have one word or a short phrase to capture each core priority, making them easier to remember and cite?
- ☐ Does each of your core priorities have a clear outcome: a clear "what" by "when"?
- ☐ Are the goals associated with your core priorities meaningful *to you*?
- ☐ Do your core priorities link to your team and organization's priorities?
- ☐ Do your team members know and support your core priorities?

YOUR CLEAR CORE PRIORITIES

By now, you should be crystal clear on your core priorities — the foundation of your Workday Warrior system. I know you have questions about all your other work — you have several non-negotiable supporting tasks. As well, you likely have several other tempting opportunities that could just as easily qualify as a core priority. I call these "future priorities," and in the next chapter, I'll show you how to manage them all. And then the fun continues, when we talk about a tool to manage all of your responsibilities — a tool that will change *how* you work.

3

How to Deal with Your Other Work

There is no magic in magic, it's all in the details.
— Walt Disney

I WALKED INTO THE OFFICE AND SAW SHAWN SURROUNDED by piles of receipts. Shawn was normally easygoing and neatly dressed — the kind of person who conveys confidence in everything he does. But that day he was frazzled and had a pained expression on his face. He correctly interpreted my unspoken *What is this?* thought. He blurted out, "I'm behind on reclaiming my expenses — by about fifty thousand dollars."

At the time Shawn and I were both consultants, flying from one city to the next and quickly accumulating thousands of dollars in expenses. Our company's policy was to submit our expenses each week so we could be re-imbursed by our clients before our credit card bills came due.

This wasn't a fun task. Nor was it inspiring. But it was a necessary task, required to maintain our personal cash flow and help pay the bills. So most of us consultants diligently completed this administrative task late into most Friday afternoons.

But Shawn had been dodging accounting for his expenses for four months. There were always more urgent tasks to complete; that is, until he hit the breaking point — he couldn't afford to personally fund these work expenses any longer.

BALANCING CORE PRIORITIES WITH EVERYTHING ELSE

Some people, like Shawn, gravitate to the big opportunities. These are the visionaries, the dreamers, the bold thinkers. They spend all their time on their core priorities and tend to create impressive results. But as the saying goes, too much of a good thing can be bad. And surprisingly, this applies to our core priorities as well. As Shawn learned the hard way, we can't ignore certain tasks without consequence. Sure, you may know some senior people who have the luxury of ignoring certain tasks — it may be practically im-possible to get them to respond to an administrative email. But this works only because they have an army of people supporting them by attending to the details. Unfortunately, few people have so many resources to lean on. The rest of us can't justify avoiding our expenses.

Other people take an opposite approach to Shawn's. They gravitate to the pragmatic tasks. They excel with clearly defined, list-based tasks. Their days tend to be filled with countless details, which they expertly knock down without breaking a sweat. They often like their desk clean and their inbox clear before they start working on any bigger task or goal. This ap-proach works exceptionally well for certain roles, such as executive assistants and billing clerks. But this fully pragmatic approach doesn't work as well for their more vague, long-term goals. Sometimes they struggle to find the time to achieve their bigger goals because they consistently bump the discrete tasks to the top of their list. They are often viewed as a valuable team member — the go-to person who helps everyone else. But since they aren't finding the time to advance big, impressive goals, they aren't usually the prime candidate for the next promotion.

Most of us need time for *both* our core priorities as well as our supporting tasks. In a perfect world, we would spend all of our time on our three core priorities. Imagine what we could do! But the reality is we have *other work* that needs our attention. Some tasks are simply unavoidable. We can't exclusively drive toward our core priorities. We need to stop and fill up with gas once in a while.

> We need time for *both* our core priorities as well as our supporting tasks.

Conversely, we can't fill our day with only our supporting tasks either. We need to find the right balance between our core priorities and our supporting tasks.

The problem is non-core activities can easily consume our day and derail progress on what matters most. I'm sure you can relate if you have days consumed by miscellaneous emails, tangential requests, and low-impact tasks. So how do we handle the endless stream of work buzzing outside the boundaries of our core priorities? It's helpful to put this "other" work into three distinct categories since each warrants a different approach:

- Supporting tasks
- Future priorities
- Distracting tasks

Supporting tasks

Let's return to Shawn. At the time he was helping one of his clients work through a merger. This project had consumed his attention for several months, which explained the delinquent expenses. But he had clearly avoided his expenses for too long. Expenses were one of Shawn's supporting tasks. Like Shawn, we all have a variety of similar jobs that we can't perpetually ignore. These supporting tasks are the operational and administrative tasks required for us to do our work and run our life.

These supporting tasks vary but might include upgrading computer programs, helping a colleague, managing personal finances, maintaining your house, and, yes, submitting your expenses. Some of your supporting tasks are quick and simple. Others are bigger and more complex.

> Supporting tasks are the operational and administrative tasks required for us to do our job and run our life.

We can't ignore these tasks. If we do, like Shawn did, they tend to snowball, becoming major problems that demand immediate attention, often at the worst possible time. Yet at the same time, we can't let attending to these supporting tasks come at the cost of devoting time to our core priorities. Such tasks should *support* versus overtake our core priorities. In part 2, we'll discuss strategies to effectively manage our supporting tasks. For now, it's enough to simply distinguish them from our core priorities.

Future priorities

When it comes to new pursuits, I'm like a kid in a candy store. My eyes sparkle, and I want it all. *Now.* But all too often I've experienced the dreadful feeling of being overloaded, not unlike nursing a sore tummy after indulging in too many treats. I now understand that I can't have it all — *at the same time.* This caveat, *at the same time,* is crucial. While we can do *anything*, we can't do *everything.* We need to concentrate our efforts to make the most of our time.

Of course, it's easy to say no to activities we absolutely do not want to do. *Bungee jumping? No thank you. Mud wrestling? Nope.* The bigger challenge is saying no to things that pique our interest. *Oversee that new product launch? Lead that committee? Join the board for your industry association?* I wouldn't blame you if you were tempted to say yes. I know I often am. And then there are all those great ideas you keep dreaming up. The entrepreneur in me can't help but think about new ideas, new projects, and new opportunities. My mind loves to walk down the yellow brick road of all the things I want to do. But just because something is a good opportunity doesn't mean it is a good opportunity to pursue *now*.

So, what do we do when another incredible opportunity knocks at our door? Can't we just say yes and log a few more hours to keep moving forward? Sadly, no. Refer back to chapter 1 any time you're tempted to dilute your efforts.

Our core priorities only have room to shine when we are clear about what we are *not* doing *at this time*. The key is to put all initiatives, outside of your core priorities and supporting tasks, on hold. These are your potential future priorities.

Any goal that is not one of your three core priorities is a contender for being a *future* priority. Your future priorities may include several tempting projects and pursuits that you are super keen to dive into. You may get pressure from others to get started on them now. But you and I know this is a suboptimal strategy. I'll arm you with some strategies to manage other people's expectations in part 3.

Ultimately, we need a solid "do not pass" line between our core and future priorities. This includes any research, reflection time, meetings, or emails related to future priorities. As good as these future priorities are, they can also be major distractions. Any time invested in a future priority comes at the cost of our core priorities. So, Workday Warriors, postpone all work related to future priorities.

> Just because something is a great opportunity doesn't mean it is great to pursue *now*.

Sometimes it helps to have a wise adviser remind you not to invest time in a future priority right now. This could be your boss, a mentor, or a friend. I have a two such colleagues who help me resist the allure of new priorities: my business partner, Susan Pons, and my mentor, Sarah Morgenstern. They are both very good at saying, "That's a great idea, Ann. Let's park it while you're focused on your core priorities." Honestly, despite me teaching this stuff, their reminders are golden.

Again, just because something is a great opportunity doesn't mean it is great to do *now*. You are not saying no to a future priority forever. You are simply saying no right now. Stay on course with your core priorities. Resist the temptation to be pulled down random paths. Otherwise, you'll risk getting lost in the forest.

Ironically, the fastest way to get to your future priorities is to spend absolutely *no* time on them right now. Zilch. Nada. Nothing. Instead, fast-track your current core priorities. Get them done. Then elevate one of your future priorities to the rank of core priority.

Our core priorities are not our forever priorities. Once we achieve our current goals, we have capacity to pursue new ones. In the meantime, we need to think about these additional goals as future priorities, contenders for being core priorities *in the future.*

You may also be wondering, Can you ever swap priorities? The answer is a cautious yes — if a *can't-resist* opportunity presents itself, you can absolutely swap out one of your three core priorities. But the key word is *swap*. If a future priority warrants your time and attention *today*, you can choose to let it displace one of your core priorities. While it can be strategic to nimbly switch focus when that once-in-a-lifetime opportunity comes along, you need to take something off your plate before adding something new. I recently had the opportunity to contribute a chapter to a book that eventually became a bestseller. I had to jump on this timely opportunity. So, I swapped it for one of my core priorities — for a week. Then I resumed progress on my original core priorities.

But swapping core priorities is not a decision that should be made casually. It's hard to make meaningful progress if we keep changing directions. So be cautious before elevating a future priority to a core priority. It's important to not discount all of the effort required to untangle from that downgraded core priority: renegotiating deadlines, cancelling meetings, and resetting expectations. All of those tasks take time and effort, and only after overcoming these barriers can we free up the time to welcome this new core priority.

Tread carefully with time-sensitive opportunities. Consult with one or more of your advisers. Sleep on your decision. Listen to your gut. Sometimes, these hate-to-miss opportunities are actually carefully disguised distractions.

This approach to priorities holds in both our personal and professional lives and applies to both big and small projects. Small projects may only displace a core priority for a short time, but the fact remains, they still displace one of your core priorities. For example, whenever I plan a birthday celebration for one of my family members, I need to park another core priority — my photo digitization project. I can return to the photos after the birthday party and when the dust settles. But if I'm honest, I'm often tempted to leave that original project undone to tackle a new bright shiny object. But I remind myself of the power of concentrating my efforts. This commitment avoids multiple piles, multiple half-completed projects, and all the frustration that ensues when I try to tackle too many projects at the same time.

> Future priorities are enticing and tempting. But they are not your *core* priorities.

Future priorities are enticing and tempting. But they are not your *core* priorities. The only action you need to take is to capture them on your future priorities list. You don't even need to add deadlines to your future priorities. After all, you are not committed to any of your future priorities at this time. Don't even worry about ranking them right now. Opportunities tend to shift. When you're ready to swap out one of your core priorities, you can decide at that time which future priority warrants the promotion, that is, when you can scan the abundant landscape of your future priorities to identify your next conquest.

Distractions

After we have identified our core priorities, future priorities, and supporting tasks, we tend to have a handful of remaining activities that don't seem to fit in. These are the fringe tasks. The miscellaneous tasks. The tasks that we may be tempted to spend far too much time indulging in. I'm talking about our distractions. Distractions include all of the low-value tasks that don't align with our goals or values. Not surprisingly, we face many distractions throughout each day. Our attention is our most precious commodity, and many savvy marketers are experts at enticing us to shift our attention over to their products or services.

But we also willingly invite distractions into our day — we ask our team to copy us on every email or we reclaim delegated work. In the latter case, that delegated work may be one of your colleague's core priorities, but it is a distraction for you. Sure, one of your core priorities may be to develop your team, which is a fitting core priority for every leader. But doing the work of team members for them and constantly looking over their shoulder by reviewing every email is impeding their growth (and distracting you from your core priorities).

Other more obvious distractions include clicking on online pop-up windows, checking for new messages every few minutes, and parking your phone beside you while focusing on another task. Distractions can also be more carefully disguised — diving down into the rabbit hole of research can occupy enormous amounts of time.

The average person spends almost two and a half hours a day or almost nine hundred hours a year looking at social media.[1] If you are a marketing manager or a television producer and social media aligns to your core priorities, keep scrolling! But chances are, this large amount of time doesn't align with your core priorities. There is no doubt that social media is captivating. It sure has a knack for holding our attention, sometimes for far longer than we planned to give it. I've been there before — scrolling practically mindlessly for far too long. Yes, social media is a great way to catch up and connect with friends, family, and others in our community. But nine hundred hours a year? At what point does social media tip over into the realm of being a distraction?

There is no need to track your distractions on a list, like we do with our core priorities. But you *do* want to be fully aware of what these distractions are so you can eliminate them from your day. Clearly identifying distractions helps prevent unconscious lingering over low-value activities during your prime time — the time when you are most productive. After all, any time absorbed by a distracting task takes time away from your core priorities. The best way to deflate the power of distractions is to crowd them out. In part 2, we'll talk about how your routines will prioritize your focus on more important activities.

We naturally manage our distractions when we are meeting with other people. We don't answer phone calls or check email. We give them exclusive access to a precious commodity: our attention. Similarly, when we *must* get a task done *now*, we shut the door and park our phone. The key is to harness this same concentrated attention we freely grant to others and urgent demands. When we bring this concentrated focus to every day, we attain a higher level of productivity.

Do distractions have *any* value? Is it ever acceptable to simply indulge?

Yes. And *absolutely* yes!

Distractions do not need to be avoided all the time. We don't need to be productive every moment in our day. Mindless, simple pleasures can be a great way to take a necessary break in our day. Micro-breaks spent scrolling through social media, chatting with a friend, playing with your dog, or whatever you fancy, can be just what you need to help renew and refuel during your workday. We all need this essential recovery time. What you choose to do during this time is completely up to you. We'll come back to the power of breaks in part 2.

⌛

We've talked about four types of activities: core priorities, supporting tasks, future priorities, and distractions. Each of these categories is associated with a countless array of tasks, tasks we can't expect to track in our memories or in some haphazard fashion. We need a system — a robust priority management system — to thrive as a Workday Warrior. The next chapter — one of my favourite chapters in this book — will show you how to build this.

Get ready to roll up your sleeves and create your version of a tool to help focus your attention and make the most of your time. I'm talking about a tool that you will soon wonder how you lived without. I'm talking about your Main Action Plan.

4

Your Most Essential Productivity Tool

Your mind is for having ideas, not holding them.
— David Allen

ASHA WAS A LAW STUDENT LIKE MANY OTHERS. SHE ENJOYED learning about the law and loved university campus life even more. She grew up watching her mom, a prominent litigator, prepare for trial. She dreamed as a young child of being a lawyer. She even dressed up as a lawyer for Halloween one year.

Once Asha started law school, she found it came easy to her. The law was clearly in her blood. Asha was incredibly social and loved to debate what she learned about in class with her classmates in the evenings in the campus pub. She visited with a different group every night. No one could keep up with

Asha socially. The other students had to protect time to study, something Asha didn't seem to struggle with.

The majority of Asha's courses had 100 percent final exams. In other words, the only mark that counted was the one test per course at the end of each semester. This situation was a procrastinator's dream: no quizzes, papers, or other assignments throughout the semester. But of course, Asha and every other student was encouraged to keep up with the readings, attend lectures, and study throughout the semester.

Despite the advice of every professor, Asha largely avoided the library. Most students who scrimped on studying produced subpar results, forcing them to pursue other career paths, but Asha managed to do well enough, despite not logging as many hours studying as her peers. Asha was one of the lucky ones. She kept up, absorbing information seemingly by osmosis, by quickly skimming the materials, attending class, and paying attention. When exams came along, she wrote them and did quite well (much to the frustration of her classmates who worked quite hard for similar results).

Fast forward a few years. Asha was a second-year associate at an international law firm. Her early career success and rave reviews were starting to fade. Asha was missing deadlines and generating sloppy work, not meeting the high standards required to practise law at this level. Asha's poor performance wasn't due to a lack of effort. In Asha's defence, she was now investing a lot of time in her work, unlike in her school days. Like her colleagues, she could be found at her desk long into the evening. The partners couldn't figure her out. Asha was clearly smart; she was well-spoken, good with clients, and liked by her colleagues. Asha said she was committed to her career and expressed interest in making partner one day. But the sad reality was that Asha struggled to manage her work. The firm was starting to question whether Asha would make it. Even sadder, Asha was starting to question herself.

Several of Asha's senior colleagues and mentors offered her some helpful feedback. They wanted to see her succeed. But when little changed, the HR director decided they needed a superhero. Instead they settled on recruiting a productivity consultant. A few days later, I walked into Asha's office.

Asha's head was in her hands. She was the first to admit her approach wasn't working anymore. Despite her best intentions, she was alarmingly behind on her work. And in an environment where every deadline counted, she struggled to get her work done on time. Her systems didn't seem to be helping her. Her inbox was filled with messages requiring action; her computer was framed with random sticky note reminders; her desk was covered with haphazard piles. Asha had reached a time ceiling. She could no longer find enough time to do what she wanted.

To some extent, we all lean on natural talents early in our careers. This works well enough when we are busy *but not that busy.* When we are merely *pseudo*-busy, we don't need the best work habits. Good enough is good enough. Sure, we face occasional intense time constraints, but somehow, we manage to get most things done.

Time ceiling: When you can't find enough time to do what you want to do.

Eventually, though, most of us hit a point when we run out of time, when we can't find enough hours in the day to do what we want to do, when the way we used to work no longer works.

This is our time ceiling. Asha had met hers, and the same is true of everyone my team and I coach. As I look back over my career, and if I'm honest, I know I've pushed up against my time ceiling many times myself.

A breaking point may be prompted by an all-consuming project, promotion, or new side hustle. Our personal life can also precipitate a time ceiling — caring for an aging parent, tending to a sweet new baby, or tackling a massive home renovation may be the final straw. We know we've hit our time ceiling when we feel we're crumbling under the pressure. There just doesn't seem to be enough of us to go around.

It's normal to hit a time ceiling once in a while. However, if you've been bumping up against one for as long as you can remember and if you're tired of feeling out of control, it's clear you are due for a change, a change that will help you raise your time ceiling without throwing extra time at the situation. You need a new system. You need a Main Action Plan.

WHAT IS A MAIN ACTION PLAN (MAP)?

At its essence, productivity is about using your most precious resource, your time, in the most effective way. (Although keeping your inbox clear at the same time is a nice bonus.) Productivity helps you make meaningful progress on your most important goals.

In chapter 2, you identified your most essential work. Your brightest gems. Your three core priorities. Knowing what these are is essential. But we also need a system to track all of the associated tasks and organize our day-to-day actions so we can achieve our goals. All too often, I see that people have filed away their incredible plans, which sit untouched until next year's goal-setting exercise. Days become consumed with reacting, and goal setting starts to feel like a make-work project. But it doesn't have to be like this.

I'm about to introduce you to the ultimate priority management system – your Main Action Plan. Unlike most to-do lists, which are haphazard, incomplete, and ineffective, your MAP is a tool designed for elite performers, for Workday Warriors. Your MAP integrates your long-term plans into your day-to-day action.

Your MAP tracks your tasks, deadlines, commitments, and goals. But it goes so much further; it assists you in organizing and prioritizing your work. It also prompts you to take action, meet your goals, and fulfill your commitments, all while navigating many other tasks vying for your attention. Your MAP is a tool that keeps up with your busy career and equally busy life.

> Your Main Action Plan (MAP) is your ultimate priority management system. It tracks, prioritizes, and prompts action on your tasks, deadlines, commitments, and goals.

A MAP is essentially your to-do list — but it is so much better. Your MAP *replaces* your to-do list and any other disjointed systems you use to track your work. Goodbye, antiquated system. Hello, strategic partner.

Core Priority A	Core Priority B	Core Priority C
Measurable objective A	*Measurable objective B*	*Measurable objective C*
Deadline: Task *Deadline: Task* *Deadline: Task*	*Deadline: Task* *Deadline: Task* *Deadline: Task*	*Deadline: Task* *Deadline: Task* *Deadline: Task*
Supporting Tasks • • •	*Future Priorities* • • •	*Personal Tasks* • • •

Figure 3. Sample MAP template

But make no mistake — your MAP is no ordinary list. Your MAP is a proactive and effective tool. As you're about to discover, your MAP will elevate your productivity more than a simple list ever could.

Your MAP is a *strategic plan* for how you spend your most precious resource: your time. This makes it your **most critical** productivity tool. Figure 3 shows an image of what your MAP may look like, although this will vary slightly depending on which application you use to house your MAP. I'll share some options in the next chapter. The most important thing is that your MAP capture five key principles, which I'll also outline in the next chapter. You can find a digital version of this MAP template at clearconceptinc.ca /WorkdayWarrior.

TWO LEVELS OF PLANNING

We all plan at two levels. High-level, strategic planning involves identifying our three core priorities, as we discussed in chapter 2. We engage in this type of planning periodically. Once we have identified our core priorities, we stay committed to them until we have reached our goals — or until a better opportunity warrants a conscious shift.

On another level, we plan to complete detailed tasks. Each of our core priorities includes multiple steps, deadlines, and niggly details that we need to track and rank.

When you add up all of your deadlines and commitments, you may have *hundreds* of tasks. As you reflect on the sheer volume of demands facing you, it can make you feel dizzy. Even the most proficient among us can be left spinning.

Ranking this vast array of tasks requires a first-class system, especially when you're running at a rapid pace. But I rarely encounter people with an excellent system. Rather, they are typically juggling a collection of disparate, incomplete systems. They use a variety of lists, some paper and some digital. They use spiral-bound notebooks and a variety of apps. They flag emails and mark others as unread. They enter deadlines in their calendar and use piles of paper to serve as reminders. And of course, they tuck items in their memory. I even met with one executive who admitted to putting tiny pen marks on his left hand to serve as reminders. *(Seriously?)*

Such patchwork systems do not result in a strategic or reliable way of working. These scattered records fail to create any real prioritized organization and require a substantial amount of time to manage. They often contribute to reactive (rather than proactive) days and usually only add fuel to fire when it comes to our stress.

With this haphazard approach, there is a real danger of tasks being forgotten. Deadlines are bound to be missed when you juggle multiple task-tracking systems. And of course, it's hard to proactively plan ahead if you need to take inventory across multiple lists.

Your work deserves a better approach.

You deserve a better approach.

A MAP is your solution.

WHY IS YOUR MAP YOUR MOST ESSENTIAL PRODUCTIVITY TOOL?

Earlier, I compared your MAP to a simple to-do list. But don't let that fool you into believing a MAP is anything but integral. I can't stress the importance of your MAP enough. There are four critical reasons why your MAP is your most essential productivity tool.

A MAP clearly ranks our many competing tasks

In the early 1900s, Charles M. Schwab, president of Bethlehem Steel Corporation, hired Ivy Lee to help improve productivity across his company. Lee taught Schwab and his executive team a simple approach. He had them list their six most important tasks each day and then work on them in the order they listed them. As Lee said, "I want you to start at number one and don't even think about number two until number one is complete."[1]

Three months later, when Schwab saw how much this simple approach translated into incredible results, he paid Lee $25,000 (the equivalent of $400,000 US today).

> Your MAP is your most essential productivity tool.

A clear ranking is the magic behind Lee's strategy. A MAP helps us bring this magic to how we work. Haphazard task-tracking systems, with some deadlines noted here and other reminders over there, simply aren't able to give us this clear ranking.

Our MAP does several things for us. It provides us with one central record of all our work. It also simplifies how we rank our tasks. It helps us *prioritize* our tasks. But as we all know, prioritizing a wide range of important steps can be a daunting endeavour. There are several factors that affect which task needs our attention next:

- Which task is most urgent?
- Which task has the biggest short-term impact?
- Which task has the biggest long-term impact?
- Which task matters most to my boss?

- What matters most to our clients?
- What helps to relieve a bottleneck for my team?
- What am I embarrassingly overdue completing?

The challenge is when we consider *too many* factors, ranking our tasks becomes overly complex. We find ourselves perpetually triaging. *Should I do this first or that? Or maybe this other task? Ugh — they are all urgent!* This prompts us to shift our task rankings. And then shift them again.

Have you ever been immobilized by your work? This happens when you have several tasks jockeying for the number one position, and each one warrants taking the top spot. Where do you start?

When we are torn between tasks, we often jump back and forth in a way that doesn't do any task justice. Or worse, the anxiety pushes us away from what we should be doing and into the arms of procrastination.

We need a clear metric, one that helps us avoid having to frequently recalibrate. We shouldn't have to mentally rehash the order of our tasks all the time. This redundant step is the last thing we need in the midst of busy days.

Workday Warrior Action: Assign a deadline to each of your tasks. Deadlines are the most effective way to rank the work associated with each core priority.

Ultimately, we need to simplify how we rank our tasks. Simplicity provides a respite from work, which can become complicated far too easily. Thankfully, our MAP provides us with a clear and simple way to rank our tasks. That is because our MAP is built around our deadlines.

Of all the ranking metrics we could use, deadlines are the best choice. Deadlines prompt us to take all the other factors into account and decide whether a task warrants our attention *now* or *later*. Deadlines create order out of chaos. Deadlines help us rank our tasks once and avoid the time-intensive chore of having to recalibrate over and over again. Simply put, deadlines drive productivity.

When new tasks come up, we slot them into the ranking based on their deadline. If no deadline exists, we create one — and ideally, we commit this deadline to someone else. There is an art to creating effective deadlines (more on this in the next chapter).

Once we have all our tasks ranked by deadline, our day becomes radically easier. Just like Charles M. Schwab advised, we should simply work our way through our list in chronological order. A MAP practically automates our task ranking, using a simple one-hundred-year-old technique.

A MAP helps us accurately gauge our capacity

Manufacturing plants know precisely how long it takes to build a widget. They use this information to measure and fine-tune workflow for optimal efficiency. They also use it to accurately predict timelines.

We can determine how long it will take to build a physical item, especially after we have built several others, but the timelines associated with developing new products or translating ideas into commercial solutions are harder to predict. When we're doing new and creative work, it's hard to accurately gauge our capacity and to commit to realistic deadlines.

You want this analysis done by next Friday? That seems doable. Until suddenly, it's Friday and you're only half done. Has this ever happened to you? Have you ever underestimated how long a task would take? I would be lying if I said I've never stumbled into this common challenge. I am human, with a tendency to overcomplicate my work at times. Ironically, I succumbed to this dilemma while editing *this exact chapter*.

Thankfully, our MAP sharpens our crystal ball powers and helps us better estimate how long things take. Our MAP prompts us to break big projects down into discrete steps. And we are better at estimating the time required for smaller steps. These small steps provide us with more insight into what a realistic deadline is (and when we need to renegotiate timelines). So, essentially, our MAP acts like a savvy project manager. A MAP guides us to accurately gauge our capacity on both our long-term goals and day-to-day tasks.

Our MAP allows us to view all of our commitments in one place, which is a key feature. This allows us to picture the full landscape, prompting better decisions about what projects we say yes to. This complete picture helps us determine whether we have room for new commitments. Without this complete record, it is far too easy to overpromise and underdeliver. The promises are made in good faith, of course. However, most people simply don't have a good understanding of their capacity to deliver on the promises they make because they don't have a simple way to consider all of their existing work demands.

When we are better able to predict our capacity, we're more strategic about our commitments. You may be tempted to say yes to multiple opportunities. I know I am. With our MAP, which allows us to easily compare new opportunities to existing commitments, we can quickly determine if *yes* is the right answer — that isn't always the case, even when a task aligns to one of our core priorities. Sometimes the most strategic answer is a firm *no* or *not now*. Sure, it is great to push ourselves, but no one benefits from unrealistic timelines.

A MAP compensates for our imperfect memory

Our brain are incredible machines. We have only begun to understand the full power of these mental powerhouses. But despite the brain's incredible abilities, our memory is a terrible place to house our to-do list. It's tempting to think we will remember something. But in reality, we often forget details we swear we won't, leading to missed deadlines and unnecessary scrambles.

Our working memory, which is where our to-do list sits when we choose to rely on our memory, has a limited capacity. A landmark 1956 paper introduced us to Miller's Law, which states that we can hold only seven objects (plus or minus two) in our working memory at a time.[2] According to folklore, this is the reason why phone numbers were originally designed to be seven digits long.[3]

However, more recent research indicates our working memory capacity may be even less. It appears that adults are able to remember only four "chunks" of information (the number is even smaller for older adults — and children, as most parents can confirm).[4]

Chronic stress also impairs our memory (among other functions). An excess of the stress hormone cortisol prevents our hippocampus from storing new memories and retrieving existing memories.[5] Stress accelerates aging in the brain, leading to deterioration in the hippocampus and frontal cortex, the precise areas that help with memory.[6]

What about people born with a photographic memory? As it turns out, photographic memory (also referred to as eidetic memory) is a myth. Certainly, some people exhibit better memories than others. But this appears to be related to complete familiarity with the material. Even chess masters, who seem capable of memorizing countless game configurations, are considered to have contextual memory, developed after years of practice, rather than photographic memory. If you show a chess master a random configuration of chess pieces, their ability to memorize is no better than ours.

> Don't use your memory for your to-do list.

Even if you could remember all of your tasks, it doesn't mean you should. As productivity expert David Allen wisely said, "Use your mind to think about things, rather than think of them. You want to be adding value as you think about projects and people, not simply reminding yourself they exist."[7] Even Albert Einstein weighed in on this subject when he is said to have declared, "Never memorize anything you can look up."[8]

Memory is much more reliable when we only have a handful of commitments: an assignment due on Tuesday; a test on Friday; and a party on Saturday — oh, the good ol' days! But life isn't this simple anymore. Like me, you probably have infinitely more to remember now than you did in the past.

Inevitably, key details slip through the cracks when we rely on our memory. Sometimes these might be trivial, but they can also be critical. And with our work, we are expected to follow through on all of our commitments, both big and small. Remembering some (or even most) of our commitments doesn't cut it. Even if we remember 90 percent of our commitments, other people are counting on us for the remaining 10 percent. At a minimum, we want to remember enough to renegotiate a deadline when needed. An *I forgot* excuse is feeble at best and certainly doesn't reflect how we want to show up.

Even if you do remember all of your key items, this recall won't necessarily occur at the ideal time. You might be driving home from the office when you remember an overdue commitment, or the thought might burst into your consciousness in the middle of the night, prompting you to open your eyes at 2:00 a.m., leaving you worrying, unable to get back to sleep. For these reasons, I like to stress with all of our clients: don't use your memory for your to-do list.

Thankfully, our MAP steps in where our memory leaves off. Our MAP serves as our external brain. It frees our memory to focus on the current task, redirecting crucial mental bandwidth to produce the results we want. Once you establish this external brain, you'll wonder how you ever functioned without it.

A MAP keeps us focused

The research is quite clear: multi-tasking doesn't work. Sure, technology has changed the way we work. But just because we can check email, tune into a webinar, and take a call all at the same time doesn't mean we should. Focusing is a far more effective and efficient approach. Think you're a proficient multi-tasker? I used to think the same. In chapter 11, I'll share how I overcame multi-tasking and why you should too.

Distractions impose a hefty tax on our focus. For example, we could be focused on one task and then be powerlessly pulled into ruminating about all of those *other* tasks, the ones we should have done yesterday. Our MAP mitigates against these distracting thoughts. When we provide a place to park these outstanding tasks, we can put them out of our minds (for a while) and focus on our core priorities.

For both our core priorities and their associated tasks, our MAP helps our most important work take centre stage. It is fundamentally liberating to list other outstanding tasks on our MAP and release the pressure to feel like we have to get it all done now. A MAP provides us with a plan to work through our tasks at a reasonable pace.

A MAP allows us to strike the strategic balance between planning ahead and staying focused on our next, most important task. Our MAP helps us break though the noise and maintain our attention on the present activity — the best use of our time *right now.*

Only when we have clearly identified all of our tasks can we confidently choose our next task. Without a MAP to provide this clarity, many people jump from one activity to the next without taking advantage of the power of focus and without always doing their tasks in the most strategic order.

YOUR MAP IS YOUR PRODUCTIVITY FOUNDATION

Your MAP is one complete and prioritized record. It helps you maintain a focus on your three core priorities in addition to all the associated details. It is a reliable and strategic tool that allows you to proactively plan the best use of your time, which we'll build on in part 2 of this book.

Your MAP is akin to your home's foundation. We know our walls will only stand strong and survive the inevitable storms if they are built on a solid base. Your MAP is that solid base. It connects and strengthens all of the other productivity principles highlighted in this book and beyond. You can survive calm days without a MAP. But as the turbulence grows, your MAP serves as a necessary anchor. Without it, your work can crumble as easily as a sandcastle.

Ultimately, your MAP helps you make the most of your time and energy.

Once you adopt your MAP, you'll wonder how you survived without it.

Let's not allow for any more time to pass before you create your unique MAP. The next chapter is your step-by-step guide, prompting you to roll up your sleeves and build your MAP.

5

How to Build Your Main Action Plan

WHEN I WAS IN MY LAST YEAR OF MY UNDERGRADUATE degree, at McMaster University, I worked on a small passion project. I was lobbying to have valedictorians added to the graduation ceremonies. At the time, McMaster University didn't elect valedictorians and we wanted to add these dynamic student representative speakers to these events. This effort required countless conversations and presentations to multiple groups, ranging from student committees all the way up to the university board of directors.

About halfway through this journey, I had the opportunity to pitch this concept to the university president, Dr. Peter George. He encouraged me to keep going and even gave me a few tips. Making a change to the long-standing tradition wrapped up in these convocations was no small feat.

At the end of our conversation, Dr. George nodded his head and wished me luck. Then he said he would call me back to check on my progress in three months. I was happy with the interest he showed but honestly didn't expect to hear from him again. After all, I was one of over fifteen thousand students he oversaw, not to mention the more than three thousand faculty and staff who worked at the university. And of course, he had all of the other responsibilities of being a university president.

But three months later, my phone rang. Dr. George had kept his promise. Even at the time, I remember thinking, *Wow — he must have a great system.*[1]

ARE YOU READY?

We all manage a sea of moving parts, which makes it thoroughly understandable when well-intentioned details get lost in the mix. But what if you had a system that saved you from forgetting about things you wanted to remember? Are you ready to build your optimal priority management system? I can't wait to guide you through the process of building your MAP.

But before we get there, I want to make sure you've answered the question posed in chapter 2: What are your core priorities? Your MAP is grounded in your core priorities, and we can't move to the next step if you don't have these clearly defined. If you need to, go back to chapter 2. Do not pass Go; do not collect $200.[2]

LET'S BUILD YOUR MAP

With your core priorities clearly defined, we're ready to build your MAP — your Main Action Plan. I'm going to show you how to elevate your current to-do list (or other task-tracking system) and turn you into a Workday Warrior with your customized MAP.

A MAP is grounded in the five principles: Categorize; Centralize; Complete; Commit; Consult — five key Cs to help you make the most of your time.

As we go through these five principles in more detail, I encourage you to start to build your MAP. You can use the sample MAP template (figure 3) in chapter 4. Or download a digital version at clearconceptinc.ca /WorkdayWarrior.

Do we need to track distracting tasks?

Good question — the answer is a solid *No!* We do not need to track our distracting tasks on our MAP. Our MAP is designed to track the tasks we want to complete. And we shouldn't plan to be distracted. Ideally, we don't want to spend any time on low-value distractions during our prime work time.

Categorize

As we've already discussed, we have different types of work. Our array of tasks, deadlines, commitments, and goals fall into one of these categories: core priorities, supporting tasks, future priorities, and personal tasks. It helps to think about our work according to these different categories so we can be prioritizing the right work at the right time. Categorizing our work helps to offset the fact that sometimes lower-ranked tasks can make the loudest squeaks. Distractions can be louder still.

When we segment our work by category, we become much more discerning about what we say yes to. Our MAP clearly prompts us to assess all new tasks based on whether they support our core priorities. This helps us make better decisions about what we commit to doing. Any enticing opportunities that may qualify as a core priority in the future can be tucked into our future priority list, so they can patiently wait their turn.

Another benefit of categorizing our work is that we rank our tasks *within* these major categories, not *across* categories. Comparing a core priority task to a supporting task is like comparing apples to oranges. They are fundamentally different. We don't want to clutter our list of core priority tasks with a range of supporting tasks. When we're focused on our core priorities, we want to exclusively focus on them. Similarly, when we're protecting time for our supporting tasks or personal tasks, we want to work through those lists.

Not surprisingly, each of these categories should be assigned to different times in our day. For example, our core priorities deserve our peak energy times. We'll discuss this more in part 2. Separating our work into these categories helps us protect most of our work time for our core priorities. This is where our magic happens.

Centralize

As mentioned earlier, too many people have too many lists — disjointed reminders scattered here, there, and everywhere — handwritten lists, piles around their office, and notebooks filled with miscellaneous reminders. They flag emails and add deadlines to their calendar with reminders that pop up at inconvenient times. They also lean on the tempting yet unreliable *I will remember that* technique.

Like a series of bad renovations, these various lists don't integrate well. The more tracking systems you maintain, the more places you have to check and the easier it is to miss tasks. People waste time referring to multiple, oft disconnected, sources (see exercise 4). Or they skip this important planning step and jump into the most pressing task or the most recent email. Or even worse, they end up missing deadlines completely. Oops.

These disparate lists aren't strategic either. The collection of tasks is rarely prioritized — but how could they be? One can't accurately rank tasks if they are not all housed in one place. In reality, identifying what we want to do next is always a *relative* decision. Should *this* task come before or after *that* task? If there is no single, centralized place where a list of all of the tasks to be done is housed, it's next to impossible to make an informed decision about what should be done next.

Multiple task lists make it easy to underestimate our work and over-commit to deadlines. As a result, users are pretty much always short on time. Despite their efforts, they don't have a global handle on what they need to do by when and are often in a reactive state.

If you are using more than one system, you're using too many.

EXERCISE 4. HOW DO YOU TRACK YOUR TASKS?

What systems do you use to track your tasks, deadlines, commitments, and goals? Check all that apply.

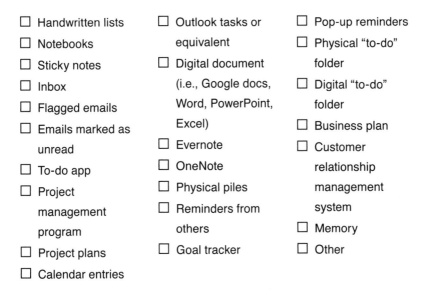

- ☐ Handwritten lists
- ☐ Notebooks
- ☐ Sticky notes
- ☐ Inbox
- ☐ Flagged emails
- ☐ Emails marked as unread
- ☐ To-do app
- ☐ Project management program
- ☐ Project plans
- ☐ Calendar entries

- ☐ Outlook tasks or equivalent
- ☐ Digital document (i.e., Google docs, Word, PowerPoint, Excel)
- ☐ Evernote
- ☐ OneNote
- ☐ Physical piles
- ☐ Reminders from others
- ☐ Goal tracker

- ☐ Pop-up reminders
- ☐ Physical "to-do" folder
- ☐ Digital "to-do" folder
- ☐ Business plan
- ☐ Customer relationship management system
- ☐ Memory
- ☐ Other

If you're like most people, there is a good chance you checked more than one of the above boxes. This shows that you would benefit from having one central record. Your MAP is that one central place to capture all of your tasks, deadlines, commitments, and goals.

Maintaining one central system allows you to rank your tasks relative to one another, gauge your capacity, and concentrate your focus on your core priorities. It also means you only need to look in one place to plan your work. All of this helps you preserve precious mental bandwidth, which you can then redirect into *doing* your work.

WHERE SHOULD YOU SET UP YOUR MAP?

There are several excellent applications that you can use to house your MAP. You could use Outlook Tasks, which integrates nicely with Outlook email. You could also use a list-making device, such as Evernote or OneNote. Or you could use a project management application such as Asana or Trello. Or you could use one of the many to-do applications available such as ClickUp or monday.com. As you can see, you have many options. Pick the one that suits you best. But regardless of which one you choose, make sure you incorporate the five principles: Categorize; Centralize; Complete; Commit; Consult.

> Our inbox is not our to-do list.

Your MAP may look different than the sample template shown in the previous chapter (figure 3). Your MAP's appearance will depend on which application you choose to house your MAP. For a comprehensive guide highlighting the benefits of these different options, as well as other notes to help you choose the best option *for you*, go to clearconceptinc.ca /WorkdayWarrior.

Complete

I've helped thousands of people create their MAPs, and I find most people have some form of a list to begin with. Often, they have several. But their lists are rarely complete. Their lists may capture some but not all of their planned work. In contrast, your MAP is a complete record of all your work, including your goals, tasks, deadlines, and commitments.

There are several problems with incomplete lists: memory must be relied on too often to compensate for their inadequacies; there is no clear task ranking; and important tasks can easily be forgotten.

Overreliance on memory

People often tuck *must-complete* tasks in their memory. They convince themselves they'll remember to call Keya back or submit the application by the 5:00 p.m. deadline. But as we discussed in the last chapter, our memories are not always reliable.

It doesn't matter how smart you are — and I have no doubt you are quite wise — juggling too many mental tasks leads to forgotten items and brain clutter. It's practically impossible to stay focused on your current task when your mind is working overtime as it strains to remember myriad other tasks.

No clear task ranking

As stated above, it is impossible to accurately rank tasks if we don't have one complete record. Only a complete list allows us to accurately rank our work, gauge our capacity, and evaluate every new idea, request, or opportunity against our current core priorities and related tasks.

Forgotten tasks

When people rely on a variety of task-tracking systems, from flagged emails to paper lists to calendar entries, items are bound to be missed. We simply don't have time to keep checking all these different places. Despite our best intentions, some deadlines silently slip past us.

⧗

In contrast, our MAP captures 100 percent of our tasks, deadlines, commitments, and goals. It captures everything we want to do today, next week, and next year. This helps us eliminate that nagging feeling we are forgetting something. More importantly, it helps us avoid the nauseating feeling we experience when we actually *do* forget a task that we fully intended to complete.

> Our MAP captures 100 percent of our tasks, deadlines, commitments, and goals.

Let me be perfectly clear: *everything* goes on your MAP. This includes any work related to your core priorities, supporting tasks, and future priorities. Short-term and long-term plans. Little tasks and big tasks. If you need to call a client next Tuesday, add it to your MAP. If you're thinking of updating your website next year, add it to your MAP. Everything you've committed to do and everything you plan to do and everything you are remotely considering goes on your MAP.

Frequently asked question

Why can't my notebook, calendar, or inbox work as my to-do list? Why isn't flagging emails a good system?

Answer: Let me start by saying that your notebook, calendar, and inbox can all be valuable tools. Your notebook is a great place to capture inspiring thoughts or notes about one specific project. Your calendar is exactly the right place to track your events, appointments, and blocked time. And of course, your email inbox is a great place to hold incoming messages until you get a chance to process them. But none of these tools has what it takes to serve as your MAP. Key tasks are bound to get lost in the midst of other notes in your notebook. Deadlines can sneak up on you when you list them in your calendar. And deadlines get lost when they are buried in an inbox flooded with countless other messages. Plus, each of these systems require you to flip, scroll, and otherwise spend extra time scanning through them to ensure you're aware of all your deadlines. This means you constantly have to recalibrate which task to do next, which is time-intensive and prone to error.

Let's come back to your inbox. Of course, simple emails can be processed right away — and these emails are easy to move out of your inbox once you have done so. There is no need to add these tasks to your MAP. But other emails require more time. These are the emails you'd like to come back to, the tasks you want to do — just not right now. These are also the emails that tend to clutter inboxes. And they sit there in the order they arrived — not the order you plan to address them. Even if you flag these pending emails, you'll squander a lot of time scanning and re-reading emails, without actually making progress with your work. Plus, messages are bound to be forgotten about when they are several screens down. I can't stress it enough: email is a great communication tool, but it is not an effective priority management system. Our inbox is not our to-do list. Instead, we want to add our tasks to our Main Action Plan.

Unlike these other tools, your MAP gives you one complete picture of every one of your tasks, deadlines, commitments, and goals. This central record is what you need to play at elite levels.

Commit

One of the best features of your MAP is that it prompts you to commit to a deadline for every task. And as we've already established, these deadlines are how we prioritize our tasks.

Deadlines have taken on a bad reputation among the overworked and overloaded. Deadlines can conjure images of unrealistic expectations and working late into the night, long past one's breaking point. But I look at deadlines completely differently. Deadlines prompt action, allow us to clearly rank our tasks, and eliminate redundant recalibrating. Deadlines are a beautiful life enhancer — something I encourage all of us to willingly welcome into our lives. Workday Warriors use deadlines to their advantage.

Deadlines drive productivity

Nothing drives productivity like a deadline. The firm commitment wrapped up in a deadline helps us make progress on any tasks we deem important enough to do. It is relatively easy to start projects; deadlines help us *finish* them. This is especially helpful for all the vague *maybe/someday/I really should* projects that can pile up around us. Deadlines are the perfect antidote for procrastination, otherwise known as *last-minute-itis* (that oh-so-human tendency).

> Deadlines prompt action, allow us to clearly rank our tasks, and eliminate redundant recalibrating.

Deadlines help us to accomplish big goals. They create accountability, which is a key driver of change. Deadlines tighten our focus, force us to streamline our efforts, and help us cross the finish line. As I type this sentence, I am laser focused on my manuscript deadline, which helps me resist the urge to jump to another project.

Deadlines provide a clear ranking

When selecting our core priorities, we choose our most meaningful and high-impact goals. But as we discussed earlier, deadlines are the best way to prioritize at the task level. Deadlines provide us with a clear and simple way to rank our discrete action items. We simply list them chronologically based on their specific deadlines.

79

Which country tops the list?

As a proud Canadian, I'd love to share the results of a fascinating study involving to-do lists.* (Yes, I used "fascinating" and "to-do lists" in the same sentence.) This multi-country study found that Canadians ranked at the top of the list for maintaining to-do lists. Incredible! But sadly, we were nowhere near the top when it came to crossing items off our list. We were more prone to collect items. Which country do you think topped the charts for rapid task turnover? Whenever I poll audiences on this question, the top guesses are Japan and Germany, two cultures known for their incredible work ethic. But neither of these countries secured the top spot. Nor did the United States, Italy, or Britain. The country with the quickest task turnover was Spain. Yes, Spain. Apparently, we can learn a lot from my in-laws' kin about doing what we say we're going to do, in a timely manner. Perhaps Canadians would have fared better in this study if they added a deadline commitment to every task on their list.

* "Survey Shows Increasing Worldwide Reliance on To-Do Lists," Microsoft Stories, January 14, 2008, news.microsoft.com/2008/01/14/survey-shows-increasing-worldwide-reliance-on-to-do-lists/.

When we take on a new task, it doesn't always make sense to add it to the bottom of our list. Some tasks warrant being done sooner than others. Instead, we can slot that task into our MAP based on how its deadline ranks relative to other tasks.

Deadlines eliminate redundant recalibrating

The order in which we work through our tasks is a *relative* decision. *Which task should I do next? This task or that one or one of the twelve other tasks that should have been done last week?*

Deadlines simplify our lives by clearly identifying what we need to do next. All we need to do is work through our list; there's no need to stop and reassess what to tackle next at every transition.

Without a clear ranking of the items on our to-do list, we have to constantly recalibrate our tasks. We spend too much time and mental horsepower deciding which item to tackle next and always feel unsure of where to turn. So many tasks deserve our attention *now* (and probably before now). Constantly having to choose what to do next make us question if we're betting on the right horse. We feel compelled to jump from one unfinished task to another, apologizing to others for delays and feeling frazzled. These redundant recalibrations are time-consuming and all too often result in errors being made.

Deadlines help us gauge our capacity

Deadlines help us gauge our capacity. They create for us a clear timeline for the next few days, weeks, and months. Deadlines give us a greater sense of what we do (and, more importantly, what we do not) have time for. We are more likely to notice bottlenecks in advance and be triggered to apply the Simplify Filter (we'll expand on this in part 3).

Ultimately, deadlines keep us focused on our three core priorities. We are more likely to say no to seemingly minor requests two weeks from now if we can plainly see it conflicts with core-priority tasks.

> Deadlines are a productivity powerhouse.

Deadlines are a productivity powerhouse. If an item is important enough to be added to your list, give it a deadline and commit to getting it done. If you're questioning whether a task is important enough to warrant a deadline, it probably shouldn't be on your list to begin with. If you don't *really* intend to do something, cross it off and move on.

The only exception, when it comes to setting deadlines, are your future priorities. This wish list doesn't require deadlines at this point. As I mentioned earlier, launching a podcast is on my list of future priorities. But I'm not committing a specific deadline to this wish-list project. Frankly, I'm not even 100 percent sure I *will* launch a podcast. When the time comes to embrace a new core priority, I will decide which of my juicy projects to promote and add any associated deadlines at that time.

Since deadlines are so important, I'm going to share even more tips. But first let's talk about consulting your MAP.

Consult

Last, we need to consult our MAP each and every day. This is *the most* important step. Our MAP stands steadfastly by our side, acting as wise counsel when we're tight on time. *Should I pivot or stay the course? Is this next task aligned to my core priority or a tempting distraction?*

We also want to update our MAP at other crucial checkpoints throughout our days: when new work comes in or when deadlines shift. We want to make these changes to our MAP in real time. We don't want to put this off until later. We may run out of time and we may not remember. If our MAP is out of date, it can no longer function at its best. The good news is that once our MAP is set up, it is easy to maintain. Updating our MAP doesn't add extra time to our day, but a complete MAP does help us use our time in the most effective way.

Ultimately, your MAP can only serve you to the extent you use it consistently. If you don't consult your MAP, you'll slip into an ineffective *winging it* approach. Or you'll gravitate back to that mishmash of lists that were retired for a good reason. If you create your MAP and then stop using it, you will have simply created a make-work project. And you don't have time for make-work projects.

As obvious as it sounds, you must consult your MAP *at least* once a day.

HOW TO SET GREAT DEADLINES

As you know, deadlines are a crucial part of our MAP. We use deadlines to rank our tasks. Deadlines are at the root of how we prioritize. Here are some valuable tips to make the most of your productivity-boosting deadlines:

Make external commitments

Do you set your morning wake-up alarm ten minutes earlier than you want to wake up? If so, what happens when that alarm goes off? Do you press snooze, knowing it's not real?

Just like these fake wake-up calls, we know self-imposed deadlines are not real. We are more likely to blow through deadlines we set on our own. We're too clever to be influenced by these squishy timelines. The best deadlines are the ones we set with someone else — such as a leader, a colleague, or a client.

Always set a deadline

The secret to achieving your goals is to attach a deadline to every task, at the precise moment you agree to doing the task. Don't wait until later to assign a deadline. That time may never come. If a task is worth doing, it is worth doing by a deadline.

Fixed deadlines are easy. We *know* we need to get our work done before a non-negotiable date, so we find a way to make it happen. The tasks without deadlines tend to be more challenging. When we know there is room to push the timeline, it is tempting to do so. But these squishy deadlines fill much of our day. For example, many meetings wrap up with no clear action items and no accountability. Sadly, such situations invite procrastination, which is always eagerly waiting to take advantage of us. Conversely, when we take charge of soft deadlines, we make an exponentially bigger impact.

I suggest you make it your personal policy to add a deadline to *every* one of your tasks. To be clear, you should do this even if (especially if) someone tells you, "It's no rush" or "Get this to me when you can." You can take matters into your own hands and be the one to suggest a date. You could say, "Okay, since it's not a rush, I'll get this to you by the thirtieth of the month." Resist the temptation to say, "I'll get this to you soon," or "Sometime next week." Instead, call out an exact date that you can add to your MAP. Don't accept a task without a deadline.

A clear deadline helps you manage their expectations and ensure there is no confusion. They might surprise you with their response, especially if they say, "I meant to say it's no rush for today, but I need it for tomorrow." Thank goodness you uncovered this true deadline in advance!

It's important to remember, though, your future priorities are an exception to this rule. You don't need to assign deadlines to these. Simply park these at the bottom of your MAP, as part of your future wish list. If and when you elevate one of these future priorities to the status of a core priority, you'll want to start integrating deadlines.

Break it down

Let's assume you agree to write a big report. It's so big that your deadline is two weeks from now, just enough time to move this mountain. But human nature tends to prevail. As much as we like to think we'll get started right away, we tend to do the work right before the deadline. Can you relate to this scenario? Are you more likely to do the work immediately after it's assigned or right before it's due? If you choose the latter, you're in good company. This approach is to be expected — after all, we're usually busy with other deadlines.

We work better with short-term deadlines. For this reason, I recommend breaking big projects down into smaller bites. Establish interim deadlines to prompt action sooner rather than later. Offer to send someone an initial draft this Friday and the final version next Friday.

Short-term deadlines are proven to boost productivity. In one study, three groups of students were asked to edit a document and circle all typos and grammatical errors. This was a long document, so all three groups were given three weeks to complete the task. Group A just had the final three-week deadline to consider. Group B, on the other hand, was given interim deadlines when they had to check in with the researchers. Group C was encouraged to set their own interim deadlines but didn't need to account to anybody.

Not surprisingly, Group B fared the best. They found the greatest number of corrections and handed their work in on time. Group A performed the worst. Not only did they find the least number of corrections, but they also handed in this assignment twelve days late.[3] Clearly, interim deadlines made a difference.

Incidentally, this is a helpful strategy when delegating work. Ask your delegatee to show you an outline or rough draft tomorrow. Check in with them and even book brief interim reviews. Don't rely solely on the final deadline. Otherwise, human nature will put the kibosh to your overall project timeline.

Renegotiate if necessary

You might be tempted to walk away without a firm deadline. Why box yourself in by setting an unnecessary completion date? What if this task takes longer than you expect? What if your time is pulled into other work?

The good news is that you can renegotiate deadlines. Sure, there are some hard, fixed deadlines. But many others are flexible. You'll gauge where you have room to negotiate and where you need to shift resources as necessary.

Of course, you'll want to renegotiate in advance. Thankfully, your MAP gives you the foresight to accurately assess your commitments, gauge your capacity, and notice the bottlenecks long before they arrive.

Everyone from time to time faces work that takes longer than expected. We do our best to set realistic deadlines, but we are often working with limited insight into what is required. We are most accurate when we estimate the work involved in micro-steps, which reinforces my advice above: break it down. Assign deadlines to each small step and you'll have a much more realistic overall timeline, one that helps you pace your work.

Overall, your clearly ranked deadline-driven MAP will keep you focused on what you need to do *now* and will help crowd control the many other tasks waiting in line.

RELEASE YOUR OLD SYSTEMS

Once you have your MAP set up (a task that takes about thirty minutes), it's time to release your old ineffective systems. You will never commit to your MAP if you have other systems lingering around. Retire those Post-it Notes. Stop flagging emails. Resist the urge to list deadlines on your calendar (even the really important deadlines you absolutely cannot forget about). Do away with reminder pop-ups. Stop drafting haphazard lists on paper and in beautiful notebooks (even if they have inspiring quotes

Workday Warrior Action: Build your MAP — Categorize, Centralize, Complete, Commit, Consult.

on the cover). Instead, add all outstanding tasks to your MAP. Your MAP will serve as your reminder. Letting go of the other memory aids may feel uncomfortable, but it is mandatory.

You must be *all in* to allow your MAP to function as it needs to. Your MAP and your tasks have a monogamous relationship. Update your MAP as new tasks come up and resist the urge to make a note here or flag an email there. If you default back to using other reminders, your MAP breaks down and no longer serves as a reliable and complete record of your work.

Categorize; Centralize; Complete; Commit; Consult: these are the five principles for building and fully utilizing your MAP, regardless of where your MAP lives. And that MAP will serve as your ultimate practical and strategic priority management tool — a tool to simplify your work and amplify your results.

Now it's time to put everything you have learned to this point into action. It's now time to build your MAP.

EXERCISE 5. RATE YOUR MAP

Is your MAP an effective priority management system? Circle the number that best applies.

MAP Principles	Low				High
Categorize: To what extent do you track your work according to major categories (core priorities; future priorities; supporting tasks; personal tasks)?	1	2	3	4	5
Centralize: To what extent do you maintain one central system to track all of your tasks, deadlines, commitments, and goals?	1	2	3	4	5
Complete: To what extent is your system one complete record of all your work, both short-term and long-term?	1	2	3	4	5
Commit: To what extent do you have a specific deadline assigned to every one of your tasks?	1	2	3	4	5
Consult: To what extent do you consult your MAP to plan each day and plan ahead?	1	2	3	4	5

YOU WILL ALWAYS HAVE A LIST

I'd like to wrap up this chapter with a liberating message: you will *always* have a list. For as long as you live, you will have tasks and activities you'll want to do. You might be groaning as you read this. Many people associate a long list with dread and overload. But I assure you — a long list is a good problem to have!

> You will always have a list.

Frankly, I think it would be sad to wake up and have nothing to do. (Actually, a brief reprieve might be a welcome relief for one or two days, but after that you may start to feel like a rudderless boat drifting in no particular direction.)

Having a list means you are growing and stretching. It means you are looking forward to new pursuits and goals. It means you are using your special gifts to help others. And we thrive when we are growing and contributing.

Stop fighting your list. Rather, lean into it. Your MAP is your strategic partner, ensuring that you are spending your precious time in the best way possible.

6

How to Plan Your Day

Make everything as simple as possible, but not simpler.
— Albert Einstein

MANY YEARS AGO, I SIGNED UP FOR A 10K RACE ALONG WITH a ten-week training program. I met with a group every Saturday for instructions and a group run. The first class was called "How to run." Frankly, I considered skipping it. After all, *I knew how to run.* I had started running when I was fourteen months old. I ran track in high school and had been a runner, on and off, for most of my life up until that point. Still, begrudgingly, I went to the class, even though I was not expecting much.

Some might say keeping your expectations low is a sure way to surpass them. While I don't usually agree with this philosophy, I certainly saw it play out during that class. I was blown away with how much I learned. For example, they showed us how to make subtle shifts in how we swung our arms and to be conscious of how high we were raising our legs with each stride. In the end, I came away from the class as a better runner. It was amazing how, by making some small changes to the way I engaged in such a simple activity, I was able to perform *so much* better.

I'd like to do the same thing with how you plan your days. I'd like to show you how to get so much more out of this simple activity. This chapter is short and sweet. But don't underestimate the power of making the most of this simple planning activity. Effective daily plans help you accumulate incremental wins — wins aligned to your core priorities. And success is mostly grounded in a series of small, cumulative wins. The way you run your day becomes how you run your life.

YOUR MAP VERSUS DAILY PLANS

We have spent a great deal of time talking about your MAP. Thus, you might question the need for a separate tool to plan each day. If so, I like the way you're thinking — simplicity is often the best solution. But we can't do away with a valuable tool, your daily plan, solely in the name of simplicity. True Workday Warriors create time leverage wherever they can. As Albert Einstein said, "Make everything as simple as possible, but not simpler."[1]

Your daily plan is an extension of your MAP.

As you know, your MAP is a complete list of all your tasks, deadlines, commitments, and goals. Think of your MAP as your mother ship. Your daily plan is like a satellite ship. Some people refer to their daily plan as a *bring forward* version of their MAP. Your daily plan is a short list of what you aim to accomplish today. Think of your daily plan as an extension of your MAP, not as a separate tool. In the same way our two hands work together, your MAP and daily plan work closely together to keep you focused on your most important work.

We build our daily plan by consulting our MAP. But our daily plan also captures new requests that need to be done *today*. Do you need to follow up on today's meeting? Add it to your daily plan. Did your leader just ask you to review a document by end of day? Add it to your daily plan. If something new needs to get done today, that item bypasses your MAP and goes right onto your daily plan.

WHY DO WE NEED A DAILY PLAN?

I don't believe I need to work too hard to convince you to plan your day. I'm guessing you're already planning each day. But let's still take a moment to identify three solid reasons why we need to plan each day.

The most important purpose of our daily plan is to help us remember to do the tasks that need to get done today. With all the moving parts we manage, it's easy for must-complete items to get lost in the shuffle despite our best intentions.

Our daily plans also keep us focused on what is most important. On any given day, there are far more activities we *could* spend our time doing. It's too easy to succumb to distraction when we are bombarded with information and requests. If we don't plan our day, we tend to get pulled and pushed around by other people and their priorities. A daily plan helps us stay focused on our core priorities, no matter how compelling an email or a link appears to be.

Finally, our daily plan helps us make good decisions about new opportunities. When new requests arrive, which happens every day, we need a simple filter to assess them. Many of these opportunities will be *good* opportunities — ones we're naturally tempted to say yes to. But it isn't always a good idea to grab at the bright shiny new object. This is where our daily plan steps in; it gives us a benchmark to use when comparing the importance of these new requests with those on our original plan. We can easily see whether tasks rank higher or lower in supporting our core priorities.

From helping us remember to focusing our attention to assessing new opportunities, a daily plan is a key tool used by Workday Warriors. It's clear we benefit from daily plans. Now let's discuss five tips to make the most of them.

Daily Plan Tip #1: Plan for Tomorrow

Let's begin by defining when the best time is to plan your day. Ironically, the best time is the day before. That's right, today's daily plan was ideally created yesterday. Similarly, the best time to plan tomorrow is today. With a solid MAP in place, this simple task should take you no more than two minutes. Keep it simple. The easier it is to plan your day, the more likely you are to build this crucial habit.

Don't wait until the morning to plan your day. This simple task doesn't need your precious morning energy — energy that would be better invested in your core priorities. You also don't want to be dwelling on outstanding tasks on your off time, when you should be relaxing and renewing your energy for tomorrow. Tomorrow may seem like it is going to be a battle, but there is something incredibly comforting in knowing you have a plan in place.

> The best time to plan tomorrow is today.

In one study, adults who spent five minutes writing about tasks they needed to complete the next day fell asleep significantly faster than those who wrote about what they had already completed.[2] The more specific their to-do lists were, the faster they fell asleep. Writing down our plan for the next day apparently helps us park our work and take comfort in the fact that we have a plan in place, regardless of what we need to tackle tomorrow.

You don't need to wait until the last possible minute, when your family is calling you to the dinner table or when your carpool friend is honking their horn outside your office door, to complete your plan for tomorrow. Rather, create tomorrow's daily plan throughout today. If you're prompted at 2:00 p.m. to work on something tomorrow morning, make a note of it on tomorrow's daily plan. Your final task of the day is to transfer over anything from today's plan to tomorrow's daily plan. Then toss today's plan in the recycle bin and give yourself a great big high-five for an amazing day.

Daily Plan Tip #2: Write it down

This may be a fairly obvious tip, but I encourage you to write down your daily plan. This is not simply a mental exercise. You don't want your daily plan bouncing around in your brain all day like a ball in a cerebral pinball machine. As soon as an *I should do that* thought pops into your mind, write it down. You don't want to rely on your memory for any tasks, as we discussed earlier. If you're going to do a task today or tomorrow, write it on today's (or tomorrow's) daily plan. If you're going to do it two days, two weeks, or two months from now, add it to your MAP.

I'm often asked whether we should literally write our daily plans with pen and paper. The answer is yes. Your daily plan can be a simple handwritten list. Sometimes I'll use a sticky note for my daily plan. Or you could even use your spiral-bound notebook — yes, the same notebook I insisted wasn't an option for your MAP. Regardless, when it comes to your daily plan, paper works. Just be sure to recycle it at the end of today. Your daily plan is not a collector's item. If today's plan still contains active tasks, transfer them to tomorrow's plan or put them on your MAP. Don't hold onto past daily plans. These create chaos you don't have time to manage.

Let me be clear: your MAP should be digitized. And if you prefer to digitize your daily plan, that also works. For example, you could highlight

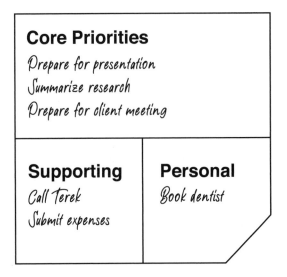

Figure 4. Sample daily planning template

the items on your MAP that you plan to tackle today. (But then you lose the joy of crossing items off your daily plan, which gives most people — and perhaps me most of all — such satisfaction every time they do it.) However, a simple handwritten list *does* work for a daily plan.

Whether you use paper or digitize your daily plan, you get bonus points for using a template. Templates are just one of many ways we can streamline a recurring process. I've experimented with many daily plan templates, and I'm showing you the version I like best (see figure 4). You can download it, among other book bonuses, at clearconceptinc.ca/WorkdayWarrior, but you can also quickly create it with two straight lines. This template highlights your core priorities, while also giving you space to list any supporting and personal tasks.

Daily Plan Tip #3: Be realistic

I've come across far too many people who have given up planning their days. These are the people whose days are so chaotic that they've lost faith in this simple tool. Too many unknowns drop in their inbox; their meetings often run late, and they are often double booked; tasks take longer than expected. All of this means their daily plan becomes more a source of guilt than of inspiration. You already know I believe daily plans are essential for even the busiest among us. But we need to keep our daily plans *realistic.*

This prompts the question: how many tasks should you list on your daily plan? Of course, there are many variables at play. How much discretionary time do you have outside of meetings? How much of your time tends to be consumed with incoming emails and other requests? How much time do each of your tasks typically require? Each of us will answer these questions slightly differently. But given these variables, I recommend aiming for the magic five: five items on your daily plan. Plus, you could add a personal task or two.

Five items may not seem like much, considering everything else you want to do each day. But you can always add more to your list if you complete the original five. On the other hand, if each task is mammoth, if your day is filled with meetings, and if you are often flooded with incoming requests, you'll want to list fewer items. You deserve to end each day feeling like the star you are. Your satisfaction at the end of each day will be closely tied to the number of items you cross off your daily plan.

On lighter days, you may be tempted to list many more items on your daily plan. But this is likely to leave you feeling distracted and frustrated. Recall, I mentioned above that I often use a sticky note for my daily plan. I intentionally use a small size — three inches by three inches— small enough to remind me *not* to list nineteen items on my daily plan.

It's good to be ambitious, but unrealistic plans create too much stress, leading to lower performance. When planning your day, always leave some buffer space. After all, many tasks take longer than expected. And new tasks will pop up. Project managers regularly double the time estimated to complete a task, and we could all benefit from this sage approach (including this author). Leave some buffer space and you'll feel much better at the end of each day.

Here's one more bonus reason to limit the items you place on your daily plan: you're less likely to overcomplicate your work. Essentially, when you place a limit on your tasks, you're more likely to streamline, scale back, and seek help for the myriad of other activities. We'll discuss this more in part 3.

> **Workday Warrior Action:** Create realistic daily plans. List your magic five. These are the top tasks you plan to complete today.

Daily Plan Tip #4: Reset as needed

Despite trying to keep your daily plan realistic, there are times when it is anything but realistic. Perhaps you were overly ambitious when you set your daily plan — I've been there. Or perhaps your colleagues and clients are sending you new requests, the kind that require your attention *now* — I've been there too.

On days like this, it's perfectly acceptable to reset your daily plan. You don't deserve to be working with an unrealistic plan, one that is bound to leave you feeling hopeless and defeated. There is absolutely nothing to be gained by dwelling in guilt and frustration over an unrealistic plan. On the contrary, we want to remain confident and hopeful. If needed, give yourself a one-minute pause to reset your daily plan and shift some tasks to other people or another time. You'll be amazed at how liberating this is in an otherwise challenging day.

Daily Plan Tip #5: Celebrate

Workday Warriors take time to celebrate what they have accomplished — and our daily plans can help us do this. Every time we cross off an item, it's as if a tiny dopamine surge adds fuel to our momentum.[3] Do you share my joy in crossing things off your list? It truly is one of life's simple pleasures. If you have ever written something down that you've already completed, just so you can cross it off, then you understand the power of celebration. I even play a little game when I'm struggling to finish a task. I claim the win, tapping into a tiny endorphin boost, and cross the task off my list — *before* I actually finish it. I know this might sound a bit like cheating, but this tiny celebration gives me the momentum I need to cross the finish line. I don't recommend using this technique often, but when I do resort to it, it reminds me how powerful celebrations are.

We also want to give ourselves a big ol' pat on the back when we finish our day and have successfully completed our daily plan. When we start our day with our magic five tasks, we are much more likely to end our day feeling good about what we accomplished. Let's not aim for perfection here. Anything over 80 percent (or four out of five items) is reason to cheer for victory. These positive emotions provide more than simply feel-good moments. Positive emotions are what keep us coming back for more. We set ourselves up for a good tomorrow when we celebrate today.

⌛

This concludes part 1. We've talked about a game-changing tool: your Main Action Plan (MAP), centred on your core priorities. As a Workday Warrior, I encourage you to rely exclusively on your MAP to track and prioritize all your work. As well, use your upgraded daily plan process to translate your MAP into daily progress. As you know, your daily plan is simply an extension of your MAP. With a solid MAP and a reliable daily planning process, your work will be forever changed, for the better, in true Workday Warrior style.

PART 2

Fortify

7

Time Barrier #2: Too Much Flexibility

What may be done at any time will be done at no time.
— Scottish proverb

Early in my career, I recall hearing a seasoned entrepreneur on the other side of the *I made it* curve describe what he valued most — flexibility. Many years of hard work had paid off, and he finally had the ability to choose what he did (or didn't do), along with when and where he worked.

I was enthralled. Flexibility seemed like the ultimate aspiration, the freedom to choose what I worked on and when.

It's tempting to think flexibility is worth aspiring to. No one looking over your shoulder. No one dictating deadlines. I admit this sounds appealing. But like many things in life, flexibility is only good in moderation. Just because something *seems* like a good thing, doesn't mean it *is* a good thing — at least not all the time.

Hold on — you're probably wondering, *What's wrong with being flexible? Aren't I supposed to drop what I'm doing to help our company's top client when they need us? Shouldn't I jump at the chance to have lunch with a friend when they're in town? Isn't it ideal to shift my work so I can attend my son's afternoon recital?*

Well, yes. And you could probably list more than a few examples of how flexibility can be beneficial. For example, savvy companies are recognizing the benefits of giving individuals the flexibility to decide whether to work in the office or virtually. In this case, flexibility grants teams and individuals the autonomy to determine what works best to meet the needs of their combined business and personal needs.

But flexibility isn't always helpful when it comes to *when* we do our work. In this chapter, I'd like to bust some myths about excessive flexibility and introduce you to a better approach to managing your time, one that is much more structured.

DO YOU VALUE FLEXIBILITY?

If you value spontaneity, I can appreciate that. For many years, I felt the same way. Like the entrepreneur I mentioned earlier, I valued the freedom I felt I had earned. I also felt that after years of hard work, I had earned the right to decide when I would do different types of work each day.

I also thought routines were for kids — they definitely seem to thrive when they have routines. The predictability gives them a sense of order and brings balance to their days. But surely, we adults don't require this strict regimen. Right?

Well, as it turns out, we too thrive with routines. There is wisdom in the saying "Everything you need to know about life, you learned in kindergarten." And I think we can all agree that kindergarten is grounded in routines.

Speaking of kindergarten, I used to love building forts back then — both outside in the snow and inside with cushions. My fellow fort-building warriors and I would work hard to create elaborate structures, designed to guard our prized possessions. Whether we were protecting snowballs or board game tokens, we would often spend more time building our respective forts than playing the game. But we were onto something: investing time upfront to fortify our boundaries is the surest way to protect what we value. Similarly, the third little piggy, the one who built a house out of bricks, knew real protection can only be guaranteed by a solid structure. This is a lesson that can be extended to our time as well.

I'll soon share how to best structure your time. I don't need to remind you that your time is constantly under attack. Your attention is your most valuable resource. So building a structure to protect your time and energy is one of the best steps you can take to prioritize what matters most.

> If you don't have enough time for your core priorities, the solution is to add more structure to your days.

If you don't have enough time for your core priorities, the solution is to add more structure to your days. Structure provides a guarantee that you will be able to fortify your schedule and protect time for what you value most. I hope you'll agree with me that this is worth giving up some flexibility.

But before we delve too far into a more structured and effective way of working (and living), let's bust some myths about flexibility.

Myth #1: Flexibility increases productivity

Flexibility often invites procrastination. As the Scottish proverb goes, "What may be done at any time will be done at no time." Nothing stalls progress more than putting off work until later. Ironically, our most wide-open days can sometimes be our *least* productive. *Why do a task now when my afternoon is wide open?* When we have too much of any resource, including our time, we are not as careful about how we use it.

Truth: Deadlines drive productivity. We are most productive when we clearly define what we'll do *and when we'll do it*.

Myth #2: Flexibility equals free time

As a busy person, you know relegating activities to your "free time" is a can't-win game. If someone cancels a meeting, you theoretically have an hour of free time. But that hour can get quickly gobbled up by any number of tasks. At best, putting tasks off to so-called free time often leads to a scramble as you struggle to fit more work into an already full schedule. Often you simply run out of time, leading to delayed timelines, lower-quality work, more stress, or all of the above. It's easy to say yes to an intriguing request, but it's so much harder to find the time to pursue that opportunity. When we don't first identify when we'll do a task, it becomes far too easy to overcommit.

Truth: The free time in which we can focus on our core priorities doesn't magically appear. We can't find time, but we can protect time. Structure helps us fortify boundaries around our core priorities.

Myth #3: Flexibility simplifies life

Imagine starting every day with a complicated puzzle. Your quest is to find a home for every piece before moving onto other things. Would you feel drained before even starting your day? This is what happens when we try to mix an abundance of tasks with unbridled flexibility.

Our daily tasks and activities are a bit like puzzle pieces. Simple puzzles, like those with a mere twenty-five pieces, are usually quick and easy to complete. But puzzles get more complicated the more pieces they have. Similarly, fitting our tasks into limited time slots gets harder and harder the more tasks we need to complete. Having to do this each and every day is infinitely more challenging. Personally, I thoroughly enjoy doing an occasional puzzle. But even avid puzzlers like me shudder at the thought of facing a must-complete, complex scheduling puzzle every morning.

Surprisingly, flexibility actually complicates life. Flexibility creates a constantly shifting schedule, one that needs to be carefully reconstructed each day. Flexibility requires us to make the same timing decisions — when to work on a project, when to meet with a colleague, when to exercise — again and again. The more decisions we have to make, the more effort we expend. Plus, we are more likely to make suboptimal decisions. Decision fatigue also quickly sets in — I'll expand on that later, in chapter 9. Making things worse, each new day's schedule needs to be shared with others when we need to coordinate efforts. The result is we spend more time sorting and less time doing. This may sound obvious but too much flexibility creates unnecessary complexity — it certainly doesn't simplify work or life.

Truth*:* A structured routine built around our core priorities simplifies our days. Routines automate the daily struggle of finding time for what we value most.

⧖

The bottom line is that excessive flexibility practically invites work overload, delayed results, procrastination, and complication. Sure, an occasional wide-open day, like those we experience when we're on vacation, can be beautifully renewing. But on a daily basis, too much flexibility, rather ironically, leaves us struggling to find enough time for our core priorities.

Think about your kitchen. Without the proper structure, spoons may be scattered, helter-skelter, in drawers and cupboards. Every time you go looking for your preferred coffee mug, it is hiding in a different location. How much time energy would you expend simply trying to execute basic tasks? Having too much flexibility is akin to having no organization in your living space. Clearly, having well-defined "homes" for our belongings simplifies life.

The same is true for our time. When we create homes in our schedule for different types of work, when we block time for what matters most before other tasks get in the way, when we lean into structure, we make the most of our time.

FREESTYLING IS FOR AMATEURS

Elite performers are incredibly talented. They achieve results that most others can't even imagine. In true warrior style, they make what they achieve look easy. But in reality, they have put a structure in place that allows them to prioritize what matters most. This is what enables them to thrive on the world stage. We don't always see this fortified structure, but it is there in the background.

Success requires more than just talent. It requires consistent focused effort. Anders Ericsson, of Florida State University, originator of the ten-thousand-hour rule, highlights this truth. As Ericsson discovered, the world's best performers refine their skills through consistent, prolonged, deliberate practice.[1] Similarly, Angela Duckworth, in her bestseller *Grit: The Power of Passion and Perseverance*,[2] describes how effort is the most important factor for achieving outstanding results. If bold goals were easy to get to, everyone would travel that journey.

But it is hard to dedicate this sustained focus with too much flexibility. A free-for-all approach leads to distraction and procrastination. Freestyling prompts us to pursue the path of least resistance — one that is rarely suitable if we want to get to our goals. Freestyling is for amateurs.

> Your routines help you establish boundaries around your core priorities so that they receive your much-deserved, consistent, and focused attention.

Note: I'm not suggesting you adopt an unyielding schedule, one you stick to with unwavering rigidity. This doesn't work. Plus, this tends to annoy everyone around you. Rather, the secret is to strike the right balance between flexibility and consistency. You do this by adding structure to your days and knowing when you're willing to flex.

Again, freestyling is for amateurs, but you're not playing at the amateur level. You are performing at an elite level. That said, if you are not doing enough to fortify your time, it's likely that you are making it harder to achieve your goals than it needs to be.

Your routines help you establish boundaries around your core priorities so they receive your much-deserved, consistent, and focused attention. Your routines help you to concentrate your efforts, something crucial if you want to achieve optimal results.

We've discussed the drawbacks of too much flexibility. Over the next few chapters, I'll showcase the benefits of routine — a productivity strategy embraced by the world's most prolific producers and soon-to-be Workday Warriors like you.

WHAT I LEARNED FROM WRITING

Before we wrap up this chapter, I'd love to share something that prompted me to stop striving for flexibility — a shift that helped me see how powerful structure could be.

Writing has been one of my core priorities for about two decades. If I was hosting a dinner party, writing could certainly make a good case for sitting at the head of the table. Practically every day, I have some sort of writing project on my list. But this list also includes many other tasks, so for many years, I was flexible about *when* I wrote.

Frankly, I thought it was good to be flexible. After all, I was still writing every day — okay, most days. I just hadn't committed to writing at a consistent time. But the truth was, when I relegated this essential task to my free time, I wasn't nearly getting enough time. And I was always worn out when I finally shifted my weary mind to writing.

Occasionally, I found it easy to start my day with writing. On those days, I would feel like a productivity rock star (a real thing in my mind). But more often, I'd be in bed beside a sleeping child working on my laptop and struggling to keep my eyes open. I pushed this core priority until after my kids' bedtime — and, frankly, after mine as well. By the time I got around to crafting something, I clearly wasn't at my best. But at least I wrote those days. There were many other days when I simply ran out of time. There were always other tasks that I let jump ahead. But this flexibility wasn't helping. I let those days run me instead of the other way around.

While I was reasonably happy to be fitting *some* writing into my packed schedule, I knew I wasn't investing enough time to achieve my writing goals. I struggled to overcome the urgent deadlines, shifting priorities, and overscheduling.

I finally acknowledged the underlying issue preventing me from writing: I was far too flexible with my time. Writing has been one of my core priorities for many years, but it sits among other priorities, ones that can easily overtake my time if I let them. For years, my writing coach, Daphne Gray-Grant, encouraged me to devote a small amount of time at the start of my day to writing, regardless of what else I needed to do that day. *"Start with your most important task, not your most urgent task."*[3]

When I finally built a morning writing routine, I brought fresh morning energy to this important task and became much more consistent. I didn't stumble upon found time; I *protected* time. I stopped indulging in flexibility, which wasn't serving me. Yes, some days I only wrote for five minutes. But other days, I wrote for much longer. Once I fortified my schedule, I started to see my results accumulate. As for the other time-sensitive tasks? I managed to fit them into the rest of the day. We are all quite good about finding time for urgent tasks. Ironically, it is the less time-sensitive tasks we struggle to find time for.

> If you are consistently short on time, the answer is to stop being so flexible.

If you're reading this book, it's because you are craving more time for what matter most to you. Ultimately, the solution is simple: the secret is to *protect* time. It's time to move away from flexibility and embrace structure — the kind of structure found in our routines.

If you are consistently short on time, the answer is to stop being so flexible. I'm about to show you how to fortify your time with a Proactive Routine. In the next few chapters, you'll learn how to best protect your prime time for your core priorities and ensure that other pursuits don't get in the way.

8

Introducing Your Proactive Routine

The key is not to prioritize what's on your schedule, but to schedule your priorities.
— Stephen R. Covey

TIME MANAGEMENT IS SERIOUS BUSINESS. SO I'D LIKE TO ASK you a very serious question. If you could pick a superpower, what would it be? Would you like to be able to fly? Hear others' thoughts? Clean your house simply by wiggling your nose? Or, like me, would you like to be able to occasionally pause time?

I vividly remember watching *Superman* as a little girl. There is a scene cemented in my memory: Lois Lane and her car get swallowed up by the ground after a massive earthquake. Superman is so distraught that he explodes into outer space and flies around the world with such force that he turns back time and saves Lois Lane's life. Countless other movies have come along since showing people frozen in time while the heroes take care of some critical work.

Watching *Superman* turn back time captivated me. I was old enough to know that this wasn't realistic, but I still thought, *I want that superpower.* Now I'm older and wiser. But I'll be honest, I still want the time-warping superpower. Granted, I'm not trying to avert a natural disaster. So I would be content to simply pause time. And only occasionally. Then, while everyone else is frozen, I would clear my list, tackle an extra project or two, watch that hot new show, and take a nap. Then I would unpause time, unfreeze everyone else. People would ask *How does she do it?* while I casually flick my hair and nonchalantly shrug my shoulders. Seriously, who wouldn't want this superpower?

It's nice to indulge in fantasy once in a while. But let's come back to reality. I believe there is a realistic approach to gaining more control over our time. Okay, maybe we can't pause time, but we can get many of the same benefits if we protect our time.

For too many years, I operated as if I could manufacture time. *Lead that project? Yes! Join that committee? Sure! Attend that event? Absolutely!* I used to believe I could do everything (and I still like this mindset). But I also believed I could do it all at the same time (a recipe for frustration and overwhelm).

My "do it all" approach worked back in the early days. Those were the days when I thought I was busy. In fact, at the time I really didn't know what truly busy looked like. But as my responsibilities grew in both my career and personal life, it became incrementally harder for me to find enough time to keep up. I hit a point where I couldn't keep throwing time at the problem. As you have undoubtedly experienced, the busier we get, the harder it is to carve out extra time. A free day or afternoon or evening doesn't magically appear.

But what if we could operate *as if* we could manufacture time? This is what the world's elite performers do. I'm talking about people across all walks of life, including the following:

- Sara Blakely, the founder of Spanx and the youngest female self-made billionaire
- Marie Forleo, prolific entrepreneur, host of MarieTV, founder of the online B-School and bestselling author
- Bob Iger, the former CEO of Disney, where he oversaw more than five times growth in their market capitalization to $257 billion
- Michelle Obama, former first lady of the United States and advocate for poverty awareness, education, nutrition, physical activity, and healthy eating
- David Suzuki, academic, broadcaster, and environmental activist
- Malala Yousafzai, the youngest Nobel Peace Prize winner (at seventeen) and an education activist

These people (and many other thoroughly impressive people) are still working with the same time constraints as you and me. Yet they appear as though they can warp time. Despite working with the same twenty-four hours a day the rest of us have, they have yielded out-of-this-world results.

What exactly are they doing differently? I've been exploring this question for two decades. How do these incredibly successful people fit so much into their days? The secret is rooted in their routines — routines built around their core priorities.[1]

> Routines are the secret of the world's most productive people.

Routines are the secret of Workday Warriors.

Routines are the secret of the world's most productive people.

Routines are their superpower. And they can be your superpower too.

WHAT IS A PROACTIVE ROUTINE?

I'd now like to introduce you to the second Workday Warrior tool: your Proactive Routine. A customized plan for your week, it is built around what you deem to be most essential — from passion projects at work to your most important life goals. This tool complements your MAP by protecting time for what you value most. It compensates for the drawbacks of excessive flexibility and has the power to transform your days.

> A Proactive Routine helps you do the right work at the right time with the right mindset.

Routines give our core priorities the equivalent of a first-round draft pick when it comes to our precious time — they give our core priorities exclusive access to the best time slots. Routines eliminate the frustration of running out of time for our important goals. Routines erase the stress of not knowing when we'll find the time. Routines mitigate last-minute scrambles and dampen the feeling that there is never enough time. Routines help us use our most precious resource, our time, in the most effective way.

Think of your Proactive Routine as a plan you will adhere to most of the time. Yes, there will be some exceptions, but for the most part, your Proactive Routine will serve as a compass to direct your attention.

MALIKA'S PROACTIVE ROUTINE

Malika is a hospital executive, overseeing resource development. In our first coaching session, Malika described her typical day: constantly racing between meetings while fielding questions from her team. She said she never had enough time to do her own focused work. In that first session, we built Malika's MAP, grounded in her three core priorities: championing a $100 million capital campaign; nurturing key hospital donors; and securing government grants. In our second session, we built her Proactive Routine.

We began by making sure Malika was paying herself first. Malika was willing to try blocking the first two hours of her workday, 8:00 a.m. until 10:00 a.m., for independent work on her core priorities. Also, she estimated she needed approximately twenty hours a week for meetings with key government partners and key donors related to the large capital campaign and other fundraising. Malika blocked off from 10:00 a.m. until 5:00 p.m. for these meetings, which gave her enough flexibility to work around the most popular meeting time slots, while also protecting time for a lunch break and some supporting tasks in between meetings. She had to carefully manage her meeting time to ensure these meetings didn't gobble up more than their twenty-hour allotment. I'll share some of the same strategies Malika used in part 3.

Malika found her energy dipped in the afternoon, and she was willing to take a break at 3:00 p.m. — something she rarely did before we built her Proactive Routine. She paired this break with a walk, oftentimes with a colleague. Sometimes they talked about work. Other times, they simply connected. Regardless, Malika soon started treating this mid-afternoon walk as a non-negotiable. Sure, she was willing to shift the time to accommodate meetings, but she benefitted so much from the connection and mental clearing that she became reluctant to give up this time completely.

Malika then focused the rest of the workday, until 5:30 p.m., on meeting follow-ups and other supporting tasks. This allowed her to wrap up her workday at a reasonable time. Before we started working together, Malika often found herself at the office long after everyone else had left for the day. But she was tired of sacrificing time with her family and keen to try something new. Her newly crafted routine included two consistent days when she worked from home: Mondays and Fridays. The predictability of this routine allowed her to plan for her home and in-office days and reclaim some personal time otherwise spent commuting.

Malika felt like the Proactive Routine we crafted around her goals was a stretch goal, and she agreed that she would need to fortify this routine to make sure others didn't broach its boundaries. But she was up for the challenge.

We met one month later. Malika described that it took about two weeks to re-align her meetings so that they fit with this new structure, which is on par with what most people experience. By the third week, she was able to align her days with her Proactive Routine about 80 percent of the time. Then, in the fourth week, the one that wrapped up just before our final coaching session, Malika enthusiastically shared that she was able to follow her Proactive Routine more than 90 percent of the time. This included consistently being home by 6:00 p.m. to enjoy dinner with her family every day that week.

Malika was thrilled. This new Proactive Routine (see figure 5) gave her time to focus on her work, time to attend key meetings, time to support her team, and time for supporting tasks. As well, her Proactive Routine fortified her boundaries between her work and her personal life, boundaries that had been blurred for far too long. Malika was able to enjoy crucial recovery time in her evenings and weekends, and she only saw this getting better. Malika was a true convert — she declared that her routine helped her rekindle her love for her work and the life she had designed. She was so energized that she joined an adult soccer league on Tuesday nights, reclaiming some time to play her favourite sport which she hadn't done in years.

> Our Proactive Routines empower us to curate ideal days.

This is just one example of a Proactive Routine. Your plan will look different as it will be customized around your goals and core priorities. Plus, you will need to remain flexible to adjust your routine occasionally. But overall, your Proactive Routine will serve as a compass, guiding you to focus on the optimal use of your time. This is a lesson I learned over two decades ago, when I was a management consultant.

Back in my consulting days, my colleagues and I used to build a framework for our final presentation on the first day of each client engagement. Then we would focus on filling in the array of missing pieces while developing the project. This strategic concept can be applied to our days as well. When we start with the end in mind, we design a plan for the most optimal use of our time. Our Proactive Routines empower us to curate ideal days.

	Monday (Virtual)	Tuesday (Office)	Wednesday (Office)	Thursday (Office)	Friday (Virtual)	Saturday	Sunday
	Sleep						
6:30–7:00	Exercise & Morning Routine					Exercise & Morning Routine	
7:00–7:30							
7:30–8:00		Commute					
8:00–8:30	Focus Work: Core Priorities						
8:30–9:00							
9:00–9:30						Personal Projects	
9:30–10:00							
10:00–10:30	Donor Meetings & Supporting Tasks						
10:30–11:00							
11:00–11:30							
11:30–12:00							
12:00–12:30	Lunch Break / Donor Meetings					Family	
12:30–1:00							
1:00–1:30	Donor Meetings & Supporting Tasks	1:1 Meetings with Team	Donor Meetings & Supporting Tasks				
1:30–2:00							
2:00–2:30							
2:30–3:00							
3:00–3:30	Power Walk						
3:30–4:00	Donor Meetings & Supporting Tasks						
4:00–4:30							
4:30–5:00							
5:00–5:30	Meeting Follow-up & Supporting Tasks						
5:30–6:00		Commute					
6:00–6:30	Meal Prep & Family Dinner						
6:30–7:00							
7:00–7:30	Soccer					Social	
7:30–8:00							
8:00–8:30							
8:30–9:00							
9:00–9:30							
9:30–10:00							
10:00–10:30	Disconnect & Bedtime Routine						
10:30pm	Sleep						

Figure 5. Malika's Proactive Routine

WHY ROUTINES WORK

Ultimately, your Proactive Routine helps you do the right work at the right time with the right mindset. Let's dive a little deeper into these concepts. After all, you may be wondering if routines really make that much of a difference. The answer is a clear yes, but I know you will need more convincing if you're going to change how you run your days. So, let me describe these reasons in more detail.

The right work

There are endless ways in which we can spend our time. The more skilled and experienced we are, the more choices we have. So, it's understandable that this abundance of choice prompts many of us to say yes to more than we should. Yet, you know how this plays out — an excess of commitments leaves us feeling overloaded, frustrated, and stressed. As you've likely learned the hard way, trying to do it all doesn't lead to ideal days or optimal results.

As we established in part 1, we won't go far if we are pulled in too many directions. We need to be selective about the paths we travel. We can't allow ourselves to chase too many goals at the same time.

Ultimately, routines help us create beautiful congruence between the way we want to spend our time and the way we are spending our time. Routines help us prioritize our most important goals — our core priorities — while managing our commitments to other people and self-regulating the tendency to want to do it all. Now. Routines allow us to be proactive about how we run our day, protecting time for our core priorities before other requests get in the way.

We can't get *everything* done. But we can focus on the right work, with the help of our Proactive Routine.

The right time

We tend to emphasize *what* to do much more than *when* to do it. But the reality is that timing matters. It matters a lot. How we spend our days is how we spend our lives. Ultimately, what we accomplish in our career, or this year, or this week boils down to how we spend our time each day. The minutes accumulate like compound interest. Our results are merely a reflection of how we spend our time from one day to the next.

Routines help us to live our life by design, with clear boundaries built around our most important work and well-being goals — boundaries that are all too often ill-defined or poorly defended. This clearly defined structure gives us the room for productive days and beautiful lives, grounded in a much better feeling of control.

When we take control over how we spend our time, we create the space to focus on what matters most. We *can* carve out time for our work before other things get in the way. We simply need to block time and fortify our calendar, to make sure we protect time for what we value, just like we do when we book meetings with others. When we proactively block time for ourselves, other people magically start to work around our schedule. This protected time helps mitigate the temptation to overcommit ourselves. Routines help us prioritize the work we most value and protect time accordingly. As personal excellence guru and bestselling author, Stephen R. Covey so wisely advised, "The key is not to prioritize what's on your schedule, but to schedule your priorities."[2]

> Our Proactive Routine gives us predictability — and our brains like predictability.

The right mindset

Our Proactive Routine gives us predictability — and our brains like predictability. Routines are like old friends whom we can always rely on: the people we turn to during tumultuous times, the ones who help us feel grounded and calm. Conversely, our brains view uncertainty as a threat.[3] Uncertainty is linked to stress and anxiety. Uncertainty makes us feel out of control and puts us on chronic high alert.

Your work likely presents you with one challenge after another. Your personal life, no doubt, does the same. All are sources of stress. And then there are other big-picture stressors — the pandemic, war, climate change, the economy. With so much out of our control, focusing on what you can control is an important way of maintaining mental health. A sense of control is one of the things we crave most in our work and our lives. No, we can't control every aspect of our days, but increasing what we *can* control is empowering. The simple act of doing what we say we're going to do builds our confidence to tackle bigger goals and step into our greatness.

Routines make us feel grounded; they keep us from feeling like our day is a hurricane, tossing us here and there. Routines give us a sense of calm in the middle of everything swirling around us. Routines allow us to run our days, instead of having our days run us.

Ultimately, routines help us feel less stressed, more in control, and ultimately more productive. Routines also enable us to adopt a mindset of success. Once you embrace the power of routine, you'll wonder why you didn't do it sooner. Frankly, I'm surprised this concept isn't taught more consistently across schools and organizations.

BUT ROUTINES DON'T WORK FOR ME!

You might be thinking: *Ann, this is a great theory, but routines don't work for me.* If so, you're not alone. I felt the same many years ago. People often believe they don't have enough control over their time. I often hear them say, "But I don't control my time." Or "Too many other people influence my schedule."

If you can relate to this, let me assure you I am not advising you to go to battle with your colleagues. We all need to remain collaborative in the team-based sport called work. But teamwork does not need to be at odds with our routines. We can be highly collaborative and integrate routines into our days. As a bonus, this is probably easier to do than you might think. You likely have more control over your time than you believe.

Several years ago, I was presenting this concept to a group of senior banking executives who were all feeling overwhelmed by jam-packed days. They were in back-to-back meetings and struggling to keep up with email and other work outside of these meetings. I was recommending they block time for their independent work and was receiving a lot of *That isn't possible* pushback. Then one executive spoke up and shared his secret. He described how he blocked off from 12:00 p.m. until 2:00 p.m. every day to eat lunch and clear his email. This helped him shrink his inbox, leaving fewer than ten messages in total. His equally busy colleagues were both shocked and skeptical. They couldn't believe this was possible, but the evidence was there within their peer group. He not only demonstrated that it was possible to protect some time during the day, but he also demonstrated that you could do so while performing at a high level. His department was thriving. Once his colleagues realized it was a possibility, many of them started adopting, and benefitting from, similar routines.

Another client, Vincent, was an executive assistant supporting two busy partners at a global law firm. An outsider might think that he would have little control over his schedule in this working arrangement. But, in truth, he had established systems that helped both him and the lawyers he supported.

Vincent met with each partner at a consistent time each morning to help them plan their day (and, consequently, plan his day accordingly). One meeting took place from 10:00 a.m. until 10:15 a.m. and the other from 11:00 a.m. until 11:15 a.m. Vincent arrived at the office at 7:30 a.m. and let his colleagues know these early morning hours were his preferred window for his focused work. They all agreed that the 7:30 a.m. to 10:00 a.m. time slot was an "emergency only" zone when it came to requests. Other than performing a quick "scan for urgency" through his inbox, Vincent didn't focus on email during this period. Instead, he dedicated this quiet time, when his energy was at its best, to tackle bigger projects. He declared that this was the most productive time of his day.

Not only did Vincent have a plan for the start of the day, he also had an end-of-day routine. He wrapped up his work at 4:30 p.m. every day, long before the partners peeled away from their desks many hours later. He asked the partners to send him any new work by 3:00 p.m. if it needed to be completed that day. Of course, they continued to send work after 3:00 p.m. — and all through the evening — but they all agreed that requests coming in after 3:00 p.m. could be completed the following day (unless an urgent need arose). Yes, there were exceptions, and Vincent, of course, was flexible as the need arose. Sometimes he worked late, and sometimes he jumped on urgent tasks first thing in the morning. But those occasions were exceptions. Most of the time (Vincent estimates 80 percent), his days aligned to these routine parameters.

Vincent's routine didn't just benefit him. The partners found his routines helped *them* structure their days and be more productive. They started to protect their own focus time in the morning to tackle big projects. They spent more time planning ahead, which led to fewer last-minute scrambles. They also started to define more consistent evening boundaries to identify clear personal time.

WE CAN STILL BE FLEXIBLE *AS NEEDED*

I'd like to be clear I'm not suggesting our routines be set in stone. We definitely need to adjust our routines from time to time. If the president of your company calls for a meeting at 12:00 p.m., I don't suggest you say, "I'm sorry — this is when I take my lunch break." Clearly, you can swap activities as needed.

There are many valid justifications for shifting our routines. Projects change. Budgets change. Schedules change. But no one would point to these as reasons not to plan! Instead, we want to plan for what we can control so we're better prepared for what we can't control. Upfront planning keeps us focused and effective. A structured plan helps us decide how to best adjust and evolve, as needed.

Your routine can (and should) be flexible. But it is truly remarkable how the rest of the world can fall in line with your routine once you establish your boundaries. You'll be amazed at how often the president (among others) catches herself first. "Oh wait — I remember you do your power walks at noon. How about we chat at 1:00 p.m. instead?"

ROUTINES SIMPLIFY OUR DAYS

Let's face it, work can be hard. Anything that simplifies the workday is welcome. A routine does just that. Routines quickly become self-sustaining, which makes our lives easier. Routines let us experience more flow, with less reliance on discipline or willpower.

Managing any constrained resource needs a plan. If your time is constrained, you will benefit from this strategic plan around how you fill your days. In the next chapter, we'll dive deeper into the magic of routines and describe how routines allow us to tap into one of the most powerful forces shaping our lives: habits.

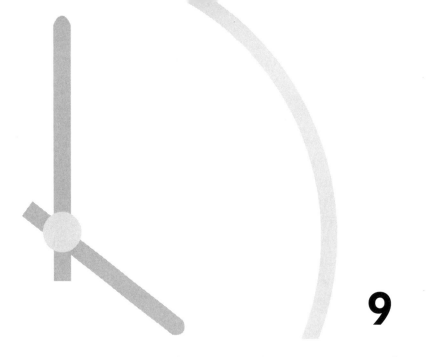

9

Habits Drive Results

Small daily improvements over time
create stunning results.
— Robin Sharma

AT MY TENTH BIRTHDAY PARTY, MY MOM HIRED A BUDDING
magician, one of her grade eight students, to perform. This was a big deal
at the time — children's birthday parties were much simpler than they
are today.

But I had a magician, so I felt I was living large. At the time, I dreamed
of being a magician. I studied magicians any time I got the chance. I wasn't
content to simply enjoy their performance. I wanted to know what was going
on behind the scenes.

Making sense of the seemingly impossible magical feats they performed wasn't easy. This was in the days before Google and YouTube, so my

imagination and library books with poorly explained "how to" instructions had to fill the gaps. But I pored over any materials I could find. I wanted to know *how* the magic tricks worked.

I'm guessing you like to know how things work as well. So, if I'm going to convince you to embrace routines, I need to pull back the curtain and show you exactly how the magic behind routines works.

In this and the next two chapters, I'll summarize three research-backed principles that highlight why routines are much more than smoke and mirrors. Let's begin by discussing how routines build habits, which is essential, because these habits help us create the results we crave at work and in life.

OVERCOMING THE KNOWING/DOING GAP

In many cases, the biggest barrier to achieving increased productivity — and many other goals — is the disconnect between knowing and doing. We may know an activity is good for us, but that doesn't mean we consistently *do* it. We all know exercise is good for us. But we also know there are many people who don't have regular exercise habits.

By now you know what your core priorities are, but knowing what you should spend your focus time on doesn't mean that you actually spend that time on them. This time isn't always easy to find. I'm guessing the main reason you're reading this book is to learn how to find more time for what matters most, both personally and professionally.

The good news is our routines help us protect this time by building deliberate habits for the work on our core priorities. And these habits drive the results we want. Habits help us to overcome our resistance to change. Habits provide our goals with the scaffolding they need. And habits compensate for our unreliable willpower. I'll expand on these benefits now to stress why we need deliberate routines to build positive habits.

Change is hard

Change is hard at first. You may have experienced unease if your boss has ever added a mystery meeting to your schedule. Your immediate thought (plus practically every other thought between now and the meeting) may be a variation of *Oh no — what's wrong?*

As mentioned in chapter 8, we much prefer certainty and the predictability of what comes next. Certainty feels safe. Certainty feels comfortable. So our brains naturally seek out patterns to better predict what comes next. Neuroscientists call our brains "prediction machines." This is why we often like an idea the more times we hear it. It's also why we naturally repeat certain activities and gravitate toward habits.

Change is hard, partly *because* of its newness. But over time, as we repeat a new activity, we become more comfortable with it. As we settle into a new routine, that routine becomes part of our life; that routine becomes a habit. Routines allow us to overcome one of the biggest barriers preventing us from getting to where we want to go: our reluctance to change. Once our routines are firmly established, we naturally cozy into their predictability, like a warm cuddly blanket on a stormy night.

Goals don't guarantee success

This might sound harsh, but having goals, even simple ones, doesn't guarantee you'll achieve them. James Clear, author of the bestselling book *Atomic Habits: An Easy and Proven Way to Build Good Habits and Break Bad Ones*, said, "Winners and losers have the same goal."[1] Every Olympian wants to win the gold medal. Every interviewee wants to get the job offer. Every applicant wants to be accepted into the elite school.

> Routines build habits and habits create results.

I'm not suggesting we do away with goals. Goals are still necessary. They inspire us, motivate us, and keep us focused. But goals alone are not enough to create the results we want. Goals merely describe where we want to go — our final destination, our ideal outcome. But we won't reach our goals unless we consistently do what it takes to get there.

Clearly, our goals need support systems to bring them alive. Routines give our goals this crucial support by prompting us to repeat the activities and form the habits needed to achieve our goals. Routines build habits and habits create results.

Willpower is unreliable

You may be familiar with the famous marshmallow study of delayed gratification led by Walter Mischel of Stanford University. Researchers conducted a test with a group of children, in which they were given marshmallows and told that if they waited to eat them they would receive a reward. Years later, when researchers followed up with the children who resisted eating the tempting marshmallows, they were found to be more successful than the children who indulged.[2] Willpower was found to be a better predictor of success than IQ.

Willpower can help us to do incredible things. For this reason, willpower has received a lot of attention over the years. It's tempting to think if we work hard enough and resist temptation, we'll achieve our goals. The above study has received some mixed reviews and obviously many factors are at play when we make a decision — especially a childhood decision involving marshmallows. But we know that resisting distractions is an important part of achieving our goals.

But willpower is not something we want to rely on. Willpower is like a muscle that tires with use. Imagine walking into your home after a long run, your leg muscles aching for a rest. If a friend calls and suggests going for a walk, you'll likely say, "Sorry, I'm exhausted." Like our muscles, our willpower fatigues with use. As great as it is, it's a limited resource. We only get so much each day. After we've taxed our willpower "muscle," we need time to recover and replenish our reserves. Your gas gauge may read full at the start of the day, but you can only go so far before you hit empty. Your daily supply of willpower (and motivation) may start strong but quickly fades.

The busier and more stressful our days are, the quicker we burn through our willpower reserves. These are the days I find it impossible to resist the chips if my hubby opens them at 10:00 p.m. My best intentions about healthy eating are tossed aside late at night. When my willpower reserves are low, I succumb to what my colleague and well-being coach Marla Warner calls the "what the heck" effect.

Willpower is not consistently reliable. So, we can't expect to apply willpower to everything we want to do in a day. Relying on willpower alone puts us at a disadvantage. Everything feels more difficult. Everything takes longer. Nothing flows easily.

Yes, willpower can be exactly what we need to push through near the end of a meaningful challenge. But we don't want to squander our limited willpower on repetitive decisions or rely on it solely to reach our goals. We want to save our willpower, like any precious resource, for when we need it most.

⧗

We've talked about what doesn't work: relying on goals alone or willpower exclusively. Rather, we want to build deliberate habits. When we perform a new task, a neural pathway is formed in our brain. If we perform that task enough times, we no longer have to think about how something's done. The action becomes automatic.[3] At this point, a habit has been formed, and it serves as an effective, reliable, and energy-conserving way to achieve our goals. As we've already discussed, our routines build deliberate habits around our core priorities. But we haven't yet discussed precisely *why* habits are so powerful. Let's do that now.

WHY ARE HABITS POWERFUL?

I'm sure you've heard the common expression that we are creatures of habit. A study led by Duke University researchers found that 40 percent of the actions we perform each day are driven by habits rather than the result of decisions.[4] Tony Schwartz, CEO of the Energy Project, highlights research estimating that up to 95 percent of our behaviours are driven by habits.[5]

Out of habit, we brush our teeth, regardless of how tired we are at the end of the day. Habits compel us to eat the same thing for breakfast, travel the same route to work, and wear the same six articles of clothing over and over again, forgoing the other ninety-four things hanging in our closet.

It's clear we rely on habits extensively throughout our day. But why, exactly, are habits something we naturally gravitate toward? Why are habits so powerful? Let's pull back the magic curtain. I'll now describe why habits consume less energy and how habits automate decisions.

Habits consume less energy

Leaning on habits consumes less energy than does relying on discipline or willpower. Following habits is like skiing in well-established cross-country tracks, which is *so* much easier than carving out a new path in fresh snow.

When we are first learning a new skill, like how to swing a tennis racket, our working memory is busy figuring out the complicated sequence. But as we repeat the steps, our brain builds up neural pathways to support these steps — much like those skiing tracks. The more times we pass through the tracks, the deeper the grooves. Whether you're swinging a golf club or facilitating a meeting, activities become easier over time as our neural pathways become more established.

Habits enable us to do activities automatically. Once we fully learn a skill, we can complete it without consciously thinking about it. Leadership expert and bestselling author Robin Sharma refers to this as the automaticity point in his book, *The World-Changer's Manifesto.*[6] When we hit this point, we free up precious cognitive resources, which allows us to both think and perform at a higher level.

> Habits enable us to do activities automatically.

I'm sure you see this automaticity in many aspects of your life. Professional athletes at the top of their games practise basic skills over and over again to achieve automaticity. Experts overlearn their subject so that they can handle practically any situation almost automatically. This allows them to focus on the details, the nuances that set them apart, and allows them to perform at elite levels.

Once we learn something in depth, we can be more fluid and flexible. We can use our knowledge to adjust to each unique situation. The more robust your routines are, the better you'll be able to navigate exceptions. This is what well-established habits enable you to do — and do so almost effortlessly.

Habits overcome decision fatigue

Habits allow us to overcome decision fatigue. Researchers estimate that our unconscious brains gather eleven billion bits of information every second. Yet, our conscious brain can only process fifty bits of information at a time.

It's no surprise our neural circuits are overloaded — this is particularly true on busy days and during stressful times.

On top of this, we are bombarded with an excess of decisions every single day. It's estimated that adults make thirty-five thousand semi-conscious decisions each day.[7] (Children make an estimated three thousand decisions every day.) According to researchers at Cornell University, 226.7 of these decisions are about food alone![8] (I'm not sure where the 0.7 comes from — should I eat part of this grape? But let's move on.) And as busy people know all too well, as our careers expand, so do our choices.

Some of these decisions are big decisions and others are minor, like Should I wear blue socks or black socks today? Should I respond to this text now or later? But a select few decisions are pivotal: Should I approve this product launch? Should I take a hard stance in this negotiation?

The point is that we face exponentially more decisions every day than we can effectively navigate. Not accounting for time sleeping, we make slightly more than two thousand decisions an hour. This translates into one decision roughly every two seconds. Every one of these decisions depletes our mental resources to some degree.

Habits automate decisions

Decisions consume energy. A lot of energy. We need to compare options, weigh the pros and cons, consider possible outcomes, consult with others, and maintain our focus. We also need to make several choices as we work through the avalanche of information available to us through a few simple online searches. Is the new info useful? Does it relate to something already being considered or does it suggest a new option? If so, is this alternative worth looking at? The list goes on. We might think we want a lot of choice, but deciding requires time and mental effort. To make matters worse, if we do end up choosing from an abundance of options, we tend to be less satisfied with our ultimate choice. The more time we spend comparing our options, the greater our expectations. After making a choice, we're left with lingering doubts about whether we made the best choice. If we don't feel we made the best choice, we experience anxiety, regret, and self-blame.

Decisions also require us to forgo one desirable choice for another. Many people encounter the difficult decision about what to work on next on a daily basis. There are so many pressing tasks vying for their attention. It's no surprise they feel mentally tired at the end of a day filled with decisions! They have decision fatigue.

Not all decisions are equal, of course. The more important the decisions are, the more time and effort we invest in them — all of this depletes our cognitive resources. This problem is especially the case with a new job, a high-risk project, a challenging conversation, or a tough negotiation. Not surprisingly, we hit our decision threshold sooner on stressful days.

At the same time, our brain is primed to conserve energy, so it is more likely to avoid the work required to make a decision when it is mentally exhausted. Every time we face a decision, we are more likely to procrastinate. And the more choice we have, the less likely we are to make a decision and act. Since this is so common, there is an actual term for this: decisional procrastination.

In the most famous study of decision fatigue, the Israeli parole board was found to make worse decisions as the day went on. Jonathan Levav, of Stanford University, and Shai Danziger, of Ben-Gurion University, reviewed 1,112 decisions made by Israeli judges over ten months to determine whether decisions to grant parole showed a clear decline as the day went on.[9] Around 9:00 a.m., prisoners had roughly a 70 percent chance of being granted parole. By mid-afternoon, their chances of being granted parole dropped to roughly 10 percent. As the number of decisions they had to make accumulated, the judges became more and more inclined to avoid making a perceived risky decision. They were more likely to preserve the status quo and not grant parole.

This study, which gained widespread attention, shows the stark contrast between what we expect — consistent, objective, and impartial decisions — and what played out — decisions significantly affected by an unrelated factor: time of day. This study makes it clear that the quality of our decisions and, by extension, our work, does not remain consistent throughout the day.

All of this discussion about decision fatigue highlights the importance of eliminating decisions, where we can. Our routines do just that. Our routines eliminate the countless *What should I work on next?* decisions that can quickly contribute to fatigue. Routines also help us make better decisions about how we use our time. Routines help us overcome decision avoidance, decision procrastination, and the making of quick but subpar decisions.

Overall, the habits reinforced through our routines help us mitigate the drain of decision fatigue. Routines automate our decisions.

⧗

Decisions don't just consume energy; they also require us to exert willpower. And willpower, as discussed earlier, is limited. The more we resist certain desires, the more we deplete the willpower we could use for future endeavours. A study involving freshly baked chocolate chip cookies demonstrate this tendency.

Psychologist Roy F. Baumeister, author of the bestselling book *Willpower*,[10] and colleagues tested this willpower depletion. They told study participants that they were going to measure how well the participants tasted certain foods and thus they were asked not to eat for three hours before coming to the lab. As you can imagine, participants arrived at the lab hungry.

Baumeister and his colleagues were not, in fact, interested in the participants' ability to taste; the researchers were really measuring the effects of resisting a desire, which taxes willpower.[11] When participants arrived at the lab, they were greeted by the smell of freshly baked cookies. Then they were asked to sit in a room in front of a table laden with these hot, tempting chocolate chip cookies. Participants were instructed to resist eating the cookies and instead eat the radishes that were also on the table. (Participants were told the cookies were for another group — even Baumeister admitted this was a tad mean.) For the sake of comparison, the researchers included two other groups: one was allowed to eat the cookies and another control group had no food to choose from — they simply sat at an empty table for the same length of time as the others.

Then, and this was the interesting part of the study, participants were asked to work on geometry puzzles. They were asked to trace geometric figures without retracing any lines or lifting their pencils. Unbeknownst to them, these puzzles were unsolvable. The participants were told they would be judged on whether they completed the tasks and not on the number of attempts or how long it took them. If they wanted to give up, they could ring a bell.

The question was, How long would they persist before declaring defeat? Unfortunately, it continued to be a subpar day for the radish group. They made far fewer attempts and gave up much sooner, after 8.35 minutes, than those who ate the cookies right away. They invested less than half the time on the puzzles compared with the chocolate-indulging group (18.9 minutes) and the no-food control group (20.86 minutes). The radish group had depleted their willpower when they resisted the cookies and had less willpower remaining to apply to the difficult puzzles.

It's easy to see how this lesson translates to our work and why we're more likely to procrastinate when we are tired. We can overcome this natural human tendency by leaning into routines that build habits around our goals. Our routines eliminate the need to make decisions about the timing of our work — decisions that make demanding roles even more difficult.

This is just one example of over one thousand studies showing the effect of seemingly unrelated decisions on future decisions. Resisting a desire drains future willpower reserves and leads to decision fatigue. When it comes to self-control, we draw from a single well.

We think the effect of deciding what to eat for breakfast only affects this single meal. But it also affects the decisions we make at work. Every decision we make reduces our daily decision-making capacity, as well as the mental reserves we need to tackle challenging tasks.

Similarly, the more decisions we make, the less self-control we have. Merely making decisions, even relatively small decisions, taxes our executive resources. And this degradation shows up in seemingly unrelated activities. The more decisions we make in the first half of our day, the less decision capacity we have for the last half of our day. Savvy executives, who know they have several important decisions to make each day, avoid getting bogged down by insignificant decisions or decisions that can be made by someone else. They delegate and move on.

How many decisions?

You are probably wondering how many decisions you can *effectively* expect to make each day. Of course, many factors come into play to answer this question, and we likely all have better days than others. Some factors, such as stress and complexity burn through our decision reserve faster than others. As psychologist Barry Schwartz says, "The more complicated a decision is, the more it wears you out."[12]

Regardless, decision fatigue is practically inevitable given the volume of choices we encounter each day. Once we pass our decision threshold, we begin making subpar decisions, such as

- going along with someone else's decision, even if our gut tells us it's wrong;
- defaulting to any decision just so we don't have to think about it anymore;
- making an impulsive decision and choosing something we wouldn't normally choose. (Incidentally, this is why those last-minute cash register purchases are so tempting at the grocery store. We're fatigued after making countless decisions while walking through the store.);
- spending far more time on a simple decision than we need to because we don't have the mental bandwidth to process it efficiently;
- procrastinating on making a decision;
- delegating the decision to someone else, which isn't an issue when they are more than capable of assuming responsibility or when any option works. But it is a concern when decision fatigue prompts us to abdicate important decisions;
- succumbing to distractions when we know they pull us away from our core priorities; and
- choosing simple over complex tasks because we don't have the energy to dive into bigger, more important work.

Making matters worse, decision fatigue is closely related to overall mental fatigue. When we are mentally exhausted, even simple steps feel as though they require more effort than we can muster.

- Challenges feel more challenging.
- It's harder to plan.
- We find it hard to focus, and we are more susceptible to distractions.
- It's harder to process information and remember information we just heard. ("I'm sorry, can you please tell me your name again?")
- It feels like our days run us instead of the other way around.
- We feel physically fatigued. This is why it is hard at the end of a tiring day to push ourselves up off the couch, resisting the Netflix prompt to watch another episode.

ROUTINES BUILD HABITS

President Barack Obama recognized the drain of excessive decisions. In an interview with acclaimed author Michael Lewis, Obama said, "I'm trying to pare down decisions. I don't want to make decisions about what I'm eating or wearing. Because I have too many other decisions to make." [13]

Obama went on to share that he ate the same thing for breakfast every day and wore only gray or blue suits. Similarly, Mark Zuckerberg consistently wears a gray T-shirt, and Steve Jobs streamlined his wardrobe to black turtlenecks and jeans in an effort to simplify. If you prefer more variety, you could do what one of my executive clients does. She lines up her suits, much like you would see on a conveyor belt, and simply wears them in order. Or you could lay out your clothes the night before to avoid tapping into precious morning energy. All of these approaches eliminate decisions and preserve cognitive resources.

Whether you're making a decision about what you wear, what you eat, or how you work, we can all take inspiration from these examples. The more

The more decisions we automate through routines, the easier our days become.

we routinize our day, the more capacity we free up for big thinking, big action, and big results.

To make the most of our finite decision-making capacity, we need to closely monitor where we are investing cognitive resources. If we spend too much time on insignificant decisions, we have less energy for the decisions that actually matter. The simple solution is to automate or eliminate low-value and unnecessary decisions. We don't want to squander our limited supply of decisions.

Thankfully, our brains created shortcuts to process this vast array of decisions and conserve energy. We find patterns. We establish habits. We create routines.

Our habits and the routines that support them help us to eliminate decisions. Our routines, built around deliberate habits, allow us to fortify the actions we know we need to do to focus on our core priorities.

Our routines, built around deliberate habits, help us to pare down our decisions for when we need them most. Routines lower our activation threshold by eliminating the need for us to make unnecessary decisions. The more decisions we automate through routines, the easier our days become.

As Verne Harnish, founder of Entrepreneurs' Organization, wisely stated, "Success equals the sum total of all the decisions one makes."[14] But this doesn't mean having to struggle through the same decisions over and over again. Our routines help to automate key decisions by fortifying boundaries around our core priorities.

James Clear also talks about lead measures in *Atomic Habits*. As Clear points out, "Your net worth is a lagging measure of your financial habits. Your weight is a lagging measure of your eating habits. Your knowledge is a lagging measure of your learning habits."[15]

To create the results we want, we need to focus on our lead measures — our habits. Habits shape our lives by prompting us to do the work to create the results we crave. Our results are merely the product of our habits.

⧖

As is clear from the examples above, habits are incredibly powerful. And as we discussed, our daily routines allow us to tap into the power of habits. Every Workday Warrior builds routines around their deliberate habits to get the results they want. This isn't a New-Age secret. We've known about the value of habits for a very long time. As seventeenth-century poet John Dryden said, "We first make our habits, and then our habits make us." Going back further, to the fourth century BCE, Aristotle said, "We are what we repeatedly do. Excellence then, is not an act, but a habit."

Routine Principle #1: Routines build habits to generate the results we want.

We are creatures of habits. Habits consume less energy than discipline and willpower. And finally, habits diminish decision fatigue. Combined, these explain why our deliberate habits, grounded in our routines, help us make the most of our finite time.

In the next chapter, we'll discuss another convincing reason why routines are so powerful — they make the most of our daily energy oscillations.

10

Energy Oscillates

If it's your job to eat a frog, it's best to do it first thing
in the morning. And if it's your job to eat two frogs, it's
best to eat the biggest one first.
— Mark Twain

IN OUR FIRST MEETING, GEOFFREY, A THIRD-YEAR LAWYER, AD-
mitted he did most of his own work after the typical workday ended — after
a long day of meetings, emails, general follow-up, and reacting to other
people's requests. Then, after an intense and draining day like this, he would
settle into his own work over a take-out dinner.

Not surprisingly, he was tired in the evenings, which made it hard to
focus and produce the high-quality work his clients and partners required.
So he ended up working longer hours to make up for his sluggish productivity. Late evenings bled into working weekends that overtook sleep, exercise,

and relaxation. It got to the point where Geoffrey felt he was working all the time.

After struggling to keep up with this flawed approach, he used one of his lifelines and called me for productivity help.

⏳

As is often the case, we intuitively know something to be true and then science shows us the irrefutable proof. We've all heard the saying "timing is everything." Deep down, we know timing matters. And an army of scientists have proven this through countless studies. *Chronobiology* is the study of our biological rhythms, including our daily energy fluctuations. It has taught us that we are more productive when we align our work to our daily internal clock.

WHEN TO VERSUS HOW TO

We experience peaks and valleys throughout our days. You may start your workday with a burst of energy but then slip into an afternoon slump. You may be keen to watch a game after dinner but fall asleep before the first commercial break.

Not surprisingly, aligning our work and personal goals with our energy makes us more effective. There are better (and worse) times to tackle different tasks. So paying attention to *when* we do certain activities can provide great benefits. Blogs, podcasts, videos, and books like this one are filled with *how to* advice. But as a busy person, you generate bigger results when you complement this *how to* knowledge with key *when to* strategies.

Despite how crucial timing is, there isn't nearly enough emphasis placed on *when* to do certain types of work. When we are pulled in many directions, our days take on an *every day is different* flavour. Meetings may overlap with our morning commute. Reactive emails edge out our own deep work. We believe every day is unique, so we build our calendar with the free-form creativity of an artist rather than the strategic deliberation of a scientist. But the truth is that applying much more rigour to how we structure our day will help us to achieve optimal results.

The best compilation of "when to" research that I've found is in the bestseller *When: The Scientific Secrets of Perfect Timing*,[1] by the wise and engaging author Daniel H. Pink. This book draws on over seven hundred scientific studies from the fields of psychology, biology, anthropology, and economics to confirm the ideal timing for our work and our lives, based on our individual chronotypes. I'd like to share a summary of his findings and recommendations, as it provides us with great insight into how we can best align our routines to our energy.

DAILY ENERGY FLUCTUATIONS

We all experience natural fluctuations in our cognitive energy throughout the day. Pink describes three distinct energy phases:

- Peak: This is when we are most attentive and best able to avoid distractions. This is the best time to do our focus work, to concentrate on our core priorities.
- Trough: This is our energy slump, which occurs approximately seven hours after waking. This is the best time to work on our easier, less thought-intensive tasks.
- Recovery: This is when our energy has another surge. It's important to note that while we may have regained some of our energy, our level of attention is down. During this time, we are less able to manage distractions, but we are *better* at free-flow thinking. This makes it our ideal time to work on creative, insight-rich tasks, as our most innovative ideas are likely to bubble up to our consciousness.

For most of us, as Pink describes, our energy follows a predictable pattern throughout the day, with a peak in the morning, a trough in the afternoon, and a recovery in the evening. But this cycle varies depending on your chronotype. Which of the following three types sound most like you?

Early birds

You're probably familiar with the term "early bird" — this term refers to people who naturally wake up with the sun, without any need for an alarm clock, and are as chipper as can be. As Pink describes it, approximately 15 percent of the population have their midpoint of sleep between 1:30 a.m. and 3:00 a.m. They naturally wake up earlier than most and are raring to go. I've been married to a true early bird for more than twenty years, and it continues to amaze me how effortless it is for him to wake up, often without the alarm clock I rely so heavily on.

Early birds experience their peak energy in the morning and their lowest energy in the afternoon. This trough occurs approximately seven hours after they wake up. Then they recover their energy again in the early evening (see figure 6).

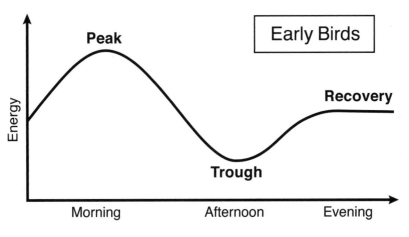

Figure 6. Early birds

Night owls

Another 20 percent of the population are night owls. Their energy patterns are a mirror image of the early birds. Night owls have an energy peak in the late afternoon and a recovery period in the morning. While morning isn't their *best* time, it still comes in at a respectable second place. They still have more energy in the late morning than during the afternoon trough that plagues everyone (see figure 7).

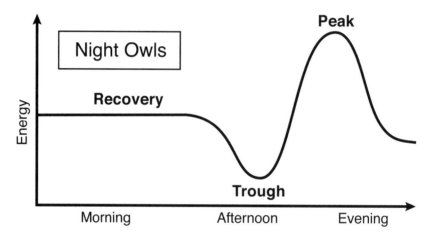

Figure 7. Night owls

Third birds

The majority of the population, approximately 65 percent, experience the midpoint of their night's sleep between 3:30 a.m. and 5:30 a.m. Pink terms this group *third birds*. Just like early birds, their energy levels peak in the morning (although later than is typical for early birds), dip in the afternoon, and recover again in the early evening. Their energy fluctuations look a lot like those of the early birds but are shifted, starting later than early birds. I fall into this category, although I wasn't always like this.

WHAT IS YOUR CHRONOTYPE?

I was a finely tuned night owl for the first forty years of my life. I was super-energized and productive into the wee hours of the night. But mornings were a struggle, which gives me great empathy for our teenagers, who find early mornings painful. Like a magician, I could miraculously transform the loudest of alarm clocks into a low, blissful hum, sometimes sleeping through an hour or more of a loud blaring alarm. Throughout high school, I remember my mom prompting me several times to wake up for school. Then, during the years I spent living in university residence, I would stumble behind my friend Shelley as she led the way to morning class while I struggled to clear my mental fog. (Those daily 8:30 a.m. science classes weren't ideal after late nights.) And now that I'm married to an early bird, I try really hard to use my nice voice when he prompts conversations before my morning coffee. *(But seriously, can't we just talk later?)* He used to offer me some advice that worked for him: "Simply pretend you are waking up to go golfing." *Um, no.* That didn't work then and certainly doesn't work now. And I *like* golf! It's just that few things can compete with sleep in my world. No, early mornings are not my best time.

I have always admired early birds — they get such a great start to their days — something we can all benefit from. Thankfully, our biological rhythms can evolve during our life. I still have aspirations of one day graduating to become an early bird, but I haven't yet become a member of the 5:00 a.m. club.

Our biological rhythms are powerful. Sure, I can wake up early if I must, but I'm not at my best. And we can all tweak our waking hours by altering our sleep habits, but our inborn energy patterns are not something we can easily flip. Conversely, when we work with our own natural energy fluctuations, we make the most of our time. Knowing the specifics of the broader population is less important than knowing your own chronotype. Once we identify when our individual peak, trough, and recovery periods are, we can align our routine to make the most of our energy fluctuations.

What is your chronotype? What are your natural energy patterns? When is your energy highest? Lowest? Are you an early bird or a night owl? Or do you perhaps fall somewhere in between, like me, as a third bird?

Once you identify your chronotype, which is as simple as noticing when you are most inclined to sleep, you'll better understand when your energy peak, trough, and recovery periods are. And you'll be better able to align your work to your energy. Let's now explore some core principles we can all build into our daily routines.

MAKE THE MOST OF ENERGY-RICH MORNINGS

Mornings are precious. Our energy tends to be abundant in the morning. This is true even if you're a night owl — of course, your ideal workday would start later than an early bird. You'll still start your workday with a fresh burst of energy.

Not only is our energy high in the morning, but our willpower is also at its highest then — we haven't yet burned through our reserves. Plus, we have not yet begun to suffer from decision fatigue. Finally, our control over our day tends to be highest in the morning. Sure, we may have some *do immediately* tasks to address first thing in the morning. But for the most part, we have more wiggle room at the beginning of our day than we do the end of our workday, when we are more likely to have hard stops. On all but the most intense days, we can still carve out time in the morning for important, instead of urgent, activities.

> Make the most of your peak energy by protecting this time for your core priorities.

The best step you can take to make the most of your peak energy is to protect most of this time for your core priorities — and this rarely includes reactive tasks like email. McKinsey research indicates that executives estimate their productivity is five times greater during their peak times.[2] Yet, these same executives estimate they spend a mere 10 percent of their time working on their most important goals when their energy is at its peak.

The world's most prolific producers sing the praises of mornings. The golden morning hours also benefit children. In a 2016 study of Danish students, researchers found the students performed best on the standard-ized tests in the morning and then saw their test scores decline with each passing hour.[3]

How can you take full advantage of the golden morning hours? Here are some practical ideas.

Begin with a core priority

Mornings, when most of us are at our peak, are the ideal time for analytical and focused work. This is often what we need for our core priorities. The way you begin your day dictates how the rest of the day will flow. Start with your hardest task, and every other task will be so much easier. Mornings are precious, regardless of your chronotype. Be proactive and start your day focused on a challenge related to your core priorities. This could include some intense focus work, an important decision, or a detailed project. If you are in a client-facing role, this could be a meeting with your top prospect. If you are a leader, this could be reviewing a detailed report prepared by your team. If you are an analyst, this could be some complicated data crunching.

Eat your frog

You may be familiar with another strategy: eat a frog for breakfast. Yes, a frog. Before you judge this questionable culinary choice, hear me out. A frog is simply a playful reference to your hardest task. The task that has been weighing on you. The one you had hoped to finish two months ago. The one you want to continue avoiding.

We all have that one item on our list that we dread — the one that feels just too hard. Our temptation may be to put it off until the end of the day. But by the end of the day, we're often too tired to tackle the tough task. So, we put it off until tomorrow. And then the next day.

But eating a frog in the morning pairs our sun-kissed, fresh morning energy with a task that has a high activation threshold. Once we complete our hardest task, the rest of our day runs so much more smoothly.

Your frog is often correlated with one of your core priorities. After all, would you commit to performing such a difficult task if it wasn't? But for the sake of clarity, I'd like to add a caveat to this strategy: Start your day with your hardest task *as long as it aligns to one of your core priorities.* The bigger and more important a task, the more you should aim to complete it in the morning.

Make yourself unavailable

We live in a world of constant connectivity. Wherever we are — sailing the ocean or flying thirty-five thousand feet above the Earth — we can usually access Wi-Fi. As a result, too many people have slipped into an "always on" way of working. They are constantly scanning their email, texts, chats, social alerts, and more. But just because we *can* be instantly accessible doesn't mean that we should be. As we will discuss in the next chapter, multi-tasking makes *every* task take longer.

If we are constantly on alert, we can never carve out the focus time we need for deep thinking and high-quality work. What we need to do is protect our attention and manage our interruptions. The best way to do this is to turn off our alerts — on all of our devices. Don't let incoming messages rule your day. You should be the one deciding when you check these tools. I'm not suggesting you avoid email for hours or days at a time. Just don't let alerts interrupt your focus work. Instead, check for messages between your focus sessions, on *your* timeline. If someone needs you more urgently, they will call. They will find you.

> If we are constantly on alert, we can never carve out the focus time we need for deep thinking and high-quality work.

Similarly, you can manage other interruptions, such as when people approach you with *Do you have a minute?* requests. Yes, if these requests are urgent, you can stop what you're doing to help. But in all other situations, you don't need to give up your focus time. You could shift these conversations to your lower energy times. "I'm booked most of today. Can we talk after 4 p.m.?"

One senior banking executive told me he used to encourage people to swing by his office after 6:00 p.m. He said this with the loveliest British accent and always made people feel welcome, even when he was postponing their conversation. Often, before those postponed conversations took place, his colleagues ended up solving their own problems. He said it was incredible how many of these meeting requests disappeared. If these late-day conversations do occur, you'll be amazed at how efficient they can be. Or maybe they will be more casual and conversational, which is a great way to strengthen your connection. Of course, you want to balance these conversations with your personal goals. Don't offer times that conflict with your family time. But if you're otherwise waiting for junior's hockey practice to finish, you may be open to connecting with a colleague.

Managing your interruptions is a Workday Warrior superpower. This is especially important during the morning; this is when your energy level is either at its highest or close to it. Morning is the best time to handle analytical tasks requiring a logical, focused, and disciplined mind. Don't squander this time by being fully accessible. Close your door. Silence your phone. Block your calendar. Grant your core priorities the same gift of undivided attention that you give to other people in meetings.

And listen up, early birds, if you start your workday earlier than most, you can extend your morning focus time by starting earlier than the rest of us. *Please* don't squander too much of this precious time on reactive tasks such as email.

Bump your meetings

I've told countless people and I'll tell you, too: don't give away your precious morning hours to meetings. If your day truly is consumed by meetings, try blocking your first hour for focus work. Then, where possible, shift your meetings to the afternoon or, at least, late morning. I'm especially anti-Monday morning meetings. Why are so many teams intent on squandering this precious time with a meeting that is better suited for later in the day? The answer surely points to a flawed belief that we can push our individual work until later and still be just as productive.

We'll discuss some options to address these morning meetings in part 3. After all, you and I both know mornings are prime time for independent work. In the meantime, can I invite you to join forces with me and push back those misinformed morning meeting requesters?

How to handle early East Coast meetings when you live on the West Coast

Cynthia worked on the West Coast. Many of her clients and colleagues worked on the East Coast and started their workday about three hours earlier than she did, which meant she consistently woke up to multiple new emails and requests. She felt obligated to tackle these at the start of her workday and also to take part in several morning meetings with her East Coast colleagues (who were already into their afternoons).

There was an obvious problem: Cynthia's peak work time, the ideal time for her focus work, was being consumed communicating with her East Coast colleagues. This kind of conflict is faced by many who work in teams that are spread across multiple time zones. It isn't always easy to align our focus work with our peak energy. But that doesn't mean that there are no solutions to the problem, that all hope is lost. Cynthia was doubtful she could do much about this situation. But once she put a routine in place, she was pleasantly surprised to see how well her plan worked.

Here are some strategies that helped Cynthia — and they may help you, too, if you find yourself in a similar situation:

Shift your hours. Cynthia was a natural early bird, so she decided to start her workday at 7:00 a.m., giving her three hours of independent work time before the bulk of her meetings started at 10:00 a.m. PST / 1:00 p.m. EST. Thankfully, her colleagues liked the idea of shifting internal meetings to the afternoon.

Pay yourself first. Cynthia was committed to protecting more of her prime morning energy for her independent focus work. She consistently blocked off 7:00 a.m. to 8:00 a.m. to focus on her core priorities. She blocked off another hour between 8:00 a.m. and 12:00 p.m. and simultaneously limited herself to no more than two hours of meetings during this time. She also limited the time she spent on email and other reactive tasks to one hour, which took some discipline — it would have been easy to spend the rest of her morning being reactive. But she agreed that most of these reactive tasks could wait until later in her day.

Tackle big goals during quieter times. By Cynthia's mid-afternoon, her East Coast colleagues were wrapping up their days. This gave her some relatively quiet time, making it easy to shift her focus back to working independently on her core priorities. Thankfully, Cynthia was in her recovery phase at this time, and she found this to be another richly productive time.

Stop aiming for perfection. Cynthia agreed to celebrate success if she could protect her early mornings for three out of five days each week. This gave her much more time to focus on her core priorities than she had had in the past, granting her more control over her work and the reward of more satisfying progress on her most meaningful goals.

Sure, Cynthia still woke up to multiple emails and meeting requests, but she found her colleagues and clients were much more open to working around her independent focus time than she had first expected. Overall, Cynthia was thrilled with how effective her Proactive Routine was, despite being three hours behind most of her East Coast colleagues.

Afternoon meetings, on the other hand, especially those that promote connections within a team, provide exactly the energy injection we need during our afternoon troughs. This is especially true for the extroverts on your team; they will get an energy boost from meeting with others.

Personally, I aim to book my meetings in the afternoon. Yes, I still have some morning meetings, but I do my best to push those meeting as late in the morning as possible. My ideal routine protects my morning hours so that I can use that blissful morning energy to focus on my core priorities. Admittedly, I do have a high level of control over my schedule as a business owner. But I still need to coordinate schedules with many others. If you think you can't shift your meeting times, I encourage you to test this belief.

No doubt, you'll find that exceptions are warranted, too. If the only time that works for everyone else is 9:00 a.m., you can make an exception. But if your executive team meets every Wednesday at precisely 9:00 a.m., I suggest you exert your excellent persuasion skills to help them recognize the merits of protected mornings. Be a role model and help guide them toward making the most of their fresh morning energy as well.

You may also want to make an exception to the no-early-morning-meeting rule if you're trying to get a favourable response from someone else. In this case, book a meeting during the first part of their workday. If you meet during their prime time, you're more likely to get the answer you want. But in practically every other case, bump your meetings. You make the most of your prime energy when you protect your mornings for your core priorities.

RAMP UP QUICKLY — EVEN IF YOU'RE A NIGHT OWL

If you are a night owl, you might not be ready to burst out the gates. You might need a bit of time to settle into your workday. You might benefit from some quick wins that allow you to ramp up to your peak productivity. These quick wins act like jump-starts, giving you the spark you need to get going and build up some momentum. But I still recommend you limit the time you spend on small tasks in the morning. Once you've settled into your rhythm, shift over to one of your more challenging tasks.

If this sounds like a workable compromise for you, here are some practical guidelines to make the most of your mornings:

- Pre-identify your wins. Before your day even starts, identify some tasks you can easily accomplish at the beginning of your day. You can flag tomorrow's quick wins during today's daily planning ritual, which will help you start strong.

- Be proactive. As tempting as it is to dive into email and direct messages, avoid opening the door to these reactive activities. Instead, commit to crossing items off *your* list first. You're still applying the "eat your frog" concept. I'm simply suggesting you eat smaller frogs than the early birds.

- Watch the clock. As you know, even night owls have a burst of fresh energy in the morning. You want to graduate from your small frogs to your big frogs rather quickly. Perhaps give yourself a time limit of fifteen or thirty minutes dedicated to quick wins. Then dive into a bigger task so you can join the ranks of the early birds with meaningful progress early in your day.

GIVE YOUR AFTERNOONS A BOOST

We've talked a lot about making the most of your prime morning energy. But afternoons can be quite productive as well — especially after a lunch or afternoon break. Here are some suggestions to give your afternoons a productivity boost.

Focus after a break

> As a Workday Warrior, you can use breaks to your advantage.

After a break, we have a fresh burst of energy. As mentioned earlier, this benefits all chronotypes. The study of decision fatigue experienced by the Israeli parole board that was discussed in chapter 9 found there was an exception to their waning energy as the day went on. After breaks, the quality of their decisions spiked back up.

As a Workday Warrior, you can use breaks to your advantage. Protect some focus work time after any of your breaks or lunch. This is another time when you may be more energized, which is always a good time for focus work. With that said, the nature of your break may alter this. For example, a calorie-dense lunch may precipitate an afternoon energy dip, especially for early birds who have been awake for so much longer than the rest of the population.

Consider taking a nap

I travelled to Spain many years ago. One of the things that most amazed me was how the cities shut down during the afternoon siestas. Practically everyone, it seemed, went home for a big lunch (their biggest meal of the day) followed by a restorative nap.

Our energy levels are lowest approximately seven hours after waking. This is our afternoon trough. And this energy dip occurs with all chronotypes: early birds, night owls, and third birds. For this reason, we want to avoid making big decisions or doing strenuous work in the mid-afternoon.

The Spaniards have figured out how to best navigate this energy fluctuation. Post-siesta, they are more alert and have better cognition — siestas even help them to have better long-term health.[4] Not surprisingly, many other countries, from Italy to Japan to the Scandinavian countries, also embrace their afternoon naps.

The afternoon siestas they enjoy don't make them less productive; in fact, it seems those short breaks help to boost their productivity. Naps have long been recognized as a powerful way to recharge, even if they aren't very common in the workplace. Naps offer all the same benefits of our nighttime sleep: increased alertness and less stress; sharper cognition; better learning; more patience; and more. In fact, twenty minutes of sleep in the afternoon provides more rest than twenty minutes of snooze-induced sleep in the morning.[5]

Experts advise us to keep our naps between fifteen and thirty minutes, as sleeping longer sends us into deeper stages of sleep, from which it's more difficult to awaken. Also, longer naps can make it more difficult for you to fall asleep at night, especially if your sleep deficit is relatively small.

If you're intrigued by the thought of an afternoon nap but concerned about sleeping for too long, try a "nappuccino." Yes, a nappuccino. The way it works is this: drink a cup of coffee (yes, the kind with caffeine) and then settle in for a 20–25-minute nap. This is approximately how long it takes for your body to absorb the caffeine. Once the caffeine kicks in, you'll wake up refreshed and raring to go.[6] But of course, I still suggest setting an alarm to safely avoid sleeping longer than you intend.

Make it easier to work through your trough

Let's face it, naps are usually viewed as a rare luxury in North America, where people trudge through their days despite any dips in energy. As effective as naps are, they aren't always possible. Frankly, some people struggle to fall asleep in the middle of the day. Others struggle to wake up again once they do fall asleep. Thankfully, there other opportunities that allow us to work through our trough in an effective way.

- Tackle easier tasks: Your afternoon trough is ideally suited for smaller, easier tasks. This is a good time to catch up on the non-urgent emails or administrative tasks that you strategically side-stepped during your prime morning zone. What simple, mundane, or repetitive tasks do you want to complete today? Save these for the afternoon.
- Save your fun tasks: While your morning is a great time to eat a frog, your afternoon is a great time to play with the tasks that you enjoy the most. These are the exact tasks that energize you when your energy is waning.
- Book a meeting: As mentioned earlier, meeting with other people can be a great energy booster, especially for

extroverts. In this case, schedule that virtual coffee with your new team member during your afternoon trough. Similarly, schedule afternoon team meetings, and focus the agenda on connecting and celebrating, which is something every high-performance team prioritizes. Just be conscious of who you're meeting with and what you need from them. Introverts won't want to see or hear from you until their energy picks up again.

- Play some tunes: Several studies confirm that listening to music can suppress fatigue and increase our energy levels, as well as improve our mood and make us feel more powerful.[7] It's no surprise that gyms crank music and runners don headphones streaming their favourite playlists. Perhaps consider grabbing your own set of headphones and making this part of your afternoon routine when your energy is lower.

Finish strong

We have another opportunity to fortify our routine at the end of our workday. This is a time when boundaries are often vague, with a blurred line between our work and personal lives. This fuzzy boundary has only got worse for so many who have transitioned from working in an office to working in their living room. Instead, we want to define clear boundaries around when we are and aren't working. Otherwise, it's all too easy for work to go on and on. We'll expand on this more in the next chapter.

Of course, you need to decide when your ideal work hours are. If your energy surge blends into your personal time, you don't *have* to keep working. You can still have a productive day, even if you don't perfectly follow your energy patterns. Sometimes we are better off with "good enough."

GOOD ENOUGH IS BETTER THAN NOTHING

As a working mom, I sometimes shift my working hours. This is especially true in the summer, when the kids are out of school and every week varies depending on their camp/activities/part-time job/volunteer commitment/ social plans. I inevitably have to adjust to a summer routine and flex it as necessary. Not surprisingly, my summertime working hours are constrained. On the one hand, I love that I can prioritize our kids. But I can't ignore my work commitments in the summer. So I creatively integrate work into my life. I look for unclaimed pockets where I can reclaim some work time — such as when I'm sitting in the hockey arena parking lot waiting for practice to end. (Yes, hockey season extends straight through the summer in Canada.) And sometimes, I'll work a bit after dinner is cleared away and the rest of my family is settled into their evening routine.

> **Routine Principle #2:**
> Routines allow us to align our work to our fluctuating energy in the most effective way.

As you know from above, late in the day is not peak energy time. Not surprisingly, I feel a bit sluggish and tired in the evenings. It's easy to succumb to procrastination temptations and think, *I'll push this off until tomorrow during my prime time.* But we don't always have the luxury of working during our not-so-ideal times. You absolutely can and many times do. It will feel harder. It will require more discipline. But the goal is to be conscious of these trade-offs you're making.

Sometimes, despite my best efforts, I find myself tackling tough challenges during my lower energy periods. But I'm happy to report this happens less and less, the more committed I am to the strategies I outline in this book. (No, I don't apply them perfectly all the time. Life happens and I am human.) But these slips renew my resolve and awareness of how powerful these strategies are — starting with clear core priorities and adding a Proactive Routine aligned to my fluctuating energy.

Once again, we can tackle tough challenges during low energy times, but it helps to recognize this as a suboptimal strategy. Of course, we want to keep this mismatch to a minimum. But whenever we find ourselves in this situation, we can use it as motivation to get better at proactively structuring our day around our ideal energy.

The point of this story is to focus on what we can control. When you have a choice (and this occurs far more often than we think), align your work to your energy. And give yourself grace when life doesn't flow exactly as you plan. Your workday doesn't need to be perfect to achieve perfectly amazing results.

Ultimately, routines help us make the most of our natural energy oscillations and generate the best results each day.

11

Focus Beats Multi-tasking

Multi-tasking: A polite way of telling someone you
haven't heard a word they've said.
— Dave Crenshaw

I ONLY ALLOW MYSELF TO GO TO COSTCO A FEW TIMES A YEAR.
As a working mom of four, I don't get out much, so this always feels like
a special outing. On these rare occasions, I make sure I have lots of time
to explore the treasures in each aisle. We are a family of six, and there are
always justifiable reasons to replenish household items. Costco seems to
have everything — the jumbo pack croissants; the great deal on movie
passes; all of those enticing books. And you just can't beat that deal on
socks or all those snacks near the checkout. I recently went to Costco
with a friend, so we had *two* carts. But most of the contents in both carts
were mine.

I once recall telling the cashier, "I only came for two items." She nodded her head with a sympathetic and all-knowing expression. Apparently, I wasn't the first to succumb to Costco's tempting purchase options. But still, I knew I needed to rein it in. After all, my budget is finite, even if the can't-pass-up deals are practically infinite.

Indulging works when we have an abundance of resources. If money is no object, we can order everything on the menu. Extra appetizers for the table, please. And a round of your special drink for my friends, too. But when money is tight, we need to be much more restrained. We need to carefully consider how we use scarce resources.

Our time is a finite resource, yet too many people treat their time as if it were an endless resource. Just like there are no ends to where we can spend our money, the opportunities for where we can spend our time are limitless.

Parkinson's Law:
Work expands
to fill the time
allotted to it.

Busy people have endless demands on their time. But just because they've been invited to sit on three boards while juggling a growing team and family doesn't mean they should. We can only divide our attention in so many ways. Yet far too many people overcommit themselves as if they had all the time in the world. I've been there before, and I understand their frustration about a new initiative seeming like a great idea — it likely is a great idea, but the problem is that turning the idea into action requires work. And I'm sure that I'm not the only one who sometimes underestimates just how much work it is.

WORK EXPANDS

In the previous chapter, we explored our energy fluctuations. Sometimes we're full of vigour and other times we struggle to answer a simple email. Similarly, our work expands and contracts. This phenomenon is otherwise known as Parkinson's Law: work expands to fill the time allotted to it.

We have all experienced surges in productivity as looming deadlines approach. But other times, without the pressure of looming deadlines, it can be hard to re-create this superheated pace. We all know how easy it is to overcomplicate work when we have oodles of time. The truth is that our productivity is inversely proportionate to the time available. The graph in figure 8 illustrates my experience with this phenomenon.

Figure 8 presents a rough approximation of the inverse relationship between productivity and time available. This relationship will vary depending on the task. It should be noted that there exist situations where too little time constrains productivity. This is particularly true if insufficient time is reserved to explore new ideas and solve complex problems.[1]

But the point remains that our work can easily expand — the more time we have to complete it, the more time we spend on it. Not surprisingly, research finds that near-term deadlines prompt people to get started on their work sooner rather than later. On the other hand, long-term deadlines practically invite procrastination.

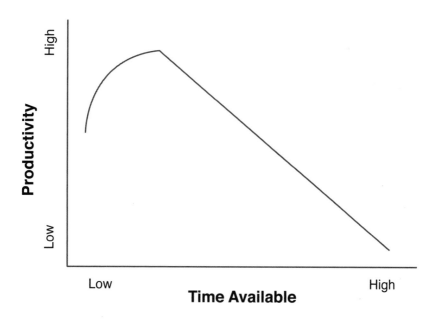

Figure 8. Inverse relationship between productivity and time available

The inverse relationship between productivity and time available can be seen in many situations — from working on small projects to large-scale efforts. The forty-hour workweek was adopted in 1926 when Henry Ford scaled the workweek down from forty-eight to forty hours. He did this believing that with a shorter workweek productivity would improve. He was correct.[2]

Similarly, several companies (such as Microsoft and Basecamp) are experimenting with four-day workweeks, without noticing a decrease in productivity or revenue.[3] Even some municipal governments in Ontario, where I live, are considering, or experimenting with, four-day workweeks as a response to the burnout felt during the pandemic.[4] Initial results point to a more energized and productive workforce. Obviously, this strategy isn't conducive to all roles, but it does reinforce the point that more is not always more when it comes to work hours.

LESS IS MORE

While work can expand, our routines can help. Our routines build micro-deadlines into our days, allowing us to contain our work. Ironically, granting ourselves less (not more) time helps us get more work done.

As logic dictates, we make better use of a constrained resource. Our routines compensate for the principle that work expands. Routines segment our days into smaller time frames, making us more conscious about making more moments count. But to do so, we need to protect these smaller blocks of time from one of the biggest productivity blockers: interruptions.

INTERRUPTIONS SABOTAGE TIME

As already noted, the shortest distance between any two points is a straight line. But too many people treat their work like a cross-country tour. Instead of focusing exclusively on drafting a letter, they multi-task. They check email, talk to their office mate, get up to stretch (*Haven't you heard? Sitting is the new smoking*), then check email again. On and on this goes. Before they know it, it is time to go to their next meeting. Their goal to complete the draft ended in defeat. They look back over the past hour and have little to account for their time, other than the meagre beginning of what they wanted to write. Interruptions are one of the biggest reasons why work expands.

We face countless interruptions all day long, regardless of whether we're working in the office or at home. These interruptions include email, text messages, chats, phone calls, and people dropping by our desk. These are the ones that people typically cite when I ask them to list their interruptions. But there is another source of interruptions, and it just happens to be the most common one. I'm referring to ourselves. We are the top source of interruptions we face. One study found that 44 percent of all interruptions are self-imposed.[5] It might be tempting to blame others. *If they could just leave me alone, I could get my work done!* But I've come to realize that I am often the one inviting any so-called interruptions. If I want to avoid having the time I spend on tasks persist far beyond what they need, I need to take control of my interruptions and commit to focusing.

> We are the top source of interruptions we face.

FOCUS BEATS MULTI-TASKING

I used to be a prolific multi-tasker. And I don't mean to brag, but I was quite good at it. I firmly believed that juggling several different tasks at the same time was the most efficient way of working. If I had two tasks to accomplish and a limited amount of time in which to finish them, I would layer them on top of one another. Now I realize how flawed this approach was.

I see people multi-tasking all the time. For example, they keep email open on a second monitor all day long. Every time a new message arrives, they shift their attention over to their inbox. They may tell themselves it only takes a moment, but the research proves otherwise.

Consider this simple exercise, inspired by a similar exercise from *The Myth of Multitasking* by Dave Crenshaw.[6] Try writing out these two lines of text:

W O R K D A Y W A R R I O R
1 2 3 4 5 6 7 8 9 10 11 12 13 14

This is a straightforward exercise, and it usually takes people approximately 7–10 seconds to complete.

But now I invite you to try this a second time, except this time try toggling back and forth between letters and numbers. Write W, then 1, then O, then 2, and so on.

This second variation produces the same output: letters on top and numbers underneath. Yet it takes people approximately twice as long to complete this task, a simple multi-tasking simulation. Plus, people tend to make more mistakes when they jump back and forth between the lines. They might mix up two letters or miss a number altogether. They also frequently report feeling frazzled during this second scenario.

> Focusing is faster, easier, and less stressful than multi-tasking.

This simple exercise demonstrates what the research is quite clear about: focusing on one task at a time beats multi-tasking.

Focusing is faster.

Focusing is easier.

And focusing is less stressful.

Focusing on one task at a time offsets the phenomenon of work expanding. Focusing on one task at a time fuels us to reach our goal faster and make the impact we know we can make. Of course, it's unrealistic to think we can sequester ourselves for hours at a time. We need to remain responsive to our clients and colleagues. Yes, we have work that requires our focused attention. But we also have emails, phone calls, and other miscellaneous items to address. What is the best way to balance focus work with accessibility?

HOW TO MANAGE INTERRUPTIONS (WITHOUT GOING SILENT)

If there is one thing that Workday Warriors need to fortify themselves against, it is interruptions. We face a non-stop barrage of interruptions throughout the day. And we can't simply ignore interruptions. If your boss sends an email, it doesn't pay to pretend it doesn't exist.

But if we are going to be able to protect our valuable focus time, we have to address the elephant in the room: you may be addicted to email. This isn't true for everyone, but the problem is worth exploring. One study found that the temptation associated with checking social media (and I argue that email is a close relative of social media in the workplace) is stronger than the temptation associated with alcohol and tobacco.[7] Now that's addictive! If I were sitting beside your desk and we kept hearing your email alerts arrive, I would want to check *your* email.

As a Workday Warrior, you need to fortify yourself against interruptions. I recommend turning off all of your alerts, including those on your computer, tablet, smartphone, watch, and anything else that alerts you to messages. Otherwise, these alerts continue to eat away at your time. Once you turn off these alerts, make sure you minimize your email — or turn it off altogether. Remind yourself that constantly diverting your attention prolongs your work and erodes your quality.

We can also stand up when someone comes over to our desk to talk to us. It's incredible how powerful this "stand up" technique can be. Standing up gives us options, including being able to subtly escort someone away from our desk ("Do you want to walk with me while I refill my water?") to contain the interruption. It's practically sneaky when you realize how effective this interruption-busting strategy is.

There are also other interruptions to navigate. You don't have to monitor chats and texts all day long. And you can let unscheduled calls go to voice mail — especially the numbers you don't recognize. Sure, if your colleague calls just before heading into an important meeting, or your child's school calls, you probably want to pick up those calls. But a few brief interruptions won't sabotage your time. It's the non-stop barrage that threatens our time; it's the non-stop distractions that we want to guard ourselves against.

WHAT IS YOUR FOCUS ROUTINE?

The best way to combat interruptions while protecting valuable focus time is to adopt a focus routine. For example, you might commit to focusing on one task for forty-five minutes, followed by fifteen minutes dedicated to email and other miscellaneous tasks. Or you might adopt a fifty-minute/ten-minute focus routine (see figure 9). Or a twenty-minute/ten-minute focus routine. Or another variation better suited to you. Your focus routine may vary by the day, depending on how much time you need to complete a task and the unwritten rules of your team's response time expectations.

Regardless of the exact way in which you organize your time, a focus routine is a true Workday Warrior strategy. To make this work, you want a clearly delineated line between your focused work and collaborative work. Otherwise, you are multi-tasking, which is practically inviting your work to expand unnecessarily.

50/10 Focus Routine

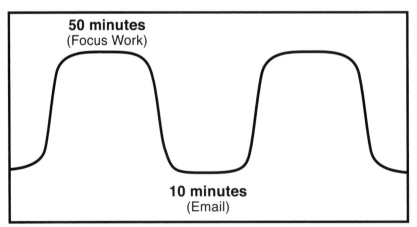

Figure 9. Sample focus routine

HOW TO FORTIFY YOUR FOCUS TIME

As I mentioned above, we are our number one source of interruptions. We choose to check email. We choose to stand up and walk away from our desks. We choose to shift our attention. So when we are trying to protect our focus time, it helps to fortify ourselves against the temptation to be distracted. There are three questions you can ask yourself to help mitigate the threat of self-imposed interruptions.

What is my goal? The first step is to define your goal for each focus session. You want to make this goal as specific as possible. Simply working on a project isn't enough. Instead, clearly state what you want to complete. Is it part one? A complete draft? A final product? This allows you to focus your attention on a clear finish line.

What is my duration? The second step is to define a duration. For example, are you giving yourself thirty minutes? Forty-five minutes? Sixty minutes? This clear time allocation directly addresses the problem of work expanding. We are much more likely to stay focused when the clock is ticking down.

What is my reward? Finally, you want to identify a reward to treat yourself with when you've reached your focus goal. This reward could include any range of indulgences. But I stand by the fact that there is one reward that works better than any other when it comes to our work — I'm talking about the reward of checking your email. Wait — I can already hear you groaning, so please hear me out.

While you're focusing your attention, there may be a tempting voice inside your head encouraging you to check your email. *Come on — just take a quick peak. What's the harm? It will only take a minute. There might be an urgent message waiting. Or something more exciting than what you're doing now.* Instead of indulging in this time-sucking email distraction, stick to meeting your focus goal. *Then* you can indulge in email. Open up your inbox and play to your heart's content. If you're still denying that email is a rich reward, you can absolutely find another suitable one. But the next time you wrap up a focus block, consider what you turn to immediately afterward. If it is your email, then this is probably an effective reward.

THE POWER OF BREAKS

Focusing on deep work helps us contain our work and avoid having it expand unnecessarily. But this doesn't mean we should focus for hour upon hour at a time. Our minds and our bodies function best when we take periodic breaks.

The most productive people take regular breaks. They don't work straight through hour after hour. One study led by DeskTime, a time-tracking app, found the most productive 10 percent of its users worked for an average of fifty-two minutes and then took a break for seventeen minutes.[8] Yes, it's random, but this is what their research found. These super-productive people treated their work time as full-on focused sprints. Then they completely stepped away from their work for fully restorative breaks. I'm not suggesting your breaks need to be exactly seventeen minutes. A short break — between five and ten minutes — may be enough to reset your focus.

> The most productive people take regular breaks.

Remember that study I referenced in chapter 10 about Danish students and declining test scores as the day wore on? Turns out that a twenty- to thirty-minute break was enough to counteract the effect, with their test scores returned to those seen at the beginning of the testing period.[9] This is in line with other research that shows breaks help us replenish our energy and recover from decision fatigue.[10] Right after a break is a great time to tackle a challenging task. In fact, if you need to do something difficult, try taking a break first.

Varying your activities can also serve as a break. You could get up and talk to a colleague, meditate, or go for a walk in between focus work. Or plan a walking meeting. These get the blood flowing, pump fresh oxygen to your brain, and fuel a more creative discussion. Or you could check email or do another supporting task. As they say, variety is the spice of life, and the choice is yours.

⧗

Let's return to Geoffrey, who we introduced in the previous chapter. Geoffrey wasn't surprised when I encouraged him to shift his independent focus work from the evening to his morning. But he didn't think it would work. He had heard this advice before but hadn't had success with adopting it. Nevertheless, he was willing to indulge me, even if he was skeptical.

We started with small steps. Geoffrey was naturally an early bird (when he wasn't working until the wee hours of the morning). He committed to the earlier bedtime that his body craved. This allowed him to start his workday day at 7:00 a.m. fresh and raring to go. Most of his colleagues didn't start working until closer to 9:00 a.m. So this gave him two solid hours of relatively uninterrupted time when he was at his prime.

Geoffrey initially pushed back when I recommended he ignore email for the first hour of his day. "But I have to respond to people right away! My clients expect this. And my partners will think I'm not working if I don't jump on any emails that came in overnight!"

Routine Principle #3: Routines keep us focused and fortify against our work expanding unnecessarily.

Ultimately, Geoffrey agreed to protect one and a half of these early morning hours for his own independent focus work (and the remaining thirty minutes for email). He was amazed at how much more he accomplished during this prime time — and how easy it was to implement.

After this initial success, he agreed to block the first hour after lunch for his own work (with a short "scan for urgency" through his email at about the halfway point). This gave him another reliable block of focus work.

Sure, he made exceptions on certain days, such as when a big deal was closing or when a non-negotiable meeting overlapped one of his focus sessions. But Geoffrey estimated he was able to stick to his routine over 90 percent of the time. What helped him succeed with routine? I believe it was his recognition that a routine was possible.

As for Geoffrey's clients and partners? The only shift they noticed was how much more productive he was. Geoffrey didn't receive a single comment about his email response time — his biggest concern.

⧗

Busy people *do* have enough time — as long as they are clear about their core priorities, as presented in part 1 of this book. Proactive Routines help all of us shift from time scarcity to time abundance.

Habits drive results; energy oscillates; and focus beats multi-tasking. These three principles cumulate in an irrefutable case for the benefit of routines. A Proactive Routine will help you to do the right work at the right time with the right mindset.

The next few chapters will help you create your unique Proactive Routines. You are only a few steps away from transforming how you run your days.

12

Define Your Time Budget

Where you are going to spend your time and your energy is one of the most important decisions you get to make in life.

— Jeff Bezos

LARRY'S OFFICE LEASE WAS UP FOR RENEWAL. HE HAD BEEN putting off the task of reviewing the contract for weeks. After all, he didn't go into business to review contracts. Yes, this was a necessary task, but it wasn't directly related to his core priorities. He owned a printing shop and focused most of his time on his clients, marketing, and his team.

But he couldn't put off attending to the contract any longer. Ultimately, he had to take his focus away from his core priorities and attend to this supporting task. And it happened at the worst time — on a day when he was also racing to meet many pressing client requests. But his lease was expiring at the end of the day — the same lease that had been sitting patiently on the corner of his desk for weeks. He couldn't ignore it any longer. This important task was now an urgent task.

Larry was navigating a challenge we can all relate to — he hadn't budgeted his time well enough. Larry prioritized his clients first, which many people do, including me. But Larry neglected to save *any* time for important supporting tasks. This is a common trap to fall into.

You may not need to review lease contracts in your job, but you definitely have other supporting tasks. These are the tasks that still need to get done, even if they are not directly tied to your core priorities. These may include anything from updating your website to preparing for a performance review to booking a flight.

> The greatest predictor of your success is how you spend your time.

How do we navigate the inevitable tug-of-war between our core priorities and a myriad of other fringe tasks — our supporting tasks that still need to get done? This is what your Proactive Routine is designed to reconcile. This tool will help you make the most of your time and build on the important work you did in part 1.

BUILDING YOUR PROACTIVE ROUTINE

Now it's time to build your Proactive Routine — a key tool for Workday Warriors. I can't wait to walk you through the simple steps you need to take to achieve your goal. As you learned in the previous chapters, routines lead to success; routines help you protect time for what you value most; and routines empower you to make the most of your time. Routines help you become a Workday Warrior.

Yet in my experience, few people fully embrace a Proactive Routine. I hope you will choose differently. After all, the greatest predictor of your success is how you spend your time.

YOUR TIME BUDGET

The first step in building your Proactive Routine is to define your time budget. You already know what a financial budget is: a plan for how you want to spend (and save) your money. A time budget is quite similar — it's a plan for how you want to spend your time. And because this book is focused on your work life, we'll talk about your time budget for work (although a time budget for your personal life can be just as helpful when trying to craft your ideal life).

If your MAP is your foundation, think of your time budget as the frame for your home. It needn't be fancy, but it is essential for providing structure for your time, just like a financial budget is for your money. With that said, there are two big differences between a time budget and a financial budget.

> **Time Budget:**
> An ideal plan for how you want to spend your time.

The first difference is that you can't *save* your time. Your time will pass, regardless of what you choose to do with that time. While you can save your money for a rainy day, you can't tuck away extra time for a future crunch period.

The second distinction between a time budget and a financial one is that everyone possesses the same amount of time at the start of each day. While there are vast differences in the amount of money people have, everyone has the same 1,440 minutes each day. Once again, it's up to you where you spend your time. But once today is done, your time is gone. Tomorrow, you'll get a fresh supply of minutes to spend.

There are, of course, drastic differences in how people spend their time. Some use it to create widespread global change for the better. Other people can hardly account for what they have done since breakfast. I know you're on the more impressive end of this spectrum, but I'm guessing you still want to do *more* with your time. Your time budget will help with that. It prompts you to target your time so you can achieve your goals.

INPUT VERSUS OUTPUT

Let's say you allocate $10,000 for a renovation project. Your supply of funds for this project is $10,000. Sure, you could invest more money in the project, but this is what you are prepared to spend. As for time, this is a do-it-yourself renovation, and you plan to dedicate twenty-five hours to this project. This is your time supply. Of course, you could spend more time on this renovation, but that wouldn't be ideal — you want to complete this project before your in-laws come to visit.

Similarly, we have a time budget for our work. If you plan to work from 8:00 a.m. until 5:00 p.m., with a one-hour lunch break, your time supply is eight hours a day or forty hours over five days. You could work extra hours, but that isn't ideal.

Both of these are examples of budget inputs: the resources you plan to invest — from money for a renovation ($10,000) to time at work (forty hours).

But all budgets have an input and an output; the output is your goal or what you are trying to achieve. You need to decide how to allocate your budget inputs, your supply of time and money, to best achieve your goals. For the renovation, you would need a wide range of materials, but you only have a finite supply of money. Similarly, you only have so much time to finish this project, despite the many discrete steps, so you may not be able to complete everything on your wish list.

Your time budget is a reflection of your inputs and outputs: the amount of time you dedicate to your work (your time supply) and what you want to do with that time (your time demand). As with any budget, trade-offs will be required to balance your inputs and outputs, your supply and demand.

WE THRIVE WHEN SUPPLY EQUALS DEMAND

The free-market system is driven by supply and demand forces; there is always some flux and sometimes the balance between supply and demand can become skewed. But market forces work to equalize them. Similarly, our time supply and demand is often in flux. Our schedules can feel under attack when the there is a significant imbalance between our supply of time and the demands placed on it. For busy people, it is often demand that outpaces supply — there is too much to do and not enough time. And this disequilibrium never feels good.

If a project demands two hours of work, you need to make two hours available. If you only have one hour to complete the work, you cannot expect to complete the task. To solve this problem, you can do one of two things: increase your time supply or decrease the time demands of the project. You can work all through the night, or you can scale back, streamline, or seek help, which we'll discuss more in part 3. But whichever approach you use, you need to find a way to balance your time budget. This is exactly what Workday Warriors do — and they do it every single day.

Yet, most busy people perpetually live in an uncomfortable disequilibrium. They are always busy. Always running. Their time demand consistently exceeds their time supply. If your work supply is eight hours and your work demand is twelve hours per day, you can't help but feel stressed, overloaded, and frustrated. You could be the most efficient person in your organization, but you can't escape the fact that your work demand is far greater than your time supply. This is an unsustainable disequilibrium.

An unsustainable disequilibrium:
Supply < Demand
Not enough time and too much to do

The longer this inequity persists, the more likely you are to feel frustrated and compelled to pour more and more time into your work. Eventually, this leads to burnout. Busy people often say, "I need more time" or "There just isn't enough time!" You might have said something similar. I know I did before I reset how I work, and if I'm honest, I'm still tempted to say it once in a while. The difference is that now I know how to equalize my supply and demand, which shortens these imbalances.

While a small, short-term disequilibrium between supply and demand can be manageable, a large and chronic one is unsustainable. You may not have put it in this way, but your prime goal in reading this book is probably to equalize your time supply and demand.

We can't perform at our best until we balance this equation — when the time we dedicate to work equals the time required for our best work. Plus, we want to be happy with the amount of time we invest in our work and equally happy with the results we're generating. We don't need this equation to be perfectly balanced all the time, but we need these two sides of the equation to be equal *most* of the time if we want to thrive.

A balanced time budget:
Supply = Demand
Time dedicated to work = Time required for your work

Making work *work* is all about making supply equal demand. We know this intuitively, and we are naturally compelled to reconcile any unsettling disequilibrium — and we can do so in one of two ways. But before we go there, let's define your time supply and demand.

DEFINING YOUR TIME SUPPLY

Half of your time budget reflects your time supply — the amount of time you invest in your work. So let's dive into this important part of your time budget. Let's discuss your current time supply, your ideal and your *realistic* ideal.

Your current time supply

How much time do you currently invest in your work? This depends on what it takes to advance your core priorities, support your leader, serve your clients, partner with your colleagues, and achieve your goals. To calculate your current time supply, consider the hours of your typical workweek. Make sure to include all the tiny bits outside of your traditional working hours. Do you scan your phone while eating breakfast? Do you work on projects after putting the kids to bed? If so, add this time to your overall supply, even if it is a mere fifteen minutes. This time quickly adds up each week.

At this time, we are considering only your time dedicated to work. For now, do not include time you take for breaks and personal tasks. These breaks are essential, and we'll spend more time talking about them in chapter 13. But let's not count them toward your work time supply — the time you invest in your work.

Once you identify your current time supply, it may be even more obvious to you that this amount of time is not ideal, especially if you are working more than you want — longer workdays; evenings; weekends; vacations. Sure, you knew these long hours weren't ideal before doing this exercise. Frankly, this is probably what prompted you to read this book. But it becomes oh-so-much clearer when you see it written down. Plus, you're better able to make a shift when you know exactly what you're dealing with.

Your ideal time supply

Let's now consider your ideal time supply. I encourage you to take some liberties here. Don't be constrained by what you've done in the past. For example, maybe you want to work twenty hours a week and have three months of vacation each year. You may prefer a four-day workweek with ten-hour workdays. You may prefer to take Wednesdays off but are willing to work on Sunday mornings. For a moment, allow yourself to dream of what your ideal workweek could look like. It's okay if your ideal is not entirely possible — most roles have fairly established work hours. But you'll never be able to shift away from an undesirable time budget if you don't allow yourself the chance to imagine what your ideal looks like.

Once you've explored what may be possible, I encourage you to settle somewhere between your current and ideal time supply. I call this your *realistic* ideal time supply.

Your realistic ideal

Your current time supply may not be ideal, and your ideal time supply may not be realistic. So let's discuss a third option: your *realistic* ideal. You might think this sounds like an oxymoron. But I prefer to think of it as a stretch goal. It's your best-case scenario: an attainable plan that allows you to thrive, both professionally and personally.

Your realistic ideal time supply gives you just enough time for your work, while also protecting the time you want for your personal life. I encourage you to set your realistic ideal time supply as close to your ideal as you can. In chapter 6, I encouraged you to incorporate a buffer in your daily plan so you can accommodate the inevitable incoming requests. But when it comes to your time supply, I don't recommend you include a buffer. If you do, Parkinson's Law will kick in and your work will expand to fill all of that bonus time, as we discussed in chapter 11. I'd rather see you function with a wee too *little* time. That will keep you focused on your core priorities and more resistant to tangents. You'll be less likely to dance with future priorities. You'll stop meandering down the path of distraction. You'll also be forced to apply the Simplify Filter, a key Workday Warrior tool which we'll discuss in part 3.

⌛

Now it's time to put pen to paper. Use exercise 6 to define your time supply: your current, ideal, and realistic ideal for a typical week. Some variation from one day to the next is to be expected. But you can usually identify a close-enough estimate over a week.

Don't worry about perfecting your time estimates right now. Set "good enough" as your goal. Done is better than perfect. Plus, you'll be able to refine this over time as you pay closer attention to what works best for you.

EXERCISE 6. DEFINE YOUR TIME SUPPLY: THE TIME YOU DEDICATE TO YOUR WORK

Time supply inputs	Current (hours per week)	Ideal (hours per week)	Realistic ideal (hours per week)
How much time do you have available for work between when your workday starts until it ends?			
Do you work before your work-day starts (e.g., Check your phone over breakfast; read on the bus, etc.)?	+	+	+
Do you work in the evenings (e.g., focus work, email, calls, etc.)?	+	+	+
Do you work on the weekend (e.g., focus work, email, calls, etc.)?	+	+	+
How much time do you take for lunch, breaks, or personal ac-tivities during your workday?*	-	-	-
Are there any other factors that impact your supply of work hours?	+ / -	+ / -	+ / -
Total			

---

* I encourage you to take breaks during your workday. Breaks are essential, both personally and professionally. Breaks support our well-being and also allow us to renew our energy. After a break, we come back to work more refreshed and pro-ductive. Workday Warriors recognize the power of breaks and prioritize them every day. With that said, you should not include this personal time when you calculate the total time you invest in your work.

CALCULATE YOUR TIME DEMAND

Now let's calculate the other side of your time budget: your time demand. You might find you could work a solid twelve hours a day, six days a week, just to feel like you are keeping up. In that case, twelve hours may reflect your *current* time demand. But this may not match your ideal time supply. And as we've already established, a disequilibrium between your time demand and your time supply doesn't allow you to perform at your best.

Before we equalize your supply and demand, let's consider a more precise estimate of your time demand. There are two ways to calculate your current time demand: one takes several weeks; the other takes a few minutes. You could certainly spend the next two weeks tracking your time; the result would provide you with valuable insight into how you spend your time. For this reason, I include time tracking as a Workday Warrior strategy in part 3. But for the sake of this exercise, you don't need to track your time. In the spirit of keeping things simple, I suggest you just spend a few minutes estimating your current time demand. As you do so, I'd like you to consider the time you dedicate to your core priorities, supporting tasks, future priorities, and distractions. I'll highlight some factors to consider as you calculate your time demands over the next few sections.

As you think about your different types of work, I invite you to fill in exercise 7. But please don't overthink this exercise. Don't worry about getting this perfect. You'll quickly see whether you need to make any adjustments once you implement your Proactive Routine, which we'll discuss in chapter 14.

EXERCISE 7. DEFINE YOUR TIME DEMAND: THE TIME REQUIRED FOR YOUR WORK

Types of work	Current		Realistic ideal	
	Core priorities (hours per week)	Supporting tasks (hours per week)	Core priorities (hours per week)	Supporting tasks (hours per week)
Independent focus work	_____	_____	_____	_____
Meetings (plus any required commuting or travel)	_____	_____	_____	_____
Informal communication (email, texts, chats, unscheduled calls, etc.)	_____	_____	_____	_____
Subtotals	_____	_____	_____	_____
Total time demand	_____		_____	

Note: I did not include a set of columns for your ideal time demand. Sure, it may be ideal to assign 100 percent of your work time to your core priorities. But since we've already established this isn't realistic, you can go straight from your current state to your realistic ideal.

Time demand: Core priorities

Let's begin by considering the time demands for your core priorities. As mentioned above, it may be perfect if you could spend 100 percent of your work time on your core priorities. This is certainly appealing. After all, this is the work you value most, and it makes the biggest impact. But this isn't realistic. You and I both know how hard it is to shield ourselves from outside forces. Perhaps you can occasionally carve out time to hide at an isolated retreat, free from interruptions. But this probably isn't a frequent option. Plus, as we've already discussed, some of your time needs to be protected for supporting tasks, including planning, reporting, team bonding, et cetera.

If you spend too *much* time on your core priorities, you'll make impressive progress, yes, but your systems are likely crumbling around you. You may feel you're on the brink of chaos. Oh yes, and there is a good chance your colleagues will be frustrated (even if they don't appear to be so) since they will often have to pay the price when you don't invest enough time in supporting tasks. They often have to chase you down to get simple answers, and they may have to cover your share of the tasks designed to help the greater good.

On the other hand, if you spend too *little* time on your core priorities (a much more common experience), you will end up frustrated with your slow progress. Your inbox may be clear, but you won't have enough time for your big goals.

To help identify a close-enough time estimate for your core priorities, consider the three *ways* you work: focus work, meetings, and informal communications. For each of the three ways of working, consider how you currently spend your time, along with your realistic ideal.

- Focus work: Approximately how much heads-down, independent, focus work do you need for your core priorities each week? In my experience, practically every one of us needs at least some independent focus work time. I have yet to come across someone who didn't.
- Meetings: Approximately how much time do you spend in meetings related to your core priorities each week? The more senior you are, the more time you tend to spend in meetings. Similarly, if you are in a client-facing role, most of your time could be spent in meetings.
- Informal communication: How much time do you spend communicating outside of meetings? This includes email, texts, chats, unscheduled calls, casual conversations, and other discussions related to your core priorities.

Time demand: Supporting tasks

Let's now turn to your supporting tasks. As we discussed in part 1, supporting tasks are necessary for your role — they still need your time and attention — but don't directly relate to your core priorities. I'd like you to consider exactly how much time is necessary to invest in your supporting tasks. But to do so, you must know what you're dealing with. See the below exercise for a list of tasks that may qualify as your supporting tasks. But don't be limited to this list. You may have other supporting tasks that are not included here.

Some of these tasks will be more relevant to you than others. Conversely, some of these items might relate to your core priorities, in which case you should not include them in your time budget for your supporting tasks. For example, if you are a marketing manager, social media may be one of your core priorities. But this may be a supporting task for someone in another role.

> Supporting tasks are necessary to your role but do not directly relate to your core priorities.

You might be surprised to see strategic planning on the below list. You might wonder why such an important step is relegated to the ranks of a supporting task? You are right — it *is* an important step. But it is a step that *supports* your core priorities — thus, it is a supporting task. And we need to budget time to this important supporting task, among others.

It's important to note that the same type of work can be associated with different things, like your core priorities or your supporting tasks. For example, you'll have some meetings about your core priorities and other meetings about your supporting tasks, The same is true for independent work, email, chat, texts, and more. So, we can't just make a broad sweeping statement that email is a supporting task. Yes, sometimes it is. But other times, email helps us to advance our core priorities. I'm not suggesting you count and categorize every email and meeting. I'm simply encouraging you to roughly estimate how much time you need for your supporting tasks (see exercise 8).

EXERCISE 8. WHAT ARE YOUR SUPPORTING TASKS?

Which of the following reflect some of your supporting tasks? Use this list to help you define your realistic, ideal amount of time to spend on these supporting tasks each week.

Meetings
- ☐ Team meetings
- ☐ Town hall meetings
- ☐ One-on-one meetings
- ☐ Company events

Business growth
- ☐ Business development
- ☐ Marketing / social media
- ☐ Writing / blogging

Team & Communication
- ☐ Email, texts, and chats
- ☐ Casual conversations
- ☐ Team support
- ☐ Partners
- ☐ Feedback conversations

Strategic planning
- ☐ Goal setting & reviews
- ☐ Executive updates
- ☐ Reporting
- ☐ Financial management
- ☐ Daily planning

Professional development
- ☐ Training
- ☐ Performance reviews
- ☐ Reading
- ☐ Conferences

Community
- ☐ Volunteering
- ☐ Networking
- ☐ Industry associations

Administrative tasks
- ☐ Time tracking
- ☐ Meeting logistics
- ☐ Expense submissions
- ☐ Contract reviews
- ☐ Facilities management
- ☐ Vendor management
- ☐ Commuting
- ☐ Business travel
- ☐ Technology updates
- ☐ Organizing
- ☐ Scanning / digitizing

Other
- ☐
- ☐
- ☐

WHAT IS YOUR IDEAL TIME SPLIT?

Now that we've discussed both your core priorities and supporting tasks, you're likely asking what your ideal time split is. Like any good consultant, I'll answer that question with a declarative, "It depends." It depends on your role and what you are trying to achieve. Everyone's time demands are different. Your core priorities may require a different amount of time than my core priorities. Overall, I recommend you reflect on what your Goldilocks balance would be: not too much and not too little time for both your core priorities and supporting tasks. But alas, I recognize this doesn't get you closer to an answer on your ideal time split.

Thankfully, there are some indicators that 60:40 *may* be a good split — 60 percent of your work time for your core priorities and 40 percent of your work time for your supporting tasks. Brendon Burchard, author of *High-Performance Habits*,[1] surveyed over twenty thousand people to identify what high performers do differently. He found that the most effective people dedicate 60 percent or more of their time to their core priorities, or their prolific quality output, as he calls it.

> The most effective people dedicate 60 percent *or more* of their time to their core priorities.

Similarly, time studies led by Mark Ellwood, of Pace Productivity, found that great performers spend approximately one hour a day more on their core priorities than do good performers. Good performers dedicate four hours a day (or 50 percent), whereas great performers dedicate five hours a day (62.5 percent) to their top priorities.[2]

Based on these findings, the best split of your work time may be 60 percent or more for your core priorities and 40 percent or less for your supporting tasks. But ultimately, you need to determine the ideal ratio for your role. How much time do you need to achieve the goals associated with your core priorities, both personally and professionally?

Sixty percent may not seem like enough for your core priorities. But we can't ignore those supporting tasks. Most people require at *least* two hours a day for their supporting tasks. In fact, supporting tasks are often clamouring for much more of your time. But just because you could spend more time on your supporting tasks doesn't mean you should. Forty percent of a forty-hour workweek corresponds to just over three hours a day. Perhaps think of this as your upper limit for your supporting tasks. If you work more than forty hours a week (as many professionals and executives regularly do), you'll get the biggest payoff by investing the extra time in your core priorities. We want to protect 60 percent *or more* of our work time for our core priorities. As a Workday Warrior, consider setting three hours per day *or fewer* as your time budget for your supporting tasks. Just keep in mind that you can't eliminate your supporting tasks completely. As Larry, who I mentioned at the beginning of this chapter, learned the hard way, our supporting tasks still need our time and attention.

Time demand: Distractions

The final variable to consider in your time budget is your distracting tasks. These are all low-value tasks that don't align with your goals. Distractions can be obvious ones, like cat videos, or subtle ones, like attending unnecessary meetings and giving interruptions unfettered access to your focus time. Not surprisingly, you don't want to allocate any of your work time to distracting tasks. Sure, if you're bored and looking for things to fill your time, you could indulge in distractions. But I'm pretty sure "boredom" is not one of your challenges. People who struggle to fill their time tend not to read productivity books.

Now, you don't need to be militant about your distractions. If you occasionally succumb to a distraction, you can still have a productive week. But if you spend more than a little time on distractions, you likely have a bigger issue to consider. You may not be investing enough time in well-being; as a result, your weary mind doesn't have the strength to resist things vying for your attention. Or you might not be inspired by your work, in which case you may be due for a mindset or role change.

To successfully curtail our distractions, we need to know what they are. Personally, one of my biggest distractions is diving into the rabbit hole of the internet. The topics that take me captive tend to creep up on me in a sneaky way. I'll begin by looking up one piece of research related to a core priority. Then I click on a related link. Then another. Before I know it, I'm caught up in a topic far removed from what I came searching for.

In part 1, I encouraged you to identify your distractions. It's worthwhile to revisit this exercise as you define your time budget. After all, distractions can be sneaky and quite good at consuming more of our time than we want to give them. Consider using exercise 9 to identify your distractions. Remember that a distraction for you may be a core priority for one of your colleagues.

Your distractions may include scrolling through social media, attending meetings that your colleagues are more than capable of managing, doing work better suited to someone else's role, frequently revisiting decisions that have already been made, refining a process that is already good enough, and more. Does this mean you should never do any of these activities? Not at all. Sometimes a small amount of time spent on these activities is justifiable. But any more than that becomes a distraction.

> High-performance teams prioritize team connections and relationship building.

Some activities are purely distracting, so you want to avoid spending any time on them. And of course, there are many activities that you may pursue during your personal time but not during your work time. If you choose to check your social feed on a break or to relax in the evenings with your Netflix bestie, go for it! Restorative breaks make you more productive (while also boosting your well-being) — we'll discuss this more in chapter 13.

Clients will often ask me whether casual conversations with their colleagues count as distractions. When you add up time spent on random social banter at the start of every meeting, the quick "Do you have a minute?" conversations, and all other casual chats, the minutes rapidly accumulate. But I don't think of this time as a distraction. These chats are essential team interactions that strengthen trust and elevate team performance. High-performance teams prioritize team connections and relationship building. If your team has a hybrid model, with some virtual and some in-person work, you'll want to protect even more time for casual connections during your in-person time.

EXERCISE 9. WHAT DISTRACTS YOU?

Which of the following activities distract you? How can you reduce the time you invest in these activities during your prime working hours?

- ☐ Spending too much time on social media
- ☐ Browsing the internet without a clear goal
- ☐ Over-researching topics
- ☐ Attending certain meetings
- ☐ Reclaiming delegated work
- ☐ Redoing others' work
- ☐ Revisiting decisions
- ☐ Refining good-enough processes

- ☐ Asking others to copy you on every email
- ☐ Constantly monitoring email, chat, and text or other forms of multi-tasking
- ☐ Gossiping and other unproductive conversations
- ☐ Worrying and doubting yourself
- ☐ Other

Time demand: Personal activities

You might notice that personal time is missing from exercise 9. That is because breaks are not distractions. We absolutely do want to take breaks during our workday. Breaks help us restore our energy and come back to work more renewed and focused. Plus, we can't ignore the fact that we need to book dentist appointments, pay our bills, and talk to our suppliers, and we can't always shift these personal activities outside of our traditional working hours.

So yes, take a lunch and other breaks. This is a crucial Workday Warrior strategy. Just don't include this personal time in your work time budget. We'll discuss our personal time more in our next chapter — a chapter dedicated to paying ourselves first, doing such things as looking after our own well-being. For now, while we focus on your work time budget, we are simply looking at your time dedicated to work (although a time budget can work equally well in your personal life if you are feeling stretched there as well).

Time demand: Future priorities

Now let's consider how much time you should dedicate to your future priorities. But of course, you already know the answer to this. We talked about this in part 1. That's right — absolutely no time at all. Zilch. Nada. Nothing. This applies to future priorities in your work and personal life.

As we've already discussed, any time you give to future priorities will dilute progress on your core priorities. So use your time budget as a reminder to push off all work on any future priorities until you are ready to promote one of them to a core priority.

Completing this part of your time budget is so easy, I'm going to do it for you. I haven't even included room for your future priorities in your time budget template. If you're tempted to override my recommendation, I invite you to consider whether your core priorities are getting enough of your time and attention. If the answer is no, put your pen down and step away. Your time invested in future priorities should remain at zero.

BALANCING SUPPLY AND DEMAND

Now that you've defined your time supply and demand, you may be facing a common dilemma — your time demand exceeds your time supply. We all face pressure to do more. Like an elastic, our time demands strive to stretch us further. But our time supply is the counterforce, pulling us back after we hit a certain threshold. It's not surprising that we feel stretched too thin when our time demands are too, well, demanding.

So yes, we need to balance our time supply and demand. Clearly, an imbalance is not a sustainable situation. But I don't need to tell you that. No doubt, you are reading this book because you want to find a solution to this problem. As you now know, you have two options to balance your time supply and demand.

Option A: Increase supply

We've discussed the first option of increasing your time supply. You could throw time at the problem; you could work longer hours. Wake up earlier;

stay at work later; log on again after the kids go to bed; work on the weekends; work on vacation; cancel plans with your friends so you can work. Not surprisingly, this option leads to burnout and, of course, necessitates countless personal sacrifices.

This is the option most people default to. I should know. After all, I did this for far too many years. And while this option may work for a short-term sprint, it is not a sustainable long-term solution. But you already know this. Thankfully, we have another option.

Option B: Decrease demand

Option B is to reduce the demands for your time. This is exactly what you're learning about in this book. I'm not implying you should play small. I'd rather see you use all the strategies in this book to amplify your efforts. As we already discussed in part 1, you make the most of your time when you focus on three core priorities. Now, in part 2, we are building your Proactive Routine, which will help you use your time supply in the most effective way. And as we'll discuss in part 3, we'll consider more opportunities to scale back, streamline, and seek help.

WHAT IS YOUR BALANCED TIME BUDGET?

Now it's time to answer the question we've been building toward: How many hours do you need to balance your work time supply and demand? Consider your realistic ideal for both your supply and demand. You may stick to the standard forty-hour workweek. Or you could set that number higher or lower.

Regardless, you need to identify the number that best supports your goals at this time — and a number that balances your supply and demand. You can always revisit your time budget in the future as conditions change. But for now, we'll use this amount of time to build your Proactive Routine, which we'll dive into in the next chapter.

If you're struggling to balance your supply and demand, it is likely because your demand is too high. I assure you there is hope. In part 3, we will

Your Balanced Time Budget:

Your Time Supply = Your Time Demand

_____ hours/week = _____ hours/week

discuss multiple ways for you to scale back the demand on your time. The best part is that these options won't dilute your impact. In fact, as a Workday Warrior, you can often accomplish more with less time.

YOUR PROACTIVE ROUTINE

Now that you've balanced your time budget, it is time to apply it to your Proactive Routine. I'm sure you've been mentally crafting your routine, but now it's time to pull it all together. We'll do this together in the next chapter. It's time to pay yourself first.

13

Build Your Proactive Routine

How you spend your time defines who you are.
— Oprah Winfrey

WHEN I WAS TWENTY-FOUR YEARS OLD, I WAS RELATIVELY new to being financially independent from my parents. I had graduated from university, backpacked across Europe, and recently settled into a career I loved. I was renting an apartment and juggling all the expenses that life brings. I was also thinking about some of the bigger expenses looming — including home ownership, which seemed so out of reach at the time.

Right around that time, I heard David Chilton, author of *The Wealthy Barber*,[1] speak. I vividly remember Chilton introducing the concept of paying myself first. I was captivated. Chilton recommended we *first* put money aside for savings and investments before spending in other categories. This concept made perfect sense and I started applying it to my modest income immediately.

Paying ourselves first is good practice when dealing with any scarce resource. This couldn't be any more true for our most precious resource: our time.

PROTECTING SPACE FOR BIG ROCKS

Around the same time I heard David Chilton speak, I also heard a powerful analogy — one that I've thought about many times since. It was a story of a professor who was standing at the front of her class with a glass vase on her desk. She poured in some water, then some sand, and then some pebbles. She also had a few big rocks on her desk, but she couldn't fit them in the vase. There was no more room.

She asked the students how she could fit the big rocks in, and they correctly told her to start again. But this time, put the big rocks in the vase first. Then add the pebbles, sand, and water. The teacher did as instructed and had no trouble fitting the big rocks in the vase. As a bonus, she managed to fill in the gaps with a lot of the pebbles, sand, and water. She couldn't fit in all of these "extras" but that wasn't the goal. The goal was to find space for the big rocks. Similarly, if we want to find time for our core priorities — our big rocks — we need to add them to our routine first, before other tasks fill our time. We need to pay ourselves first — with both our money and our time.

We'll now transition to building your Proactive Routine around this crucial concept: paying yourself first. This will ensure that your core priorities and personal well-being get first pick for your limited time.

BUILD YOUR PROACTIVE ROUTINE

Step 1: Define your work hours
In the previous chapter, you identified your total supply of work hours. You may have set your time supply as the standard forty hours, assuming you work full-time. Or you may have decided to invest more time in your goals.

In some industries and some roles, of course, the time expectations are much higher. The exact number of hours you commit to working is a personal decision, one that requires you to strike the ideal balance between your time supply and demand based on your goals.

Now it's time to take your fixed supply of work time and allocate these hours across your week. When are you planning to work? Your work hours may not fit into the neat and tidy 9–5 schedule that is a relic of long ago. And in our modern world — with global teams spanning time zones and devices that are constantly connected — people can literally work anywhere and any time. This is both good and bad.

On the plus side, this flexibility offers a great opportunity to align our work to when it best meets our combined business and personal needs. If your role allows for some flexibility, you may choose to shift some of your work hours to better suit your life. On certain days, I pick up my kids from school at 3:30 p.m., which I value doing. Sometimes I'm able to quickly return to my work; other times, I step right into my chauffeur role and don't get back to my work until their activities wrap up later in the evening. But I'm perfectly content to shift my work hours to balance my family needs.

Not all roles have as much flexibility. Your hours may be fairly set, based on the nature of what you do. If that's the case, you may appreciate the clearer boundaries between your work and life. The downside of the increased flexibility is that the line between work and life has become quite blurred for many. The fact that we can work anywhere and at any time often means we are working everywhere and at all times — alongside roommates, children, or barking dogs. Thankfully, clear working hours help us tap into the upside of flexibility while avoiding a frustrating overlap between work and life.

In plotting the boundaries of your work, you will clearly identify when you choose to work (and when you choose not to work). The professor's vase mentioned above created boundaries for its contents. Similarly, a clearly defined workday creates boundaries for our work. It helps to avoid a fuzzy spillover between our work and personal life. Of course, you will need to be flexible in select instances. But you'll soon realize how powerful these boundaries are at containing your work.

As we're going through this chapter, I encourage you to build your Proactive Routine. You can use the template found at clearconceptinc.ca /WorkdayWarrior.

Marco's work hours

Marco, an insurance executive, described during our first phone call how work had consumed his life. Despite working around the clock, he still felt incredibly behind and knew he was underperforming. We began by defining Marco's core priorities and building his MAP, which helped him sharpen his focus and make faster progress on his most important work.

> **Workday Warrior Action:**
> Build your
> Proactive Routine
> Step 1: Define your
> work hours.

Then we focused on building his routine. Marco considered his time budget and determined that forty-nine hours would provide the ideal balance between his time supply and demand given his goals at the time.

As an early bird, Marco's peak energy was at the beginning of his workday. Marco found it easy to start his workday earlier than most, at 7:00 a.m. But by lunchtime, he was due for a break. In the past, he had worked straight through lunch — never feeling he had the luxury of stopping. But skipping his lunch wasn't helping. His productivity declined as the day wore on; he admitted he was dragging himself through the afternoons.

After a prolonged discussion about the power of breaks, Marco eventually conceded to blocking off an hour for a lunch break (see figure 10). It took some time to convince him that a break would condense his workday. But once he regularly took these lunch breaks, his afternoon productivity was so much better. He got more done in less time. These midday breaks gave him a chance to renew his energy and left him with enough stamina to work until 6:00 p.m. (and 5:00 p.m. on Fridays) — long before he used to wrap up his workday — before Marco committed to becoming a Workday Warrior.

	Monday	Tuesday	Wednesday	Thursday	Friday
7:00–7:30					
7:30–8:00					
8:00–8:30					
8:30–9:00					
9:00–9:30			Work		
9:30–10:00					
10:00–10:30					
10:30–11:00					
11:00–11:30					
11:30–12:00					
12:00–12:30			Lunch		
12:30–1:00					
1:00–1:30					
1:30–2:00					
2:00–2:30					
2:30–3:00			Work		
3:00–3:30					
3:30–4:00					
4:00–4:30					
4:30–5:00					
5:00–5:30					
5:30–6:00					

Figure 10. Marco's work hours

Step 2: Protect time for your core priorities

Next, we move onto the most exciting step — protecting time for your core priorities before anything else gets in your way. This is where you protect time for your big rocks *first*. With this simple step, you are adopting a productivity secret embraced by the world's most elite performers: they consistently block time for what matters most. They know this is the single best way to boost their productivity and generate the results they want.

Not surprisingly, the best time to work on your core priorities is during your peak energy. As we discussed in chapter 10, your peak energy often bookends your workday. Whether you are an early bird or a night owl, you likely have fresh energy at the start of your workday and another surge toward the end of your workday. You may also have an energy uptake after lunch or breaks — although larger meals can make you feel sleepy. Ultimately, you are the best judge of when you have your best energy.

> **Workday Warrior Action:**
> Build your
> Proactive Routine
> Step 2: Protect time for
> your core priorities.

Once you've identified your prime energy time, you want to protect this time to focus on your core priorities. You could cluster your independent focus time in the morning since mornings are so rich. Or perhaps you'd prefer some independent focus time in the morning and some more focus time late in the afternoon. This may be an overly used catchphrase but protecting this time will truly help you work smarter instead of harder.

In chapter 11, we talked about a key Workday Warrior strategy: focusing on one task at a time. Your Proactive Routine helps you to embrace this strategy by clearly identifying when you'll do your independent work.

You may not be comfortable ignoring new email and other incoming requests for several hours during your focus time. But you can adopt a focus routine, such as the 50/10 rotation we discussed in chapter 11: fifty minutes of focus work followed by ten minutes responding to messages. This allows you to balance high-quality independent work with timely responsiveness. I probably don't need to remind you that focus routines like this do require careful monitoring. Incoming requests tend to clamour for more and more time. It helps to remind yourself that you will have several other pockets throughout the rest of the day to address them.

Marco's core priorities

Once Marco had his work boundaries clearly defined, he identified when he would do the bulk of his focus work. Marco agreed that the beginning of his workdays, when his energy was high and his interruptions were low, was the best time to focus on his core priorities. He knew that three solid hours of focus work at the start of his day would help him make significant progress on his most important work. To protect this focus time, he pushed his meetings to start after 10:00 a.m (see figure 11). Once in a while, he accepted a meeting request before 10:00 a.m., but for the most part, he was able to protect this early morning time for his independent work.

	Monday	Tuesday	Wednesday	Thursday	Friday
7:00–7:30					
7:30–8:00					
8:00–8:30			Focus Work (Core Priorities)		
8:30–9:00					
9:00–9:30					
9:30–10:00					
10:00–10:30					
10:30–11:00			Meetings (Core Priorities)		
11:00–11:30					
11:30–12:00					
12:00–12:30			Lunch		
12:30–1:00					

Figure 11. Marco's Focus Work

Step 3: Define your meeting sweet spot

When you're dining out, do you let others dig into your yummy meal before you do? I didn't think so. But when it comes to your time, are you letting your meetings eat up your time before you've protected it for your core priorities? Giving your meetings first pick in your calendar is akin to letting an always hungry teen eat your meal before you take a few bites. Speaking from experience, there likely won't be much left over for you, even if they've just polished off their own meal before diving into yours. If this only happened occasionally, you could refill during your next meal. But if it happens consistently, you won't get the nourishment your body needs. The same is true for our insatiable meetings — we want to grant them access to our calendar *after* we've blocked time to focus on our core priorities. In other words, stop giving meetings unrestricted access to your prime morning energy.

> Block time in your calendar for independent focus work.

Let me be clear: meetings are an important part of our workday. Meetings are a crucial way to advance many of our goals. Work is a team sport, and we *want* to make time to collaborate. But we don't want these meetings to overpower our equally important independent focus work — unless your role simply does not require independent focus work (which is rare).

I'm often asked whether we should block time in our calendar for independent focus work and the answer is yes. On many teams, people have access to each others' calendars so that they can book meetings whenever they choose. This leads to meetings scattered here and there, with only choppy bits left over for core priorities. As a result, days feel like a frustrating game of tennis — you're running back and forth from one side of the court to the other, never really in control of the game. And when meetings consume more than their fair share of your day, it feels like your own work keeps getting interrupted by endless time outs. You can avoid this by blocking time for independent work.

In the last chapter, I encouraged you to define the ideal amount of time you want to spend in meetings each week. I call this your meeting sweet spot. Now, I encourage you to define when the best times are for your meetings. Some of your meetings will relate to your core priorities; others will relate to your supporting tasks. Regardless of their focus, schedule these meetings outside the time you've dedicated to your independent focus work.

Personally, I aim to book my meetings in the late morning or early afternoon. When I'm scheduling time with someone, I'll suggest times between 11:00 a.m. and 4:00 p.m. This allows me to protect focus time at the beginning and end of my day, when my energy levels are best aligned to independent work. Of course, I can and sometimes do schedule meetings outside this window. But it is refreshing how frequently others can accommodate my ideal meeting times. Overall, my meeting routine allows me to contain most of my meetings to their ideal time slots — without interfering with my core priority focus work.

Workday Warrior Action: Build your Proactive Routine Step 3: Define when the best time is for your meetings.

Let's revisit what we discussed in chapter 10: early morning team meetings — especially those that fall on a Monday. If an early morning meeting squanders your precious focus time, think about how big a drain an early meeting is for your entire team. If your team falls prey to the myth that early mornings are the best time to meet, I encourage you to lobby for a later time slot. An energizing team meeting during everyone's afternoon trough can be much more effective. Or if you can delay a meeting until late morning, everyone will be able to protect the first part of their day for valuable focus work. With that said, I concede that you need to work around what is best for your team. A sales team may find a morning team meeting to be an energizing start to their day before they spend the rest of their day meeting with clients. But in this case, they are less reliant on the need for morning focus time.

Marco's meetings and supporting tasks

After some deliberation, Marco decided that his meeting sweet spot was four hours a day, or twenty hours a week. Since he was a senior executive, much of his work was done in meetings, and many of these meetings were

	Monday	Tuesday	Wednesday	Thursday	Friday
7:00–7:30					
7:30–8:00					
8:00–8:30			Focus Work (Core Priorities)		
8:30–9:00					
9:00–9:30					
9:30–10:00					
10:00–10:30					
10:30–11:00			Meetings (Core Priorities)		
11:00–11:30					
11:30–12:00					
12:00–12:30			Lunch		
12:30–1:00					
1:00–1:30					
1:30–2:00					
2:00–2:30					
2:30–3:00					
3:00–3:30			Meetings & Supporting Tasks		
3:30–4:00					
4:00–4:30					
4:30–5:00					
5:00–5:30			Focus Work (Core Priorities)		
5:30–6:00					

Figure 12. Marco's meetings and supporting tasks

directly related to his core priorities. Marco found his meeting time was highly productive. Of course, Marco could have spent so much more time in meetings, but he needed to balance this plan with time for his independent focus work and supporting tasks. On any day, Marco needed to find ways to simplify his meeting demands. Sometimes he would agree to attend half of a meeting, or every other meeting. Regardless, he had to remain vigilant about how much time he spent in meetings. I wouldn't be surprised if meetings take more than their fair share for you as well. Stay tuned — we'll explore more meeting management strategies in part 3.

Sure, some days were more meeting-heavy than others, but Marco aimed to keep his weekly meetings to no more than twenty hours. When he allowed the time he spent in meetings to tip over this threshold, he struggled to find enough time for his core priorities and to keep up with his supporting tasks. These were the weeks when he kept working past the limits of his defined workday. He was making too many personal sacrifices, and it didn't help him feel any more caught up. Marco quickly came to realize that his meeting sweet spot required close monitoring.

Of course, Marco knew he needed to make himself available for meetings for more than just four hours a day. It would be ideal if others' schedules perfectly aligned to our schedules, but this isn't realistic. So, Marco allocated 10:00 a.m. until 5:00 p.m. for both meetings, supporting tasks, and a lunch break (see figure 12). His supporting tasks were fluid, so he tackled these in the gaps between meetings. When he contained his meetings to four hours a day, he found he had a good balance and had time available for his core priorities and supporting tasks.

At 5:00 p.m., Marco turned his attention back to some independent work related to his core priorities. He had another energy surge late in the afternoon, and he found this to be a productive time to follow up on his meetings and prepare for his next day. His only exception was on Friday, when he shut down his work at 5:00 p.m. On the weeks when he stuck to his routine, Marco didn't feel compelled to work again over the weekend.

Step 4: Protect time for your supporting tasks

After you've given your core priorities prime billing in your calendar and identified when the best times are for your meetings, you can admit your supporting tasks. You'll find these supporting tasks easily fit into the gaps between your core priorities and meetings.

The secret to fitting all of your work into your working hours is to have your supporting tasks *complement* rather than overshadow your core priorities. Of course, your supporting tasks would benefit from your peak energy, but they shouldn't be depriving your core priorities of that precious resource. Instead, I encourage you to add your supporting tasks to your routine *after* you've protected time for your core priorities. Consider putting smaller tasks in your lower energy periods, such as your afternoon trough.

Pay attention to your unique biological rhythms. Does your energy start to fade before lunch? Are you mentally fatigued toward the end of your workday? Like me, do you shift some of your daytime work hours into the early evening, when you can't help but be a bit tired? If so, these lower-energy times are best suited for your supporting tasks. But of course, your supporting tasks range in size and difficulty. If you need to tackle a tough supporting task, consider moving it to a moderate energy period. I would still recommend protecting your peak energy times for your core priorities.

Workday Warrior Action:
Build your Proactive Routine Step 4: Define when you will work on your supporting tasks.

I have coached countless clients to move their supporting tasks *out* of their prime energy periods. This is such an easy win that I continue to be surprised when they push back. They may feel compelled to respond to others or naturally like to tie up loose ends related to a variety of peripheral tasks. These intentions are terrific. But again, we don't want the time given to supporting tasks to come at the cost of devoting our peak energy to our core priorities. Rather, we want to strike the right balance throughout our day. The truth is that you can respond to others and attend to smaller tasks in short breaks during your focus time. We spoke about this in chapter 11, when we explored 50/10 focus routines and other models. If you're protecting most of your prime time for your core priorities, you can take a few minutes to attend to email and other small tasks, which may relate to either your core priorities or your supporting tasks. In this way, some of your supporting tasks can be sprinkled into the breaks between core priority focus work. Then you can protect longer stretches of time to your supporting tasks during your lower energy times.

Step 5: Prioritize your well-being

There is one other crucial area where we want to pay ourselves first: our well-being. Frankly, I would argue this needs to come before any of the elements we discussed above. True Workday Warriors recognize the need for a strong foundation of well-being, one that includes sleep, exercise, relationships, relaxation, meditation, and healthy nutrition. When we invest in our well-being, every aspect of our lives is enhanced.

But despite good intentions, many people struggle to prioritize their well-being. They skimp on sleep. They put off exercising until another day. They take shortcuts with their meals and find themselves in drive-thrus more than they want. They tell themselves they don't have time to meditate, like I did for far too many years. The irony is that those who fail to protect time for their well-being also tend to be the least productive. It's as if they are always running on power-save mode. The reality is that crucial well-being activities such as sleep, exercise, and meditation actually *save* us time. These investments in our well-being allow us to perform at our best.

Thankfully, routines can also help us prioritize our well-being. If your well-being habits could use some more attention, I encourage you to build routines around the following seven pillars of self-care:

1. Breaks and relaxation: Workday Warriors recognize that pushing away from their desk at lunch and taking other breaks throughout the day actually improve their productivity. As we discussed in chapter 11, breaks give us a chance to relax, rest our eyes, and move our bodies — something many don't get nearly enough time for. Breaks also give us a chance to refocus and recharge. Plus, breaks help to dissipate the stress that builds up when we face one meeting after another, according to a Microsoft study.[2] Breaks are essential both during and between our workdays. We can't expect to run flat out and fully recharge on an annual vacation. We recharge our devices each day and need to do the same with our own energy.

2. Exercise: Our bodies are designed to move, but our stationary jobs aren't doing us any favours. Exercise not only helps

our bodies, it also helps our mind
by improving our mental health,
lowering our stress, sharpening our
focus, and more. It's no surprise
that exercise has been called "fertil-
izer for the brain."

> Routines help us prioritize our well-being.

3. Sleep: Sleep is so much more than a luxury, as it is often
    thought of by busy people. It is when we sleep that our brains
    and bodies do their necessary repair work. Sleep sharpens our
    thinking, improves our memory, decreases our stress, boosts
    our immunity, and more. Chronic sleep deprivation, on the
    other hand, puts us at higher risks for multiple diseases from
    diabetes to strokes and decreases our performance at work.
    For all these reasons and more, high-quality sleep should be
    considered non-negotiable. Yet far too many people scrimp
    on their sleep. More than one in three Americans don't get at
    least seven hours of sleep a night according to the Centers for
    Disease Control and Prevention[3] and 50 percent of Canadians
    suffered from insomnia challenges during the pandemic,
    according to Royal Ottawa Mental Health Centre.[4]

4. Nutrition: Healthy eating helps to enhance our perform-
    ance. Nutritious foods help us focus and be more productive,
    sharpen our thinking, and be more creative, engaged, and
    collaborative. Healthy nutrition also helps to offset many
    of the deadliest diseases. Two-and-a-half millennia ago, the
    Greek physician Hippocrates said, "All disease begins in the
    gut." Despite how tempting it can be to indulge, we've known
    for generations that building routines around healthy meal
    planning and prep helps us thrive in all areas of our life.

5. Meditation: Left to its own devices, the brain can be over-
    whelmed by a dizzying array of thoughts, worries, and
    regrets. Thankfully, meditation helps us to calm the chaos
    swirling around the snow globe of our mind. Meditation
    is essential brain training that helps us focus our attention.

When we calm the jumbled array of thoughts crowding our mind, we tap into a deep state of relaxation. We also carry with us a calmer, more effective mental state in between meditation sessions. If you struggle to justify the time for this miracle practice, remind yourself that fifteen minutes is a mere 1 percent of your day.

6. Gratitude: We are inundated with information throughout the day, and our negativity bias makes us more prone to notice what is wrong. Practising gratitude, however, helps us notice the positive all around us. We can practise gratitude by engaging in such things as journalling, pausing to recognize positive events, and sending thank-you notes. And when we do, we experience better mental health, happiness, resiliency, health, relationships, and more. Being grateful for all that we have doesn't banish our problems — life isn't perfect. However, we can improve our lives if we keep in mind all that we have to be thankful for.

7. Relationships: The longest longitudinal study of happiness, spanning over eighty years, found that those with close relationships tend to be healthier and happier and live longer than those who do not have these close relationships.[5] There is no question — relationships are essential for our well-being. But it is easy to take them for granted when life gets busy. Routines that protect time for the people we value most are an essential part of a life well lived. This is true in our professional and personal lives — our relationships matter. They matter a lot.

Marco's proactive routine: Well-being

As mentioned earlier, when I first started working with Marco, he was working straight through his day, pausing only briefly to refill his coffee throughout the day. He skipped lunch and admitted he made up for it with a calorie-dense dinner late at night.

Marco protested quite strongly when I encouraged him to pause for any form of well-being break. "But I have way too much work to do! How can I stop working when I'm always behind?" Eventually, Marco agreed to go for a fifteen-minute midday power walk to start with. Soon, he started picking up a healthy lunch on his way back to the office. Then his walks got longer. Over time, he started to rely on the energy boost these midday well-being routines gave him. On days when he had unavoidable lunchtime meetings, he moved his power walk up to 11:30 a.m. and turned one of his afternoon meetings into a walking meeting. Marco started to recognize he performed at his best when he protected time for these restorative breaks. Gradually, his colleagues started to join him for these power walks. Soon many others were adopting the same afternoon walking meetings.

Workday Warrior Action: Build your Proactive Routine Step 5: Prioritize your well-being by protecting time for your self-care routines.

Over time, Marco adopted more well-being routines (see figure 13). Instead of skipping the gym in lieu of an extended workday, Marco promptly wrapped up work at 6:00 p.m. so he could fit in a short high-intensity workout at the gym on his way home. Then he joined his wife for dinner at 7:00 p.m. Yes, this dinner time was a bit later than ideal, but after a hearty lunch and an afternoon snack, he found a light dinner was more than enough.

Also, Marco guarded his evening family and relaxation time. This was radically different from the old Marco that consistently logged into work in the evening. At 9:00 p.m., he shut down his devices and parked his smartphone in the kitchen so he could start his bedtime routine. Marco agreed that any screens disrupted his sleep. Instead of scrolling through his phone, Marco reclaimed his love for reading books. Overall, Marco found his new routine allowed him to get a solid 7.5 hours of sleep each night, which was the amount he needed to feel renewed and energized.

Marco's Proactive Routine is an example of how we benefit by adding structure to our time — in both our work and personal life. Routines help us

	Monday	Tuesday	Wednesday	Thursday	Friday	Saturday	Sunday
7:00–7:30						Morning Routine	
7:30–8:00							
8:00–8:30			Focus Work (Core Priorities)			Power Walk	
8:30–9:00							
9:00–9:30						Personal Projects	
9:30–10:00							
10:00–10:30							
10:30–11:00			Meetings (Core Priorities)				
11:00–11:30							
11:30–12:00							
12:00–12:30			Lunch			Relaxation & Family Time	
12:30–1:00							
1:00–1:30							
1:30–2:00							
2:00–2:30							
2:30–3:00			Meetings & Supporting Tasks				
3:00–3:30							
3:30–4:00							
4:00–4:30							
4:30–5:00							
5:00–5:30			Focus Work (Core Priorities)		Gym		
5:30–6:00							
6:00–6:30			Gym		Relaxa-tion	Social	
6:30–7:00							
7:00–7:30							
7:30–8:00			Dinner & Family Time				
8:00–8:30							
8:30–9:00							
9:00–9:30			Bedtime Routine				
9:30–10:00							

Figure 13. Marco's well-being routines

prioritize what matters most. And as I've said many times, we can be flexible with our routine. But the closer we stick to our Proactive Routines, the more we lean into our ideal lives.

Now would be a good time to reflect on your well-being routines. Does your bedtime routine start at a time that ensures you can consistently get a restful night of sleep? When are you protecting time for exercise? When are you doing your meal planning and prep?

I'm not suggesting you adopt all of these routines all at once. Rather, work on embracing one new well-being routine at a time. Once each of these routines is established, they will consume less energy and you'll have the capacity to build another beneficial habit.

CONSISTENT DAYS OR THEME DAYS?

When building your Proactive Routine, you can adopt one of two approaches. The first is to design consistent days. There is some beautiful simplicity to be found in consistent days. You can quickly settle into a routine, and your inner circle rapidly learns how they can integrate with your routine. As we discussed earlier, routines are essentially habits. And the more consistently you follow a process, the more entrenched a habit becomes. Perhaps this is why so many writers (me included) commit to their consistent daily writing routines. As Leo Tolstoy, the author of *War and Peace* and a five-time nominee for the Nobel Prize in Literature once said, "I must write each day without fail, not so much for the success of the work, as in order not to get out of my routine."

Another effective approach you can adopt involves building your routine around "theme" days. Theme days may revolve around clients, travel, marketing, planning, writing (shout out to all my fellow authors), or court (for lawyers and anyone else who is particularly trouble-seeking).

Sara Blakely introduced theme days at Spanx when she found herself being pulled in too many directions during her tenure as CEO. She set Mondays as her free-thinking days; Wednesdays to meet with her direct reports and other key leadership meetings; Thursdays for her product and creative team (she would often be trying on products and brainstorming new ideas with them); and Tuesdays/Fridays were her swing days — on those days, she made herself available to go where she was most needed. Before Blakely introduced theme days, she found she didn't have enough time to dive deep into any of these topics and felt she didn't have the context to make good decisions. The theme days allowed her to focus on topics for longer and more effectively. She said, "I found that it helps the quality of my thinking so much to bucket my day."[6] Blakely also says her team preferred this routine. Presumably, this gave them more predictability and structure to plan their work.

Another popular theme is a meeting-free day, which gives you large, protected blocks of focus time. I've worked with many teams that have meeting-free days and people *love* them. My friend Shelli Baltman, president and co-founder of The Idea Suite, calls this the "Block It Big" approach,[7] and she relies on this when she is tackling big projects.

Ultimately, you need to decide whether you prefer a consistent routine or a routine that varies by day. Regardless, your Proactive Routine is designed around when you want to protect time for your core priorities and all other important activities in your work and life.

⧗

We've now covered the key concepts to help you build your Proactive Routine. It's time to implement. In the next chapter, I'm including some quick and helpful tips to make this go as smoothly as possible. This next chapter will help you fast-track your way to becoming a Workday Warrior.

14

Implement Your Proactive Routine

The best time to plant a tree was twenty years ago.
The second-best time is now.
— Chinese proverb

NOW THAT YOU HAVE BUILT YOUR PROACTIVE ROUTINE, IT IS
time to put it into action. In this chapter, I will share a few tips to help you
make the most of your Proactive Routine.

JUST GET STARTED

The best time to implement your Proactive Routine is now. You may want
to continue tweaking it. You may not be sure it is good enough to meet your

needs. But the only way to know is by trying it out. You don't learn to swim by standing on the shore. I recommend you jump in before you feel you're fully ready. Putting your routine into action is the only way to know if it is complete, realistic, and balanced.

You might think, *I first need to get more caught up on my work.* Or *It will take time before I can reschedule other commitments.* Yes, these statements may be true. But this doesn't mean you need to delay implementing your Proactive Routine. The conditions will never be perfect. If I was still waiting to feel fully caught up or that my routine was perfectly designed, I'd never have got around to applying this powerful productivity booster.

The best time to implement your Proactive Routine is now.

Don't let perfectionism get in your way of adopting a Proactive Routine. Don't overthink this activity. You could probably craft an excellent routine in a mere thirty to sixty minutes. Then it is time to implement your routine. Let "good enough" be your goal at this point. There will always be opportunities to enhance your routine. But for now, just get started.

The best way to start implementing your Proactive Routine is to block your calendar for your independent focus work. This is akin to setting a recurring meeting with yourself. You might have to look forward a few weeks, given previously scheduled commitments. But going forward, this will prevent others who might have access to your calendar from booking meetings during this time. It also reminds you to pay yourself first as you establish this key habit. Then block time for your well-being activities, such as exercise and relaxation, and to clear boundaries between your work and personal life. Then start to shift your meetings into the time you designated for collaborative work. These simple steps will help you slide into your routine more easily than you might have thought.

BELIEVE IN YOUR ROUTINE

I have heard countless clients declare, "My days vary too much to establish a routine." Or "There is no such thing as an average day in my role." Ironically, these clients become some of the most committed converts once they accept that routines can work for them.

Like most others, your work varies from one day to the next. You manage many unique details. But let's stop focusing on the differences. Instead, let's focus on your common elements. Surely your workweeks have many commonalities that you can build routines around.

COMMIT TO DEEP WORK

Your Proactive Routine protects time for you to focus on your core priorities. Georgetown University professor and author Cal Newport refers to this as deep work in his bestselling book, which he appropriately titled *Deep Work*.[1] Even if the rest of your workday was a jumbled mess, this protected focus time has the power to dramatically expand your impact. But this deep work requires a commitment — because there will be no end to the distractions vying for your attention during this time. As Newport wrote, "One of the most valuable skills in our economy is becoming increasingly rare. If you master this skill, you'll achieve extraordinary results."

Remind yourself that the time you block for focus work is *not* the time to open new emails. Nor is it the time to run that errand you've been putting off for too long. This is the time to dive deep into a core priority. This is the time you need for deep thinking and sustained attention.

There will be a prolonged battle between the tyranny of the seemingly urgent and your long-term goals. Ironically, we will always make time for the urgent tasks when the need is pressing. If it must get done, you will find a way. It's the important ones that stand the risk of being left to the wayside.

Keep redirecting that compelling voice in your head — the one tempting you to check your email. *Come on — just do a quick check. It will only take a few seconds. What if someone needs your help?* Remind that voice that your focus work *is* your most important work. Plus, others will find you if something really is urgent. True emergencies aren't communicated over email. They won't rely on email alone if there is a crisis.

KEEP IT SIMPLE

I've helped hundreds of people craft their Proactive Routines over the years. Some of these are extremely detailed and complex. Others are clear and simple. The most effective ones, the ones that stick, tend to be on the simpler end of this continuum. Keep this fact in mind when crafting your Proactive Routine. You don't need to define every fifteen-minute break. You don't need to define every ten-minute email batch you squeeze in between your periods of focus time. The easier your routine is to remember, the more success you'll have adopting it. If your routine is overly complex, the simple act of booking a meeting will become a chore — and one you'll be tempted to delay.

Of course, your Proactive Routine needs to meet your needs. Ideally, my late afternoon routine would follow a consistent pattern each day. But the fact that our kids' activities start at different times from one day to the next requires me to trade my work hat for my carpooling hat at different times from one day to the next. This variation is unavoidable. But other elements of my routine can be streamlined. For example, my general rule of no meetings before 11 a.m. works most days.

POST IT

While you're getting used to your Proactive Routine, you'll want to post it somewhere convenient for easy reference. This will allow you to refer to your ideal plan every time you need to schedule an activity.

You may decide to post your Proactive Routine above your desk. Or inside an office cupboard that you often open. Or perhaps tuck it underneath your transparent desk blotter. Or set it as your virtual desktop. It doesn't really matter where you post it — as long as it is somewhere highly visible. You don't want your Proactive Routine to be filed away and forgotten.

Of course, some of your routines can be loaded into your calendar, such as your recurring blocks of time focused on your core priorities. Wherever possible, it helps to automate your routine. But other aspects of your routine aren't so easy to schedule. For example, if you, like Marco, the insurance executive we met in the previous chapter, plan to keep your meetings between 10:00 a.m. and 4:00 p.m. with no more than twenty hours of meetings a week, it's harder to transfer this plan into your calendar. Rather, these parameters need to be considered with each new meeting.

> It takes about two weeks to implement your routine.

Tempting as it might be, you can't block your entire day. You need to keep some windows open to meet with others and process the inevitable incoming requests. If you block your entire day, people will start to ignore your boundaries. They'll book meetings overtop of your blocked time, and they'll knock on your closed door. You may find you have less focus time. Instead, post your Proactive Routine for easy reference every time you need to make a scheduling decision.

GIVE YOURSELF A FEW WEEKS

In my experience, it takes about two weeks to implement your routine. As much as you'd like to start fortifying your time right away, you have those pre-scheduled commitments to work around. You'll likely need to go ahead a few days or even weeks before you can start blocking your independent focus time in your ideal time slots. In the meantime, block time for your core priorities as close to your ideal time slots as possible. Also, work on rescheduling meetings to align with your Proactive Routine. If you are struggling to juggle an excessive number of meetings, stay tuned for part 3, where we'll tackle this all-too-common dilemma. In the meantime, find opportunities to shorten, postpone, or decline meetings.

SYNCHRONIZE WITH OTHERS

You may choose to share some or all of your Proactive Routine with others, such as your assistant, key colleagues, or your family. When their routines interact with your routines, it helps to synchronize. If your assistant books many of your meetings, it helps for him or her to know your plan to book meetings during certain hours. A predictable routine helps your team know when you are available for different types of work. Predictability also helps you plan for meals with your family and commit to carpooling duties. Synchronizing with others helps to co-create routines that take into account everyone's goals.

> The best routines strike the right balance between structure and flexibility.

AIM FOR 80 PERCENT

As you recall from part 1, I recommend you aim to keep your MAP in near-perfect condition. I wouldn't say the same about your Proactive Routine. We need to retain some flexibility with our routines. There are exceptions where variations are warranted. If your CEO calls a town hall meeting at 9:00 a.m., I wouldn't advise declining because that is when you do your focus work. You can shift your focus work to start at 10:00 a.m. on that day. Similarly, if your top client asks to meet over lunch, you can postpone your midday power walk.

The best routines strike the right balance between structure and flexibility. Consider it a success if you can adopt 80 percent or more of your Proactive Routine.

GET BUY-IN FROM OTHER PEOPLE

Once you are fully committed to your Proactive Routine, it helps to get buy-in from other people, especially those you interact with most often. After all, they have a great deal of influence over your schedule. I'm also not suggesting you post your routine on your social feed. Like your aunt who tells you the name of every medication she takes, this would be a classic case of oversharing. Instead, I suggest you share the highlights of your routine with your inner circle. For example, you could tell your leader that your preference is to not book meetings before 10:00 a.m. And you could tell your spouse that your plan is to work in the office on Tuesdays, Wednesdays, and Thursdays, which may prompt a discussion about how you are sharing personal responsibilities. Of course, these discussions might prompt some negotiation, and I do encourage you to design a Proactive Routine that also considers the greater good.

You can also gently remind others of your Proactive Routine whenever you are planning to meet. Don't leave the timing of meetings wide open and to the discretion of others. Don't simply offer a wide-open invitation to "find time in my calendar." Instead, give them some guidelines aligned to your Proactive Routine. You could say, "Afternoons are best for me." Even better, suggest specific days and times that fit with your routine. Yes, it takes a few extra minutes for you to coordinate the meeting, but the trade-off of keeping your routine intact is worth it. If you have an assistant, empower them to book meetings based on your Proactive Routine.

As I said, you can make exceptions once in a while. But once you commit to your routine, you'll be pleasantly surprised with how well the rest of the universe falls in line. Not many people tap into the power of routine. So, their *any work at any time* approach will often morph to fit the needs of your routine.

TWEAK YOUR ROUTINE

Routines are like closets. You can create a beautifully organized closet, with discrete homes for key belongings and easy access to your most-used items. But over time, you acquire new items and your needs change. If you don't keep up, your delightful organization starts to fall apart. The same is true for your routine. Your time-related needs evolve. You may have been recently promoted. Or maybe your key client wants you to work at their office twice a week. Or maybe your son joined a new soccer team, adding to your carpooling duties. Regardless, Proactive Routines require updates from time to time. Occasional exceptions, as we discussed above, are expected. But when these exceptions start to become the norm, it's time to tweak your routine.

This doesn't need to be an overly complicated activity. Simply work through chapters 12 and 13 again. Consider how to best meet the needs of your core priorities and supporting tasks. What is your current meeting sweet spot? How can you prioritize your well-being? What is the best plan to help you make the most of your time?

STRENGTHEN YOUR HABITS

In chapter 9, we talked about the power of habits and how our routines help to build our habits. Let's now discuss the key steps you can take, based on the latest science, to strengthen your habits and practically automate your routines.

Set a specific goal
To create a new habit, it's necessary to start with a clear and objective goal — and of course, we want to list these goals on our MAP. *Sleep more* or *spend more time focusing* are far too vague to serve as effective goals. Rather, goals should be measurable. For example, *I want to run a half-marathon by August 31,* or *I want to launch my global program by June 1.*

Declare your why

I encourage you to be clear *why* each of your goals is important to you. A compelling *So I can* statement helps you tap into the power of neurolinguistic programming: *So I can improve my fitness and feel more energized each day;* or *So I can fill this pressing need in my market.* Then, close your eyes and visualize yourself achieving your goal. I can't stress enough how important this step is. You must be convinced you can achieve your goal before you do so in reality.

Take tiny steps

Ironically, the biggest action you can take when forming new habits is to take tiny steps. B.J. Fogg, Stanford University professor and bestselling author of *Tiny Habits*,[2] advises us to "floss just one tooth" or "do just one push-up." These small steps might seem ridiculously insignificant, but they are remarkably effective. In the beginning, it's not about volume, but rather about taking consistent action. As bestselling author Gretchen Rubin said, "What you do every day matters more than what you do once in a while."[3]

It's tempting to think we need big blocks of time for our goals. But getting started is the hardest part and big steps make things harder than they need to be. Once we start, we're more likely to continue — and this consistent action is what strengthens our routines, which eventually become habits.

Celebrate

The final step to strengthening your habits is to celebrate success — and to do so with each tiny step. If you set out to tackle big steps, you may fall short of your plans. This will make you feel bad — and feeling bad won't give you the motivation to change. Instead, tap into the power of positive emotions when you complete a tiny step. This can be as simple as saying, *I did it!* A combination of these positive emotions *and* repetition is what helps you build strong routines. But initially, these positive emotions are what inspire you to commit to your routine. Success begets success.

YOU ARE OFFICIALLY A WORKDAY WARRIOR

By now, I trust you've implemented your Proactive Routine. As you know, this allows you to protect time for your core priorities, at work and in life, and make the most of your most precious resource — your time. With these essential tools in place, your Proactive Routine and your MAP, you are officially a Workday Warrior! Frankly, you could close and shelve this book at this point. Hundreds of the busy people I've led through this process feel focused, in control, and even liberated at this stage. Thus, for many years, this is where I wrapped up my productivity coaching.

But in follow-up discussions, I noticed that some people slipped back into excessive busyness. Perhaps their newfound time prompted them to take on more work, thus filling the time void they worked so hard to create. Perhaps others noticed these people's productivity gains and rewarded them with more responsibility and promotions.

Their MAPs and Proactive Routines made them more productive. But one can only offset a growing volume so much. There comes a point where it's necessary to simplify before we can amplify. This is what brings us to part 3, where I will introduce the Simplify Filter. This is the third and final tool that busy people like you need to make the most of their time.

PART 3

Simplify

15

Time Barrier #3: Too Much Complication

Simplicity is the ultimate sophistication.
— Leonardo da Vinci

IT WAS A PERFECT EXAMPLE OF WHAT NOT TO DO. EARLY IN MY consulting career as a management consultant, a not-so-subtle senior colleague tapped me on the shoulder and said, "Ann, you are overcomplicating your work. You have to figure out how to get through your work faster."

Ouch.

This was undoubtedly wise advice, but this wasn't the most constructive kind of feedback. My ego would have felt less wounded if the message had been delivered with a little sugar-coating. Plus, his input didn't help me figure out *how* to simplify my approach. It's not that I wasn't working hard.

I was logging the industry standard fifteen-hour workdays. That particular project had a monstrous volume of work, which demanded enormous amounts of time. Plus, like all consulting projects, it required a meticulous attention to detail — we were practically groomed to be perfectionists. But truthfully, I wasn't getting through my work fast enough. I was overcomplicating too many aspects of my work. Although, after several years of agonizing over every tiny detail, it was hard to imagine another way of working.

Some would call me a workaholic. But here's the thing about workaholics: other people think we *like* working all the time. This isn't true. At least it isn't true in my case. Sure, throughout my career I have generally liked my work (with the odd exception — like everyone, I, too, have had to complete some dreadful tasks). At the same time, I also love my life outside of work. I like spending time with my family and friends, exercising, indulging in my photography hobby, and watching mindless television once in a while. I even once took a sewing course — although that pursuit didn't really go anywhere.

But during my consulting years, my personal life took a backseat to my career. I felt like I didn't have much of a choice other than to log all those long work hours and forgo many personal activities. There were always more items to cross off my list and deadlines to meet. I was perpetually overcommitted and time-stretched. So yes, I suppose I was a workaholic. But it wasn't my intention to be one.

I remained stuck in this predicament for longer than I want to admit. I kept falsely telling myself that complicated work equalled high-quality work, which I know now isn't true. In most situations, a simple approach is better. But at the time, I believed I needed to keep working this way to maintain quality — something I wasn't willing to sacrifice. It is true, sloppy work doesn't cut it. But at the time, I didn't realize there was a third option, one that was not only easier but also led to better results.

So I kept working the same way I had always worked. I kept dotting every *i*, crossing every *t*, and suffering self-inflicted pain with my perfectionism and do-it-all-myself tendencies. I wasn't willing to relinquish control over anything. Yet, I still needed to get through my work faster if I wanted to rise to the next level, where I would have even more responsibilities.

It was at about that time I started recognizing that a few of my peers had found a better way of working. Yes, they were working hard, but they seemed to get their work done faster. They were producing lots of great quality work *and* finding time for a rich life outside of work. With them as inspiration, I started to consider other approaches to work and eventually conceded that there was a better way of accomplishing all that I needed and wanted to do.

> When we simplify our days, we can amplify our results.

I started to simplify.

Once I committed to simplifying, I saw my efforts pay off even more. I came to see that when we simplify our days, we can amplify our results. I became more and more intrigued by this concept and learned that there are multiple opportunities to simplify. I'm keen to share these with you.

But first, let's review our choices when we get busy.

- Work more: We can throw more time at the problem, like I used to do. As we discussed in part 2, we can increase the supply of work hours by working more. Sure, this can be okay in the short-term, but it is hardly an effective long-term approach, especially if we want a robust life outside of work.
- Do less: As we also discussed in part 2, we can produce lower quality work, downgrade our goals, miss deadlines, or avoid doing what we say we're going to do. Obviously, this isn't going to win you kudos from your boss or your team; nor, since you set high standards for yourself, will it satisfy you. It certainly won't give you that great sense of accomplishment derived from attaining meaningful goals.
- Simplify: Obviously, the first two choices are less than ideal. Thankfully, we have a third option, the most effective choice of all. We can simplify. Ironically, when we simplify, we also tend to amplify. But to get there, we need to change how we are working.

DO YOU WANT TO LEVEL UP?

As your career advances, your responsibilities grow. At the same time, your life tends to get busier. You may find your work habits, the ones that were good enough in the past, are no longer good enough at this level. The same will be true for the level above and the one after that. To reach higher (and overcome the time struggles at this level), it's necessary to change how you are working.

Myth: Complicated work equals high-quality work.
Truth: Simplifying allows us to perform at a higher level. Genius is often found in simplicity.

It's natural to keep working the way you've always worked. Personally, I have always loved diving into the details. I could hang out in the blissful minutiae of my various projects all day. But the reality is that what got you to where you are won't get you to where you want to go. Working the same way you always have won't allow you to fix the inequality between your time supply and time demands. Nothing changes until you decide to change.

Incidentally, when people hit a time ceiling, they tend to reach out for productivity coaching. And they can run up against these barriers at any stage in their career — at the beginning, just after graduation, and at any point after that. Even the most senior executives can find themselves coming up against their time ceiling. I'm about to share the elite strategies I teach to them when they hit one of these time barriers.

In part 1, we focused on concentrating your efforts on your three core priorities. Your MAP is the key tool to help you remain focused and strategic. In part 2, we focused on protecting time for what you value most. Your Proactive Routine is the tool which helps you make the most of your time. These two tools help immensely, but they still don't entirely solve the time dilemma for many busy people, the ones who still have too much to do with too little time. Even with these essential tools, you may find yourself chasing your calendar, struggling under the weight of underestimated demands, swimming in information, and sucked into the vortex of too many low-value tasks.

If you keep hitting a time ceiling and can't find the time you need, you need a fresh approach. When your time demand is perpetually greater than your time supply, you need to simplify. You need the Simplify Filter.

YOUR THIRD POWER TOOL: THE SIMPLIFY FILTER

The Simplify Filter is the third power tool in your Workday Warrior toolkit. With this, you'll expertly handle the challenge of too much work and not enough time. The Simplify Filter helps you in three ways: it prompts you to scale back by trimming your list and eliminating non-essential steps; it cues you to streamline by automating recurring tasks and standardizing processes; and it reminds you to seek help by delegating more often and developing your team.

Overall, the Simplify Filter helps you tackle today's list and rise to meet future challenges. It helps you work through constraints, manage expectations, and generate the results you want — at work and in life. The Simplify Filter helps you to free up more time for what you value most. Ultimately, it puts you back in control of your time. And when you simplify your days, you amplify your results.

> The Simplify Filter prompts us to streamline, scale back, and seek help, so we can generate the results we want — at work and in life.

SIMPLIFYING IS AN ELITE SKILL

Something that always strikes me when I'm working with senior executives: they keep things simple. They don't micromanage. They don't busy themselves with inconsequential details. They don't feel compelled to do it all themselves. They are decisive and don't need multiple meetings to discuss minute details. They don't spend time rehashing decisions and *if only*-ing. They don't strive for perfection. They are willing to take risks and accept occasional stumbles. When they fall, they don't beat themselves up. Rather, they just stand up, dust themselves off, absorb the learning, and try again. They keep their focus on their end goal and are less concerned about the path to get there.

Knowing how to simplify is a crucial skill for Workday Warriors. It can make the difference between remaining stuck versus growing and expanding your impact. There is an unspoken test of promotion-readiness: the ability to thrive at your current level. Workday Warriors do this and more.

You probably know people like this — people who seem to fit so much more into their days than others. These are the true Workday Warriors, and they have embraced the Simplify Filter.

Simplifying is an elite skill. And it's a skill you can learn.

HOW MUCH COULD YOU BENEFIT FROM THIS TOOL?

If I asked you whether you had time to spare, I'm sure you'd say no. *Heck, you barely have time to read this book! Bored* isn't a word you use very often. You could probably use some more wiggle room in your days. Thankfully, that breathing space is within reach, at least that is what the research among equally busy people finds.

One study cited in *Harvard Business Review* found an average of 41 percent of the typical knowledge worker's day was spent performing tedious, unsatisfying tasks that could be eliminated or done by someone else.[1] Following up on their findings, researchers Birkinshaw and Cohen then trained these workers to *slow down and think* about each of their tasks before completing them. Could they drop any tasks? Could they delegate any tasks? Could they redesign any tasks to be done more efficiently? In other words, they encouraged them to simplify.

The result was anything but modest. Those who were trained saved an average of 20 percent of their time, or eight hours each week. I don't need to remind you that this equates to an extra workday a week. The time savings identified in this study included six hours of desk work and two hours of meeting time. This newfound time added up to four workdays over a month and forty-eight workdays a year. Imagine what you could accomplish with forty-eight extra days this year. Incredible!

HOW MUCH WILL THE SIMPLIFY FILTER HELP YOU?

I am sure you already simplify in many ways. It's a strategy born out of necessity. Busy days require creative solutions. But you may have even more opportunities to apply the Simplify Filter fully and consistently. Every single busy person I've introduced this tool to has achieved measurable time gains. And most of these people were already performing at elite levels.

But still, I invite you to assess how much you'll gain by applying the Simplify Filter. Use this short self-assessment (see exercise 10) to gauge the extent to which the Simplify Filter will help you.

EXERCISE 10. SIMPLIFY SELF-ASSESSMENT

Circle the appropriate number for each of the following questions. Then add up your total score.

To what extent do you ...	Never				Always
Find you don't have enough time for your core priorities?	1	2	3	4	5
Race from one commitment to the next, without sufficient time to prepare?	1	2	3	4	5
Feel frustrated by your rate of progress?	1	2	3	4	5
Seem to be working harder than your peers?	1	2	3	4	5
Sacrifice your own well-being to keep up with work commitments?	1	2	3	4	5
Your Total Score:				————	

If you scored higher than 20, you are facing a time crisis. But I didn't need to tell you that. This Simplify Filter is a must-have tool.

If you scored between 11 and 19, you will also greatly benefit from this section. A few simplifying tweaks will give you a greater sense of control over your work.

If you scored between 5 and 10, you are a productivity expert. Drop everything and reach out to me. I'm sure I could learn a thing or two from you. Yes, you may feel overly busy at times. But overall, you are doing an outstanding job of balancing your goals. You could skip the rest of this section, but I have a feeling you'll read it anyways — time-management gurus like you are often keen to keep learning how to make the most of your time.

HOW THE SIMPLIFY FILTER HELPED ME

When I first started leading productivity workshops, I had about one session a month. I spent a lot of the time in between preparing for these presentations. Then the frequency increased to a few presentations a month. Then a few presentations a week. Within a few years, I was leading over one hundred presentations annually. At the same time, my audiences got bigger and more discerning. As my pace increased, I needed to change how I was preparing for each of these presentations so I could continue delivering an effective training experience.

As with any project, preparing for a presentation involves multiple steps. As is the case with many projects, these may be staggered over several weeks. Over the years, I've found that applying the Simplify Filter to my presentations has helped me immensely.

I have worked hard to refine my speaking notes, so it takes me less time to refresh my memory. They were scattered here, there, and everywhere, including in Word, PowerPoint, and Evernote files. Plus, I had countless paper folders stuffed with magazine cut-outs, printed studies, and handwritten notes. Needless to say, extracting the information I needed from all of these sources cost me an incredible amount of time. I often squandered time recreating speaking notes and sometimes lost track of compelling points. But I kept putting off the meticulous effort required to consolidate these notes in one place.

> **Workday Warrior Action:** Invest the time upfront to simplify. Where can you scale back, streamline, or seek help?

To solve this problem, my team and I created detailed participant guides that work for each of our major programs, regardless of how we customize our presentations. We also centralized our program materials in a content bank, so it is easier to prepare and find what we need for each unique audience. As you can imagine, these efforts took some upfront effort.

But investing in this upfront effort has been an incredible time saver. Now my colleague can prepare my draft presentation, saving me roughly 80 percent of the time I used to spend customizing work for each client. I still customize training programs for each unique audience, but simplifying this process has allowed me to work so much faster. Helping to make things even simpler, we introduced checklists to collect key logistical information much more efficiently. This checklist prompts a quick and focused conversation with each client to confirm the who, what, and when for each program.

As well, I have delegated many logistical tasks from preparing proposals to sending invoices. To stay focused, my team and I have even eliminated training programs that have less of an impact with our audiences. It wasn't easy to let these go since I had spent a great deal of time developing these programs, but the gains from simplifying made it worth it.

Step by step, I kept applying the Simplify Filter. The more I pushed myself, the more I found ways to scale back, streamline, and seek help. I was able to free up time without sacrificing my quality expectations. I was then able to redirect this time into doing more of what I loved, at both work and in life.

BE A MULTIPLIER

Rory Vaden, leadership expert and bestselling author of *Procrastinate on Purpose*,[2] calls people who consistently simplify, "multipliers." Multipliers, according to Vaden, ask themselves, "What can I do today that would make tomorrow better?" Multipliers seek opportunities to eliminate, automate, and delegate. They invest in creating more time tomorrow based on what they do today. They choose to simplify.

Over the next three chapters, you'll learn how you can scale back, streamline, and seek help so you can create easier days and better results.

Admittedly, many of the Simplify Filter strategies I'm about to share will take some time to implement. Obviously, we can't just wave a wand and magically change. Some of these strategies will require a bit more planning before they yield results. Other strategies provide quick fixes you can claim now. Some strategies will resonate more with you than will others. But I encourage you to experiment with all of these options, especially those you haven't leveraged much in the past.

Overall, the Simplify Filter requires an ongoing commitment to process improvement; an ongoing commitment to scaling back, streamlining, and seeking help. Over time, these small steps will add up to radically easier days and better results. If you want to make the most of your finite time, you'll want to consistently run all your tasks through the Simplify Filter. It won't always be possible to apply the Simplify Filter, but the act of considering your simplifying options is often enough to prompt helpful action. When you simplify your work, you often amplify your results.

When we play the long game, we can clearly see how this valuable tool pays off. When we consider how we can make tomorrow easier, we lean into the Simplify Filter. This time is going to pass by anyways. So, I encourage you start leveraging the Simplify Filter *now*. If I knew how straightforward it was to simplify, I would have done it far earlier in my career.

16

The Simplify Filter: Scale Back

Learn to say "no" to the good so
you can say "yes" to the best.
— John C. Maxwell

THERE'S A GOOD REASON WHY I COULD RELATE TO ENZO, THE national law firm partner I coached who sat on six *(six!)* boards while juggling a demanding career. He also had an equally busy family life. No wonder he was struggling to find time. I, too, used to raise my hand for every committee and every project. My friends once volunteered me to chair a school committee, without checking with me. Why bother? They knew I would say yes. Like this executive, I, too, had to learn this lesson the hard way: productivity can't compensate for trying to do too much at the same time. *We can only do so much at once.*

The bitter truth is that we'll never have enough time to do everything we want to do. We'll always be making choices and trade-offs. Avoiding making these choices and saying yes to everything simply invites overwhelm.

If you consistently feel overloaded, the first step is to scale back. It's not necessary to streamline or seek help with a task if it isn't worth doing in the first place. As you learned in part 1, we want to concentrate our efforts on at most three core priorities. But even when we focus on three core priorities, we can still feel overloaded. So as Workday Warriors, we want to keep exploring opportunities to scale back across each of our core priorities and supporting tasks.

But this doesn't mean we let others down, renege on commitments, or otherwise act like the doofus no one wants to work with. We can't just suddenly drop the ball when others are counting on us. But we can scale back in ways that work for both us and our colleagues. Enzo is a great example of someone who scaled back like a true Workday Warrior.

Admittedly, it took Enzo time to scale back on his board commitments. One of them was easy to give up. He had served on the board for four years and felt he contributed all he could. He gave his notice and parted on good terms, agreeing to remain a member of their association. For another board, he was able to recommend his mentee to step in and take his place. This was a great opportunity for his colleague, and Enzo felt he was leaving the board in good hands. This also helped him stay connected to this board, which he still valued, through his colleague, but in a way that required much less of his time.

The third board was a tougher conversation. This board loved having access to Enzo's expertise and network. But truthfully, Enzo wasn't as passionate about this organization. Nor did it line up as well with his core priorities. Enzo wasn't looking forward to the frank conversation, but he knew it had to be done. He was pleasantly surprised by how gracious they were when he explained he had overcommitted himself and needed to step down from the board. Apparently, they could relate as well!

Enzo was on a roll and informed the fourth board that he needed to put his involvement on pause. The timing worked well as they had just wrapped up their annual campaign. This left Enzo with two boards – still perhaps one too many but much more manageable than six. For these two remaining boards, Enzo managed expectations by making clear how many years he planned to sit on their boards. He told each board his policy was to sit on any board for a maximum of four years. This meant he had one and three years left on each respective board. Enzo committed to not taking on new board commitments until these terms wrapped up.

Enzo is such a great example of doing the *right* thing instead of the *easy* thing. Sure, it was easier to continue attending all these board meetings and doing some extra board work at the end of his workdays. But Enzo knew he was spread too thin and not doing any of them well (according to his own self-assessment). So he invested the time and embraced challenging conversations to do what he needed to do.

With Enzo as your inspiration, where can you scale back? From small tasks to large commitments, you likely have several opportunities. Here are some suggestions to help you identify more opportunities to scale back.

FILL UP ON YOUR CORE PRIORITIES

I've always had a goal to eat healthy. But let's be honest, treats are tempting — especially when you're hungry. The most effective nutrition strategy I've found is to fill up on the good stuff. Often this leaves me too full for the sugary snacks. (Okay, I admit this doesn't always work. But it *usually* does and that's good enough for me.)

The same is true for our time. We want to fill our calendar with the good stuff — our core priorities. I'm referring to the "pay yourself first" principle we discussed in part 2. Once we have blocked time for our core priorities, in both our work and personal lives, we become much more aware of how little time we have remaining for other pursuits. It's harder to say yes to peripheral activities when we realize how little time we have for any other tempting distractions or tangential projects.

This strategy might seem counterintuitive, but one of the best ways to scale back in one area is to say yes in another area. When we protect time for our core priorities *first*, we avoid getting sucked into the temporal quicksand that other activities can engulf us in. With our calendar full of core priority activities, we recognize we don't have room for those other enticing projects. Blocking time for our core priorities helps us recognize how little time we have left to run in different directions. This strategy prompts us to scale back by default.

MAINTAIN A TIME BUFFER

The meeting runs late. A top client sends an urgent request for a call *now*. Your son needs help logging in to virtual school. And the dog throws up. All at the same time. We've all been there before — unexpected events throw off our beautifully planned day.

"Unexpected" is a funny word. My clients often tell me that unexpected requests sabotage their time. They create great plans, but then they face a universal law: life happens. All of these things that must suddenly be attended to are layered on top of a schedule filled with overlapping meetings and impossible deadlines.

I like to ask my clients how often these unexpected events occur. They predictably scorn the absurdity of this question and earnestly declare, "All the time!" Hmm. In that case, these are hardly exceptions. Clearly, these new requests need to be considered in our daily plans.

> The best way to accommodate the unknowns is to maintain a buffer.

We may not know exactly *what* will throw off our day. It might be big and green. Or prickly and red. But we do know that some form of bossy and impatient request will land on our desk each day. And there's a good chance it will bring along a few equally demanding friends.

It is far more accurate to refer to these new requests as *unknowns* instead of *unexpected*. After all, we can pretty much guarantee something will come up, even if we don't know exactly what that will be. We're in much better shape if we plan for these unknowns, and the best way to accommodate them is to maintain a buffer. This creates some open space in our day to navigate around these new must-complete tasks.

How much of a buffer should you leave in your schedule each day? That depends. As we discussed in part 2, you may need two to three hours a day simply to deal with new requests (the kind that need to be completed *today*), email, texts, unscheduled calls, people dropping by to chat, and other informal communications. I would consider this your minimum daily buffer time. In fact, you may need more time.

I keep a buffer by blocking "focus work" time during my day. Based on my current core priorities, I need about three hours a day for my independent work. If I accept too many meetings, I inevitably feel pressured to compensate by shifting my focus work into my evenings or weekends. I don't mind doing this occasionally, but I like this kind of spillover to occur rarely.

Keeping in mind the time budget concept that we discussed in part 2, can you calculate how much focus work time you need each day? Are you paying yourself first and blocking this buffer time so you have a better sense of how much capacity you have for new work? This strategy has been a game-changer for me. Like the previous strategy, this helps me scale back by creating a buffer for my more important work, even if these tasks are currently unknown. Blocking this buffer time in advance reminds me of how much capacity I have for new work. This helps me scale back by reminding me I can't say yes to more work than my schedule permits.

MANAGE UP

Marlena raved about her boss, Priya. Priya was incredibly encouraging; she was loved by the firm's clients and knew everything there was to know about her job. But there was a problem. If Marlena had a magic wand, she would use it to tweak one of Priya's qualities, one that made Marlena's work infinitely more challenging than it needed to be.

Despite being a corporate executive, Priya was an entrepreneur at heart. She was constantly coming up with new ideas. Good ideas. Compelling ideas. But following up on these ideas sent her team running in too many directions. Marlena tried her best to keep up with Priya's suggestions but couldn't help feeling frustrated. She tried to push back but admitted she wasn't having much luck convincing Priya to put some of her great ideas on hold. Like many other people in many other organizations, Marlena and her colleagues were struggling under the weight of too many priorities imposed upon them from above. They needed to manage up.

In part 1, we stressed the importance of staying focused on your core priorities. Anyone who feels time-stretched knows that saying no to new work is the correct response. Doing the opposite, saying yes to everything, can only lead to disaster. Every additional *yes* will add extra meetings, emails, decisions, research, follow-up, and more to your already full days. Every *yes* likely costs you time you don't have. Every *yes* is simultaneously a *no* to something else — this may include time spent on one of your core priorities (or your sleep). Don't lull yourself into believing you can juggle a fourth priority. You're amazing but you still can't do it all. At least, you can't do it all at the same time.

> Every *yes* is a *no* to something else.

Of course, saying no is fine in theory. But it is much harder in reality, especially when an overeager boss is prompting you to say yes to another priority. Knowing you should say no and *saying* no are two separate things. It's easy to say no to bad or even semi-good opportunities. But it is much harder to turn down an excess of great opportunities. Sometimes, we can struggle to find the right words when we're put on the spot. Personally, I find it so tempting to justify new, bright shiny objects. *It's just one meeting.* Or *I feel obligated to help.* Or *This could turn into a big opportunity.*

Marlena agreed to having a few key phrases ready for the next time her boss suggested a new project. She immediately saw how hard this was going to be when I led with a hypothetical situation about a tempting opportunity. Even though this was make-believe, Marlena struggled to say, "I can't right now." Then she dropped her head in her hands and groaned. "That's it! I'm doomed to always overcommit myself!" But after a few more practice rounds, Marlena started to find the phrasing that felt authentic to her (which is so important for all of us). Her go-to line became, "That sounds amazing! I just can't give this what it needs right now. Can we revisit this opportunity next month/next quarter when we have wrapped up our other exciting project?"

If you don't yet have your preferred wording, like Marlena, you can still guard yourself against the danger of overcommitting in the heat of the moment and avoid the time equivalent of buyer's remorse by buying yourself more time. Try saying, "That is an interesting idea. Let me think about it." Or "I'd like to discuss this opportunity with my colleagues first." This strategy works well for me every time I'm tempted to say yes to something new. A simple conversation with one of my trusted advisers is often enough to set me on the right path again. If you can't bring yourself to say no now, at least buy yourself some time to reflect and consider whether this new request supports or detracts from your core priorities. I use this approach whenever I'm tempted to say yes but know my plate is already full.

You can also renegotiate if you have been overzealous and taken on too many commitments. You can re-establish your boundaries with phrases like "I need to reschedule" or "I've changed my mind" or "I have overcommitted myself — can we shift the timeline?" Of course, you don't want to neglect your commitments. If the other person is relying on you, I encourage you to find a way to follow through. But in many situations, you may be surprised at how understanding the other person is.

Marlena tried this approach with her boss the next time she introduced another bright idea. At first, Priya was insisting they squeeze out "just a little time" for the new priority. But Marlena eventually won her over by convincing her that it was more effective to focus on their three core priorities instead. Of course, Priya wanted to do it all now — that was just her nature. But she agreed to put the new idea on pause for a month while they wrapped up another project. Marlena was thrilled — and immediately felt more liberated.

SAY YES TO SOME, NOT ALL

Surrounded by friends who were ready to indulge as we all celebrated milestone birthdays at a hot new restaurant, I made a regretful decision. Or rather, I failed to decide — I ordered *two* entrees. The first few bites of each meal were scrumptious. But you know how this story ends. Despite the delight my taste buds experienced, I walked away groaning with an aching tummy.

Regardless of how many tempting options there are on a menu, we *know* we need to choose one. This is obvious. But somehow, it is easier to forget this truth when faced with the possibilities offered by a multitude of new projects, new ideas, meetings, invitations, and more opportunities.

Do you tend to say yes too often? Are you an *over* helper? Have you become the go-to person for practically every minor inconvenience experienced by your team? If so, you may cringe at the thought of saying no. Thankfully, work isn't as binary as this. Ironically, you can say both yes and no at the same time.

Scope and timelines can often be negotiated (and renegotiated). Can you do this part but recommend someone else for that part? Can you arrange to do some now and the rest later? Can you co-lead a project to share the load? Can you offer to share your expertise in a brainstorming call, without taking ownership of the project? This isn't feasible in every case, but you'll know when this is a possibility. As a Workday Warrior, I encourage you to consider every new request: how can you say yes to some but not all?

RENEGOTIATE TIMELINES

Have you ever overcommitted yourself? Sorry, that was clearly a rhetorical question. Of course you have! So have I! We are human after all. Ironically, I overcommitted myself while writing this book. But thankfully, we can renegotiate deadlines. And when we can successfully push out deadlines, we scale back on our time demands today. This often gives us some much-needed breathing space to give our core priorities the time they need. Clearly not every deadline is flexible, but you have a good sense of which timelines have flexibility.

Resetting deadlines requires a conversation, but this doesn't need to be a painful conversation. A simple request can work, e.g., "Would it work if I send you a draft tomorrow and the final report on Friday?" Often, the less you say, the smoother the negotiation. I learned this strategy from the best negotiators I have ever met: my children.

Obviously, the best time to reset a deadline is in advance, rather than beg for forgiveness afterward. We don't want to let others down by asking for an extension at the last minute or, worse, *after* the deadline. Few things frustrate colleagues more than having a team member *not* do what they said they were going to do. On the plus side, colleagues may be relieved if you suggest pushing out a deadline. Odds are, they didn't have time to tackle their part or meet with you right now either.

I will say that we want to play this renegotiation card selectively. Far better to set realistic deadlines in advance. But at crucial times, renegotiating timelines can be a lifesaver. With that said, we want to make sure we're applying this principle selectively. This brings us to the next strategy: drop the right ball.

DROP THE RIGHT BALL

Work can sometimes feel like a circus act, especially when you are juggling too many balls. But juggling may not be one of your party tricks, so it is completely understandable if one or two balls drop. But some balls are more important than others. If you're going to drop a ball, it's important to know which is most important and which is least. But this distinction isn't always easy to see when all balls feel important. Here is an analogy that can help you decide where you can scale back.

Think about all your tasks as three types of balls: glass balls, rubber balls, and lead balls. The glass balls are the tasks you *must* do. If you drop any of these, they will break, and you will pay a big consequence. These tasks include timely client requests, urgent support needed from a colleague, a personal emergency, and other things that need to be handled in the very near future. These glass balls can't be ignored.

Rubber balls are the tasks you really *want* to do. But if you drop any of these balls, they tend to bounce back up, which means you get a second chance at dealing with them. These rubber balls tend to accumulate in people's inboxes as "nice-to-dos." But you need to be careful because these balls will only bounce for so long before they go away, which has a consequence. Perhaps others will feel you're not responsive or reliable if you don't attend to them within a reasonable timeframe. Or maybe you'll lose out on a great opportunity.

Then there are the lead balls, which represent all the tasks you *could* do. If you drop any of these, they tend to stay on the ground. Frankly, this is probably where they belong. These lead balls may include tweaking your website or revamping an already good-enough process or any number of other tasks that won't make a meaningful impact on your core priorities. Between the time you spend looking after your glass and rubber balls, you don't have time for these lead balls. The sooner we recognize these lead balls for what they are — time wasters — the less we find we need to juggle. Not surprisingly, discarding these lead balls offers the first and best opportunity for us to scale back.

AVOID TANGENTS

Hindsight is 20/20. If you could go back and rank all the work you did over the past year in order of importance, you would, no doubt, move to the bottom of the list all those make-work projects that didn't go anywhere: the report that sat unopened in someone else's inbox; the project plan for the event that never launched; the agenda for the meeting that never happened. If only we knew then what we know now, we would have saved oodles of time. But if we had paused to consider the worth of those tasks when they were first brought to us, we might have recognized them as disposable.

Admittedly, it's not always easy to recognize something as a tangent when we're walking down that path. Enticing projects and detailed debates about inconsequential details can seem so important in the moment. When we're swept up in the moment, diversions feel important and significant. The truth, though, is that when we follow these tangents, we don't have enough time for our core priorities. We need to stay focused on our destination. We want to choose carefully before embarking on exploratory journeys.

Ultimately, we can maintain our focus by clearly identifying why we're doing a task. I was recently working on a large research report about hybrid working models. I found myself getting bogged down in details, such as which insights to highlight. There were so many good ones. I struggled at the bottom end of the insight list. Where did it make sense to draw the line? But when I stepped back to consider our overall goal, I realized that all of the options I was considering worked. This helped me make a faster decision and move on.

Goal clarity is the best antidote for avoiding time-wasting tangents. If you've been assigned a project, make sure you're clear about what they think success looks like. Simple questions such as, "What does success look like to you?" or "Do you have an example you'd like me to reference?" or "Can we quickly review our plan before I run my analysis?" can help you avoid unnecessary tangents and rework.

> Goal clarity is the best antidote for avoiding time-wasting tangents.

Perhaps this is why Oprah starts every meeting by encouraging others to state the purpose of getting together.[1] This keeps their discussions focused. As we've all experienced, meetings can burst apart, their focus abandoned for tangents — this is one of the reasons why meetings have such a bad reputation. But a clear reminder of the discussion goal helps keep the conversation tight. Whether you're meeting with someone else or working on your own, you want to keep a clear eye fixed on your goal.

The more focused you start, the more effectively you finish. Yes, clarifying the goal in advance takes time. And many busy people claim they don't have time to plan. I argue that they don't have time to *not* plan. Tangents may help you discover new hot spots on a city tour, but they won't help you take control of busy days.

SCALE BACK ON MEETINGS

Liquids are incredible. They magically assume the shape of their container. This is one of the principles of particle theory that I studied this last year as part of my grade seven parenting duties — the kind you aren't warned about before you have kids. It struck me that meetings have a similar quality. They are able to morph themselves to fill whatever time we make available. Of course, this is known as Parkinson's Law, which we discussed in chapter 11: work expands to fill the time allotted. And this is never more obvious than it is in meetings.

I've worked with countless executives whose days are jam-packed with back-to-back and overlapping meetings. Practically all of them look weathered and exhausted when they reflect on their meeting load. The more senior they are, the more time they spend in meetings. Thankfully, we can apply the Simplify Filter to minimize the time spent in meetings while at the same time maximizing the value of them. There are many steps you can take to turn your meetings into a bright spot in your day.

The best way to reclaim excess time spent in meetings is to stop going to them. Of course, we can't avoid every meeting. Often, a meeting is the best way to progress a goal. But just because you've attended certain meetings in the past doesn't mean you need to continue going. Can you attend every other meeting? Can you appoint someone else to lead the project (while you shift into a champion role)? Can someone else attend in your place? Can you attend part instead of all of the meeting?

The next best way to reclaim meeting time is to book shorter meetings. A nice tight meeting with focused agenda items is always more effective than a rudderless, extended one. My team and I like to book "power half-hours" to work through several topics. Of course, we sometimes need, and do, book more time. But we don't automatically default to the standard sixty-minute blocks. When booking your next meeting, ask yourself if you can accomplish what needs to be done in twenty-five, forty-five, or fifty minutes. You'll be amazed at how much more efficient the conversation is. You'll also create necessary transition time between meetings. And on behalf of all women who've birthed children, plus everyone else who relies too heavily on coffee, can we please allow time for bathroom breaks?

You can also decrease the frequency of meetings. Generally, I love the accountability of short yet frequent meetings. But sometimes we don't allow ourselves enough time to get the work done between meetings. Can you meet every other week? Or every six weeks instead of monthly? Can you combine one meeting with another? Of course, we want to maintain momentum with projects. But we can use other methods to keep up the momentum between meetings. Interim deadlines and informal check-ins can bridge the gap.

Similarly, you can reschedule previously scheduled meetings. Generally, I don't recommend the shuffle once the time is booked. With all the effort it takes to coordinate schedules, you might as well simply have the meeting. But at the same time, other people tend to be very understanding when you need to make an exception. Often, they welcome the newfound time in their day.

Most of us have opportunities to scale back on our meetings. But I'm not suggesting we eliminate all meetings. In some cases, a five-minute chat can avoid a string of emails. Plus, meetings are the best way to work through complex or emotionally charged topics. Ultimately, you need to decide when a meeting is worthwhile. At the same time, you likely need to raise the bar on how you use the time during meetings you decide to attend.

ELIMINATE TIME WASTERS

There are some activities that are full-fledged time wasters, and Workday Warriors do everything they can to eliminate them. For example, occasional venting can feel cathartic, but excessive complaining doesn't do anyone any good. It keeps you stuck in a negative thought pattern, and it drains the energy of your listener. Similarly, gossiping, showing disrespect, and offering harsh criticism create a dysfunctional environment. These habits lead to silos, mistrust, isolation, and overall lower productivity. Energy is contagious and this negativity affects everyone around you. Plus, it's just not nice.

Workday Warriors invest the time to be good team members. They build others up. They encourage. Sure, they may compare themselves to other people, but they use this comparison to channel healthy competition. They don't wallow in jealousy. Rather, they gain inspiration from others. They adopt a mutually beneficial "if they can do it, so can I" mindset. They focus on solutions and find the opportunities in adversity. They invest in making situations better. They focus on what they can control and on moving forward. Overall, they replace negative with positive behaviours, which leads to higher productivity, a better team, and even improved health.

RECONSIDER WHAT IS ON YOUR LIST

How can you adopt this philosophy with your time? I recognize you are constantly moving at a fast pace, but there is great value in taking some time to reconsider what is on your list. Are any of your commitments pulling you away from your core priorities? Which of your projects could be postponed? Which of your deadlines have some wiggle room?

Many people go through an annual planning process. But they aren't nearly as disciplined about reviewing their plan throughout the year. I recommend a monthly review. This doesn't need to be an extended process. Start by protecting one hour to consider which of your activities are having the biggest impact. Look for opportunities to scale back so you can concentrate your efforts on your most essential work. The greater the focus, the greater your results. And work is a whole lot more fun when we see meaningful results.

> Workday Warriors invest the time to be good team members.

INVITE SUGGESTIONS

If you're still overloaded after considering all of these options, you would benefit from seeking input from a trusted adviser. This may include your leader, a mentor, or even a colleague. Often, they will see opportunities to scale back that you may not. Your MAP can form the basis of this discussion. Share your priorities with them, with the goal of simplifying your list.

Sharing your MAP is a great way to synchronize efforts with your leader and your team. With the growth of hybrid and virtual teams, there is a greater need for us to communicate in a more conscious and deliberate way. "Here's what I'm working on" conversations often highlight opportunities to scale back on tangents, redundancies, and general low-value activities.

REFRAME YOUR ASSUMPTIONS

We often have more opportunities to scale back than might seem apparent when first considered. If you're reluctant to say no — you like to say yes — you may need to reframe your assumptions. You may have some blind spots concerning what's possible, perhaps the result of self-imposed guilt, an unrealistic sense of obligation, pressure from others, or a keenness to prove yourself.

Busy people often convince themselves they can't say no or they can't push back. They may believe that they need to do it all themselves or that they need to prove themselves over and over again. So, their hand is often the first to go up when a volunteer is needed. But these limiting assumptions only exacerbate overwhelm.

If you are burdened with any of these limiting beliefs, remind yourself where your greatest value lies — working on your core priorities. You simply cannot give your core priorities the time and attention they need if you say yes to countless other pursuits. You'll have more regret from skimping on your core priorities than from saying no to a tangential activity. We generate better results when we proactively and strategically scale back. Simplifying helps us amplify.

⧖

By now I hope you see that you have several opportunities to scale back. The more frequently you consider these opportunities, the more you simplify your work and life. Plus, scaling back is incredibly liberating. It's refreshing to let go of those tasks and activities you never had time for in the beginning. You might say no *for now* or you might say no forever. Whichever the case, it's important to keep in mind that scaling back creates breathing room for what matters most.

Scaling back is just one of the strategies that make up the Simplify Filter. In the next chapter, we'll explore all the exciting ways you can streamline your list. You have many more options to free up time for what matters most.

17

The Simplify Filter: Streamline

Civilization advances by extending the number of operations we can perform without thinking about them.
— Alfred North Whitehead

I'VE BEEN TRAVELLING FOR BUSINESS FOR OVER TWO DECades. During my early consulting days, I took multiple flights each week, criss-crossing North America. I now fly much less often, but I always keep my suitcase handy.

As all frequent travellers know, there are ways to move through an airport swiftly. One of the most effective strategies for fast-tracking your passage through security checks when travelling across the US/Canada border is to get a NEXUS pass, which qualifies you to work through customs much faster than non-passholders. But I put off getting it for longer than I care to admit. This was an example of how making a short-term investment (complete the paperwork and arrange for a customs interview) results in a long-term payoff (streamlined travel). I was always so busy, and I felt that I just couldn't justify taking the time to complete the necessary paperwork. I was too caught up in urgent tasks. But this meant I lost at least fifteen minutes standing in extra lines at the airport. I finally did complete the paperwork, and the time investment I made in doing so paid off in time saved by the second trip.

This is such a vivid example of investing in multiplier activities as mentioned in chapter 15. I often think back to this example when I find myself slowed down by a less-than-efficient process. Regardless of how fast I'm running, I do my best to protect time to streamline. I don't always do this immediately. I might block time for this two weeks later. But I have never regretted taking the time to pause and simplify.

This chapter will help you adopt another Simplify Filter strategy: streamline. Workday Warriors consistently look for opportunities to streamline — and I'm about to share multiple practical strategies to help you embrace this powerful time saver.

USE A KITCHEN TIMER

Years ago, I would have been quite skeptical of the idea that a kitchen timer could improve my efficiency. But the "Pomodoro Technique,"[1] invented by Francesco Cirillo in the 1980s as a university study looking to be more efficient, has changed my perspective. And I'm listing this as the first streamline strategy, since I use it on almost every one of my workdays.

The Pomodoro Technique involves the use of a kitchen timer (such as those shaped like a tomato). You set the timer for twenty-five minutes, then focus on one task until the timer buzzes. At that point, you take a five-minute break and then start on another "Pomodoro." After some encouragement, I agreed to give this technique a try, and I have been using it ever since — with some slight modifications. I use a timer on my computer, and depending on my goal, I'll set it for different lengths of time (often forty-five minutes). The technique has become an essential part of my time-management toolbox, one I use every day.

I often set a timer when I do my morning writing. This timer reminds me to stay focused on my goal (and to resist the temptation to meander over to email). I also set a timer when I'm prone to distraction, such as when I need to complete a task but am not feeling motivated. In those cases, I pretend that I'm playing a game and try to complete the task before the buzzer goes off. Sometimes, I'll even use this technique in my personal time. For example, I've started to set a timer when I click on social media. This helps me avoid endless scrolling, which can easily overtake other activities I want to do.

Workday Warrior Action: Consider using a timer to keep yourself focused.

As we discussed in chapter 11, we can boost productivity by setting time limits. Where could you use a timer to contain a project, keep yourself focused, and make the most of your time?

TRACK YOUR TIME

While a timer helps us monitor our time use right now, there is another approach that gives us a broader perspective: tracking our time. There are many benefits to tracking our time. Time tracking gives us a much more accurate picture of where we are spending our time, which helps us identify opportunities to simplify. It also shines a spotlight on the fact that we often think tasks will take less time than they do. Sometimes, simply recognizing how long tasks take prompts us to find ways to streamline. Awareness is often the first step.

Building on this, time tracking helps us see where we can reassign our time investments. Knowing exactly where our time is spent helps us to fine-tune this going forward. Even saving a mere fifteen minutes per workday adds up to five bonus hours every month. Imagine what you could do with five bonus hours.

Tracking your time for two weeks will provide you with enough information to notice the trends in how you spend your time. You can download a time-tracking template in your book bonuses (clearconceptinc.ca /WorkdayWarrior) to facilitate your time tracking.

LET GO OF PERFECTIONISM

One of the best bonus effects of both timing our work and tracking our time is that both help us to corral one of the biggest productivity destroyers: perfectionism. By paying attention to how long tasks take, we are much more likely to spot situations where we are overdoing it. This awareness often highlights how time-intensive perfectionism can be. Speaking from experience, the pursuit of perfection is a perfect way to complicate our work.

But if you want to simplify, let go of any beliefs that perfection can be achieved. Perfection is a lie. The pursuit of it leads to slower progress, more stress, and less impact overall. Yes, your "done" still needs to meet a high bar. But perfection isn't necessary, unless there is a clear right answer, such as when you are adding a series of numbers. But few situations demand this level of precision. We often have more licence available than we believe we have. I'm not advocating for shoddy work. I'm simply suggesting it makes sense to quit refining when you've hit "good enough." Once you've reached this point, done is better than perfect.

When there is any degree of subjectivity involved, perfection is unattainable. So, rather than trying to attain the impossible, adopt an iterative approach. Share a draft, test an idea, and move forward. Resist the urge to edit the same document seven times. Don't feel compelled to poll all ninety-two members of your national team. Yes, hold yourself to a high standard. But once you reach that, it's time to move on. Done is better than perfect.

Listen up, perfectionists — I'm about to serve up a message that will taste bitter: failure is your friend. Failure needs to be celebrated. Failure is one of your greatest productivity hacks in this high-speed world. We all face setbacks. We all stumble. And we learn every time. Failure is due for a rebrand. Failure is really the same as experience, but it's missing the good PR.

When we recognize this, we realize it's okay to fail — this allows us to make faster progress and receive valuable real-time feedback. If you aren't failing once in a while, you're not stretching yourself. And if you keep delaying the completion of a project because you are in pursuit of perfection, you may never get around to launching.

Not only does perfectionism serve as a drag on your own performance, it also affects others. The more you nitpick over the details, the less empowered they will feel. They'll be less confident and show less initiative when working with you. After all, you're likely to change their work. Do yourself a favour and streamline your work — stop striving for perfection.

> Stop striving for perfection.

PLAN FOR INTERIM STEPS

Way back, when I thought being a perfectionist was a strength, I would aim to perfect documents before sharing them internally with my colleagues. But several years ago, I was forced to show up with a rough draft. I simply had not protected enough time to get it in better shape before our team meeting. To my surprise, this worked in my favour. My rough draft gave us more than enough to reference during our discussion. And ultimately, we decided to go in a completely different direction. In hindsight, I see that any more upfront time spent perfecting my work before this interim review would have been wasted.

Interim steps also help to mitigate a shared human tendency: procrastination. If you are responsible for something that is due in a month, when would you start working on it? Today? Tomorrow? Or in three weeks and six days? Most people pick the later start date. This delayed action can't entirely be pinned on procrastination. We are often busy with more pressing deadlines. But we can't deny the power of a deadline. The challenge with big, long-term deadlines is that work often piles up. And when we try to tackle big tasks in small blocks of time, we almost inevitably run out of time.

Conversely, interim steps prompt action. We are more likely to take consistent steps. Plus, we remain more focused and spend less time veering off on unnecessary tangents. Savvy delegators recognize the time-saving benefits of frequent, brief check-ins with those who are doing the delegated work.

Another benefit of using interim steps is that it reduces the pressure to strive for perfection. People are more creative and more innovative when they feel safe showing up with ideas that are still rather loose. In many cases, using this approach is far more efficient than spending oodles more time perfecting work that is going to get cut or radically edited. Ironically, multiple micro-steps generate more rapid progress than periodic big leaps.

But we can't pretend we have a short-term deadline when we all know it is truly a month away. So the key is to propose partial deadlines to other people. Commit to sharing an outline on Friday. Or offer to send them Part A by Tuesday. Or book a meeting to discuss the outline next week.

The key is to manage expectations. If others are expecting a final draft the day before the final client meeting, you don't want to show up with a bulleted list of rough ideas. But when everyone agrees to partial, interim deadlines, we can often move much faster.

AUTOMATE

Perhaps the most obvious way to streamline work is to automate recurring tasks. Law firms have automated the chore of scanning volumes of case law by using technology to automatically do the searches based on keywords, saving them hundreds or even thousands of labour hours.

Many simple tasks can also be automated. One popular way to automate work is to share a link to your calendar with others. This serves to help eliminate multiple back-and-forth emails about scheduling. Many people also use email rules to automatically sort certain emails. You could also set up standard email responses for recurring questions. You may choose to arrange for automatic bill payments or automatic replenishment of your supplies. You could also try tools like Zapier or IFTTT (If This, Then That) to automate your apps. These tools allow you to automatically share content across your social media accounts or customize your automatic voice assistant or even alert you to cool updates, such as when the International Space Station is overhead where you live.

Clearly, there are many aspects of our job that cannot be automated, like reviewing reports or crafting recommendations. But where it is possible, I encourage you to consider automation.

STANDARDIZE REPEATING TASKS

It is true that no two days are exactly the same, so automating tasks isn't always possible. But still, our work has many aspects that are quite similar. I have certain tasks that I do practically every day, from answering recurring questions to reviewing key business results to booking meetings. These similar tasks are practically begging to be standardized, although I admit it hasn't always been my strength to do so. For example, when I used to send a link to one of our self-assessment tools, I would re-create the text to go along with the link. I only needed to craft a few sentences each time, but still, this time added up. I eventually stopped reinventing the wheel each time and created a record of standard text that I could easily copy and paste. I then started to do the same with other recurring messages. Each situation required a simple tweak in how I worked, but I'm now amazed at how much joy I take in not having to recreate these simple messages each time.

> Much of our work benefits when we structure, organize, and follow standard processes.

Much of our work benefits when we structure, organize, and follow standard processes. Standardization streamlines our efforts and often leads to higher quality results, especially when these standard processes are grounded in clear values and are refined over time. Standardization can elevate training, customer service, safety, and more. Standardization prompts us to invest the time to integrate the best of how we complete an activity. This can elevate the quality of our work and also help to remove bias from key processes, such as recruiting, work allocation, and performance reviews. In contrast, when we recreate something new each time, we may produce inconsistent, lower quality work.

This doesn't mean every aspect of our work needs to be standardized. Some elements require unique insights and analysis. But I encourage you to think about where you can standardize, especially when it comes to your recurring tasks. Can you standardize a process? Can you direct people to an FAQ page on your website? Can you record some videos to help onboard new team members? Can you bundle your products in three clear offerings? Can you use a template for your proposals and other key documents?

USE CHECKLISTS AND TEMPLATES

A few months after one of my babies was born, I was invited to lead a workshop not too far from home. I had led countless sessions like this in the past, so this felt like a good way to ease back into work. I squeezed back into my pre-pregnancy work clothes, packed my supplies, and headed to my client site. Once I arrived and started unpacking my bag, I realized I had forgotten my most important tool — my laptop. How could I lead a workshop without access to my presentation?

There were other times I forgot key items. I once left my wallet at home, which made it hard to get my car out of the parking garage. Thankfully, a generous client loaned me some cash (which I promptly paid back). Then, for another presentation, I forgot my computer charger and was internally praying that my computer battery would last longer than my talk. All of these examples were obvious mistakes — steps I should have easily remembered. Thankfully, I discovered the power of checklists, and these have saved me from who knows how many potential future inconveniences.

Checklists provide us with another great opportunity to streamline. I became a big advocate for using these essential tools after reading *The Checklist Manifesto* by renowned surgeon Atul Gawande. Checklists simplify recurring tasks and compensate for the mistaken belief that it's possible to keep track of many details all at once. As Gawande says, "The volume and complexity of knowledge today has exceeded our ability as individuals to properly deliver it to people — consistently, correctly, and safely."[2]

I now use a checklist in many situations. For example, I have one checklist to discuss key logistical details for every keynote and every workshop. I also use a checklist whenever I'm teaching one of my colleagues to lead our training programs. I use another checklist when I'm packing for a business trip — plus a separate checklist to pack for family trips. In every situation, I know I've saved myself from inconvenient situations like the ones I described earlier.

I find that every one of my clients has benefitted by incorporating checklists into how they work. Where could you use a checklist? Perhaps one to help with the onboarding of a new team member or to prepare for a marketing campaign or to complete a safety audit. I encourage you to build these simple lists to streamline your recurring activities.

Templates are another equally useful streamlining tool. Like checklists, templates can direct you to ask the right questions and focus on the information you need. Templates help you build on past experiences and avoid building documents from scratch each time.

ADOPT THE KAIZEN PHILOSOPHY

You may be familiar with the term *Kaizen*, which is a Japanese word that roughly translates to "continuous improvement." The Kaizen philosophy maintains that small, ongoing improvements tend to make a significant impact over time. Specifically, the Kaizen approach aims to eliminate waste, relieve overtaxed systems (or people), and make work more consistent. The Kaizen approach is often used as shorthand for the constant striving for greater efficiency and quality. W. Edwards Deming, considered one of the early thought leaders on quality management, helped to implement Kaizen in Japan,[3] and it was eventually adopted by corporations around the world. Deming emphasized that as we improve quality, costs go down and productivity goes up. Over time, this leads to better results than choosing cheaper shortcuts.

Google models this approach with its search engine. It is estimated that Google makes five hundred to six hundred search algorithm updates each year.[4] Yes, it updates its search engine more than once per day. When we commit to process improvement, we focus on more attainable steps and launching our ideas.

In the previous two sections, we spoke about standardizing processes and leveraging checklists or templates. But sometimes we want to improve a process before we use these strategies. I think we could all point to systems or processes in our work that just aren't working as well as they should be. As I mentioned earlier, I've been working on upgrading my notes related to my company's training programs. As much as I recognize the benefits of standardizing, this was an area that needed some refinement before I was ready to do so. This is a massive undertaking and it is the kind of project that will never be urgent, making it hard to justify blocking off large stretches of time for it. But it is still an important project. So I have been taking a few small streamlining steps every time I work with my notes. As we discussed in chapter 14, tiny steps add up to remarkable results.

How can you apply the Kaizen philosophy to streamline your processes? Of course, large-scale improvements take time to implement. But small, consistent steps start to accumulate quickly. Can you consolidate and simplify your reports? Can you automate the way in which you respond to website inquiries? Can you seek input from your clients and eliminate the features they don't value? Where is the excess in your operations? Where can you make incremental improvements?

STREAMLINE YOUR MEETINGS

Now let's turn to how we can streamline our interactions with others. In the previous chapter, we talked about scaling back your meetings. There also exist several ways in which we can *streamline* our meetings. The use of an agenda offers the best way to do this. Sure, agendas may stifle the fun at team-bonding events or on date night, but they are an irreplaceable way to focus business discussions.

Agendas help to ensure that conversations remain tight and mitigate against the dangerous tangents we spoke about in the previous chapter. But the key is to set realistic agendas. I see far too many over-ambitious meeting agendas. Heck, I've crafted such agendas. The thing is that when we try to tackle too many topics, we don't do any of them justice. We often have to revisit rushed discussions in yet another meeting.

As well as focusing the discussion, agendas also help us decide who needs to attend a meeting (or even if we need to attend the meeting, per the suggestion in the previous chapter). Meetings aren't as efficient when we are missing a key contributor. Without that person, it's likely that we will need to repeat the discussion later. This redundancy costs extra time. The same problem results if we have too many contributors — we often end up spending too much time rehashing the same points. Of course, there are situations where it makes sense to include more team members. In these cases, the goals of co-creation, inclusivity, and collaboration can justifiably trump that of strict efficiency. In most cases, work is a team sport, and we do need to make time for this teamwork.

Before we leave the topic of meeting agendas, I'd like to make an important point. The most effective meeting agendas allow some time for establishing or building personal connections. There is a reason why all meetings, from negotiations to parent-teacher interviews to performance reviews, start with some casual banter. Meetings are more productive when teams protect time to connect.[5]

High-performance teams recognize that small talk is a big deal, so they protect time for informal banter and team bonding. This is even more important for teams with hybrid working arrangements, where there are fewer water-cooler type chat opportunities. Unstructured chats strengthen relationships and build trust. In turn, this leads to a more effective team. So yes, set an agenda. But make sure to allow time for personal connections.

TALK ABOUT DECISIONS, NOT UPDATES

Whether you're meeting with one person or an entire committee, you want to make the most of the limited time you're with them. You can do this by focusing more on decisions and less on updates. There are so many asynchronous tools, such as email, that we can use to share general updates. Sharing updates in advance allows people to come to the meeting prepared to discuss. Debating issues, brainstorming new ideas, and finalizing plans are often most effectively done in meetings, which can be either in-person or virtual.

With that said, some exceptions are justified. If you want to draw attention to key updates or foster team bonding, you can make time for these updates during your meetings. Morale-building discussions, such as recognizing others and celebrating team accomplishments are best done when you come together, either in person or on a video call. If your team is working virtually or in a hybrid model, they will benefit from the human connections, even if they are sharing updates that could have been addressed in email.

SIMPLIFY DECISIONS

Speaking of decisions, we are required to make an extraordinary number of decisions each day, as we discussed in chapter 9. When that number becomes overwhelming, decision fatigue quickly settles in. Anything that can be done to limit the number of choices we face simplifies our days and results in us having more energy for what matters most.

Where can you streamline your decisions? Can you limit yourself to three options when making a purchase? Or three sources when seeking more information? Just because you can research every conceivable option doesn't mean you should. Ironically, the more time you invest in deciding, the more likely you are to have buyer's remorse, as we touched upon in chapter 16. To avoid this, strive for "good enough" with your decisions. Aim to satisfy versus maximize.

As mentioned in part 2, you can simplify your decisions even further by eliminating the need to make some of them and by delegating others. When you do delegate decisions, resist the temptation to micromanage. If the person you've delegated work to seeks your input, you can, of course, offer suggestions. But otherwise, consider whether you need to weigh in to reach the ultimate goal. The more you step back, the more they step up. Empower your team, and they'll take on more and more responsibility, simplifying your life even more.

DO IT NOW

One of the best ways to simplify decisions is to prompt yourself to do something now, rather than put it off until later, especially with quicker tasks. In other words, *do it now*. And this approach benefits us immensely when it comes to our email.

Many people struggle with email overload and do their best to sort through their messages to decide which ones need a timely response. But often, they find themselves spending more time *sorting* and less time *doing*. For example, people often read their emails — on their smartphone, tablet, watch, or other device — and stop there. They don't act: reply, delete, forward, et cetera. This creates redundancy later in their day since they have to go back and *reread* each email to action them. I talk about this more in my book *The Email Warrior*. After helping people become Email Warriors for many years, I conservatively estimate people waste more than 120 hours a year simply *re-reading* their email. If you get sixty emails a day, you spend roughly thirty minutes simply reading

> Apply the "do it now" technique to short tasks.

them. (It takes approximately thirty seconds to read the average email, give or take.) If you read those emails a second time later in the day or week, you're devoting an additional thirty minutes each day. This quickly adds up: 2.5 hours per week, ten hours a month, 120 hours a year (or the equivalent of three extra workweeks — time spent re-reading email). Clearly, you have much better ways to spend your time than re-reading email. I don't mean to give you the email equivalent of a sucker punch — but I do want you to recognize how much email can derail your day.

As we discussed with the previous strategy, you don't need to be on email all day long. But when you are processing email, commit to the "do it now" approach and action an email the first time you read it. Sure, you can do a quick scan for urgency between meetings. But this takes mere seconds. Otherwise, if you open an email to read it, commit to acting on it. This one simple shift in how you work will dramatically reduce the time you spend processing email.

This "do it now" approach extends beyond your inbox and applies to any task that takes five minutes or less to complete. Send the follow-up materials immediately after the meeting. Send a calendar invite as soon as you agree to meet. Put dishes directly into the dishwasher instead of stacking them on the counter. (And yes, you can share this book with your family.)

BE BRIEF

Have you ever drifted off while reading a long report? Have you ever skimmed through a long email and missed a request directed at you? Have you ever zoned out while an verbose colleague was talking during a meeting? Me neither. But let's suppose we're considering these scenarios for a friend.

With everyone so busy, we all benefit when we are all briefer. Shorter emails prompt faster replies. More concise meeting updates lead to richer discussions. On that note, the more senior the person you're communicating with, the more you want to streamline your comments. Begin with a high-level overview. Then delve into the details as needed.

Like most of the suggestions in this book that ultimately save you time, brevity often requires some upfront planning. Thankfully, you will reap the benefits when you take the time to consolidate your thoughts before speaking, or edit your email before sending, or scale back your report to focus on the highlights. Consider embracing the 50 percent challenge: aim to cut 50 percent of the words from your initial draft without losing your key messages.

I also recommend adopting the pyramid principle which I learned about in my early consulting days. The pyramid principle,[6] developed by Barbara Minto, is a tool that helps you to efficiently communicate complex issues. This approach prompts you to begin with the conclusion — an approach especially relevant when speaking with senior executives who want you to get to the point, *fast*. You want to lead with your recommendation and then briefly summarize one to three supporting reasons. Don't meander through the detailed, sequential process of how you came to this conclusion: *First, I called this person. But they were on vacation, so I did my own research. Then my dog groomer called so I had to put it all on hold …* This advice might also serve you well at the holiday mixer. As the saying goes, the best way to share a joke with an executive is to say the punchline first.

Be brief.

Another useful approach is to try speaking in threes. There is power in threes. Try some variation of this in your next meeting: *There are three reasons why I recommend we launch in Q2.* Once you've made your general point, you should then succinctly describe each reason. A wise former colleague of mine once suggested that if you can't summarize a topic using three points, you don't know it well enough. I don't believe this is always true, but the point is a good one and worth striving for any time you're speaking.

BE ORGANIZED

Some people are naturally organized. If you're the kind of person who takes your label maker to the cottage (why wouldn't you?), you can advance to the next strategy. But if you're surrounded by some piles, it is likely driven by two factors: you haven't protected enough time to get organized or you aren't naturally inclined to organize. If this is a time-based challenge, I suggest you look forward and block off some time for this time-saving outcome. Organization isn't so urgent that it needs to be squeezed into your busy season. But with every day that passes, you lose time spent looking for key information or key tools. I'd rather see you spend that time *doing* or *being*.

If you struggle with knowing where to start, you would likely benefit by recruiting some help. You could hire a professional organizer. Or you could engage a friend or colleague (like me!) who would be thrilled to help you get organized. If they are anything like me, they've been waiting for you to ask. Simply add music to the mix, rebrand it as social time, and organize your way through a fun Saturday night.

I'd like to share some simple principles to help you get started. The first is to get rid of anything you don't use. It's easier to stay organized when your shelves and drawers are not jammed full. The second principle is to create distinct "homes" for everything, from your papers to your paper clips. Get rid of catch-all piles and miscellaneous drawers. Use what I like to call the "real estate" principle. As you know in real estate, property value is primarily driven by location. There are prime locations and less prime locations. Consider this when establishing homes for your belongings. Keep the items you use most often within easy access — your prime locations. The third principle is to put things away as soon as you're done using them. Don't let those piles build up again and don't make work for later. Maintaining your systems is just as important as setting them up. Otherwise, all your good efforts crumble apart.

> Workday Warriors invest the time to be organized.

These simple organizing principles will help you leverage the time-saving benefits of organization. You'll also experience the joy of being able to retrieve exactly what you need, when you need it. Times like this always make me want to high-five myself. And when you are organized, the sun shines a little brighter. (Okay, this last claim isn't backed by research, but I'm pretty sure it's true.)

If you'd like to learn more about organizing, you can find free resources on my website, clearconceptinc.ca. I also recommend two of my favourite books on this topic: the first by Julie Morgenstern — one of Oprah's favourite professional organizers — *Organizing from the Inside Out*;[7] and the second by Marie Kondo, *The Life-Changing Magic of Tidying Up*[8] (yes — organizing *is* life changing!).

GO DIGITAL

I've always been an avid note taker. But I've also been a note *keeper*, which has led to me having multiple drawers and boxes filled with notes. Of course, this excess became hard to manage. It didn't matter how many folders I used; it became harder to retrieve information when I needed it again.

A few years before the pandemic hit, I committed myself to digitizing many of my notes (and purging the rest). Now, it is much easier to access key information; I can find what I need with a few simple keystrokes (while simultaneously experiencing a surge of glee whenever I can easily retrieve what I need). I can access the notes I created when working with a client five years ago. Or I can easily pass along my mom's forty-year-old yummy banana bread recipe. With so many of us working in a hybrid model, digital notes are even more beneficial. Digital notes can be easily accessed or shared, regardless of where we are working.

Going digital does take some time, and I'm not implying you should make the switch overnight. But consider digitizing your information going forward. Then consider recruiting some support to scan any old notes worth keeping. In my experience, teenagers can be incredibly helpful with this task, in exchange for some extra spending money.

LEAN INTO FLEXIBLE WORK

One of the biggest benefits of digitizing our information is that it allows us to work from anywhere. When the pandemic hit, most of us demonstrated incredible flexibility by switching to virtual work, literally overnight. In chapter 7, we talked about flexibility around *when* we do our work as something that wasn't helping us. But flexibility around *where* we do our work can elevate it. The global shift to virtual work provided us with clear evidence that we can be quite productive while working from home. In one study, those who worked from home spent 12 percent less time in large-scale meetings and 9 percent more time with customers and external partners. Their number of "tiresome" tasks dropped from 27 percent to 12 percent.

They spent less time on work that could have been delegated; the number of tasks they could have delegated dropped from 41 percent to 27 percent.[9] Overall, these knowledge workers made better use of their time when working from home.

Many organizations are continuing to offer flexible and hybrid working options and plan to retain these working models going forward. Where you have the flexibility to choose where you work, consider working from home part of the time. While the office provides more opportunities to collaborate — an important aspect of our work that we want to protect time for, virtual work can support more interruption-free focus work, and it may simplify your personal life. Of course, you need to consider what work arrangements work best for you and your team. Many teams are adopting a hybrid model between in-office and virtual work.

COMMUTE SMARTER

The pandemic brought with it many tragic and adverse situations, and no one would say the pandemic was a good thing. But amid this global crisis, there were some positive side-effects. For example, many people, including Mother Nature herself, benefitted from humans commuting less. The pandemic taught us that many of us can work quite well with video calls and virtual work. If you have the option of working virtually for some or all of your week, you will continue to save time otherwise lost to a lengthy commute. But you don't necessarily need to reroute this time into work. You could consider replacing it with exercise, extra sleep, or a personal project.

If you can't eliminate your commute, you may be able to streamline it, like I eventually did after resisting for too long. Early in my career, most of my clients were clustered in downtown Toronto, in towers within a few blocks of each other. Living in the suburbs, I had the option of taking a train straight into the city core. But I never felt the train schedule aligned closely enough with my schedule. Instead, I spent years driving over an hour each way, and don't even get me started with how much money I spent on parking and gas. But after a particularly painful commute, I decided to give the train a try. I finally realized that a few tweaks to my schedule would make the train incredibly convenient. Once I did this, I never looked back. I enjoyed the relaxation of reading, working on my laptop, or even taking a little snooze during this time. My commute was suddenly *adding* to rather than taking away from my day.

What options do you have to streamline your commute? Can you park your car and take public transit (giving the added bonus of lowering your carbon emissions)? Can you carpool? Can you avoid traffic by shifting when you leave your home? Can you work from home on certain days and avoid a commute altogether?

⧗

We've covered many ways to streamline your work, from automating recurrent steps to letting go of perfectionism. Many of these approaches focus on your own individual work. But now let's consider how we collaborate with others. In the next chapter, we'll turn to the third step in the Simplify Filter: seek help. This is quite possibly where you can experience the most leverage of all.

18

The Simplify Filter: Seek Help

If you want to go fast, go alone. If you
want to go far, go together.
— African proverb

AFTER BATTLING MORNING TRAFFIC FOR MORE THAN AN
hour, I had arrived at my client's downtown office with a cool ten minutes
to spare. Then I got the phone call. It was my husband asking me to check
my trunk. I immediately felt the dread when I saw our son's hockey bag —
the hockey bag he needed later that morning for his final tryout.

The few minutes I had to spare wouldn't be nearly enough for me to return home to deliver my son's hockey bag and then back to the client's office
for the meeting. I was in a real dilemma. No parent wants to be responsible
for their child not making the team they have been dreaming to make. Yet

both my client presentation and the hockey bag retrieval were at odds with one another.

I quickly cobbled together a plan and managed to get everything up to the building lobby by making a couple of trips from my car to the parking garage elevator. But then I was at a loss. There I was, with a monster hockey bag *(those things are heavy!)* plus a bulky box of copies of my first book to deliver to a client, plus my briefcase. I didn't have enough hands, yet I was all alone. I wanted help. I *needed* help. But there was no one there to help. And I was reluctant to ask any of the hundreds of strangers walking past me.

DELEGATE

The obvious way to seek help is to delegate. Delegating is a key Workday Warrior skill, and this is true whether you have one or many direct reports. But despite the clear time-saving benefits of it, many people are reluctant to delegate. Are you resistant to delegating? Do you hold on to tasks that could easily be passed off to someone else? If so, you might have some valid reasons — but that doesn't mean you should keep avoiding delegating.

Maybe you're reluctant because you think no one can do the task as well as you can. I have no doubt this is true; you likely are the go-to expert for much of your work. But does the task really need to be done at your near-perfection level? And what is the cost of you holding onto the work yourself? I encourage you to let go of the fact that you are the best person for the task. Instead, consider whether others are capable of learning it. Or consider whether they can help with some of the task. There is a good chance they will surprise you with how well they execute it, once given the chance.

Another reason you may be reluctant to delegate is because your colleagues, like you, are already too busy. You don't want to add to their already overflowing plates. But keep in mind that by delegating work to them you are not necessarily adding to their workload. They can leverage all the tools outlined in this book to scale back, streamline, and seek help with their existing work. New work prompts them to be a Workday Warrior themselves.

The truth is that we all perform at our best when we stretch ourselves. People often have more potential than they are using in their current role. Or they may lack opportunities. Or maybe they lack confidence. Regardless, you can help them overcome these barriers by giving them work *before* they are ready. Of course, you want to be there to support them. As mentioned in the last chapter, you will want to agree to meet regularly to ensure delegated work is progressing well. This avoids rework and unnecessary tangents.

> We perform at our best when we stretch ourselves.

Overall, delegating offers a tremendous opportunity to create leverage and amplify your results. So it is absolutely worth your time to consider every item on your MAP. Where can you recruit assistance? *Drafting a document? Conducting some research? Following up on client requests?* Just remember to ask for help before you need it. The longer you wait, the fewer options you'll have, as delegating does require an investment. I often say that delegating pays off over time. It is often faster to do it yourself the first time. But your returns start to multiply with every subsequent situation.

BE CREATIVE

Seeking help works great when you lead a large team. But what do you do if you don't have any direct reports? In this case, delegating requires a few more creative options. For example, can you seek help from your colleagues, partners, leaders, mentors, or others? It may take some finessing, but many other options exist outside those found in the traditional leader/team member relationship.

Creative delegating can involve requesting a favour or suggesting sharing work. For example, could you ask a peer to review your report? Or invite a mentor to co-lead a project with you? Or propose to rotate who facilitates a meeting? All of these options are great examples of seeking help.

Another way to seek help is to arrange for a trade. Is there something simple you can do for someone else — something that leverages your unique skills while saving them lots of time — in return for them helping you with a challenging task? Could you plan the upcoming team event, while they negotiate new terms with your vendors? Could you lead the board presentation while they oversee the associated report?

Another creative option is to outsource some of your work. In many cases, it is far more efficient, far more effective, and far less costly to bring in an expert. My team and I learned this the hard way after spending too much time and effort trying to finesse our online learning platform. We eventually concluded that we needed to bring in an expert, and they helped us achieve our goals practically overnight. In turn, this helped us expand our online training, which ultimately grew our business faster than if we had tried to do it all ourselves.

What opportunities do you have to outsource? Can someone else prepare your draft? Monitor your social media? Clean your gutters? Cut your veggies? From industry experts to virtual assistants to local teens, there are numerous resources you can use to outsource tasks.

DON'T RECLAIM WORK

After delegating, you can give yourself a great big pat on the back. You've already overcome the "it's easier to do it myself" barrier that many others struggle with. But don't let your guard down quite yet; your inner controller may be tempted to take back that work. When your colleague comes knocking and asking for help, there is a good chance you can solve their problem. After all, you are good at what you do; you have a wealth of experience with exactly this kind of situation; *and* you sincerely want to help your colleague. All of this makes it tempting to reclaim your work. *"Sure — let me help you complete this. Hand it back to me."*

A popular *Harvard Business Review* article, "Who's Got the Monkey?"[1] by William Oncken and Donald L. Wass, calls such work the "monkey." This article describes an all-too-common management scenario where the well-intentioned manager takes the monkey off their colleague's back and assumes responsibility for it. This shifts work from the person who should be doing the work to the person who should be overseeing the work. You can avoid this by offering to help with the monkey — suggest options or brainstorm ideas with the other person — but you want to leave the monkey in their capable hands. Otherwise, you're absorbing work you didn't have time to do in the first place while preventing them from all the rich learning they'd gain as they work through the challenge.

ACCEPT HELP

Some people are reluctant to ask for help, which makes it hard to be a Workday Warrior. But even worse, some people are reluctant to accept help when it comes knocking. Do you ever catch yourself saying, "No it's okay. I can do this on my own"? Whenever I hear myself saying this, I can't help but think of my younger toddler self saying, "No — I do it!" Sure, doing tasks ourselves in the early days helps us learn, but we eventually hit a point when it is better to work as a team.

If you're reluctant to ask for help, you likely have some justifiable reasons. Maybe you've always done it this way. Maybe you don't like troubling other people. Maybe you're trying to prove yourself. Regardless, if you're too busy, there is a good chance you're carrying too much yourself. It's time to accept help. Sure, you might be able to do a particular task faster and even better than others. But refusing help is likely blocking you from other valuable pursuits (and also blocking others from lending support and learning new skills). You cannot play at the level you're destined to play at if you're trying to do it all yourself.

Accepting help from others will not only help you perform better, it will also likely lead to a better result. Groups can be remarkably intelligent — they're often smarter than the smartest person in the group, as author James Surowiecki points out in his bestselling book *The Wisdom of Crowds*.[2] What's the lesson here? How does this relate to productivity? No matter how smart or experienced we are, we always benefit from collaborating. A team outperforms an individual almost every time.

ASK OTHERS TO COVER YOU

Another way to recruit help is to ask other people to cover you, especially when you are trying to do some uninterrupted work. For example, you could ask your assistant to monitor your email. Or you could ask your office mate to cover you while you slip into a small boardroom for some focus work. Or you could let your leader know you're planning to go offline to work on that big opportunity you're both excited about.

Remember, you don't need to be accessible every moment throughout the day. On the contrary, you have a big opportunity to model for others how protecting some focus time offers a more effective way of working. Instead of worrying about being unresponsive, think instead about how deep focus work generates better results. Also, think about how your actions will inspire others to adopt a more productive working style. A rising tide lifts all boats.

CONSIDER THE RATE

When I first launched my business, I was a one-person shop and did all the tasks myself. I created all the training programs and all the associated materials. My work with clients included doing everything from finding them to servicing them. I taught myself how to use the many apps and technologies needed to send newsletters, manage a website, and more. The list went on and on. But as my business grew, I couldn't keep up with the vast array of tasks. I needed to recruit some help. But like most small business owners, I struggled to justify paying someone for tasks I was perfectly capable of doing myself.

Then, one of my friends and fellow business owner, Lisa Stam, encouraged me to consider the rate associated with each of these tasks. Lisa told me to think of my tasks as either worth $10 per hour, $100 per hour, or $1,000 per hour. She went further to ask what level I wanted to operate at. Like most entrepreneurs, my eyes lit up at the thought of the higher paying jobs. But it started to become clear to me that I couldn't keep filling my time with lower paying jobs. Once I started to consider the rates, I was more open to seeking help.

If you're having trouble delegating, I encourage you to assign yourself an hourly rate. Then consider whether you would pay that rate for all the work you're doing. I've coached countless lawyers whose billing rate is several hundred dollars per hour. Many of the newer lawyers, who are incredibly technologically savvy, do their own document formatting and other straightforward tasks. Whenever I ask if they would pay someone hundreds of dollars to format their documents, they immediately say no. This is a clear sign that they shouldn't be doing it either. If they aren't willing to pay their rate, they should consider delegating the task.

> Would you pay someone your hourly rate to complete this task?

Obviously, there will be some exceptions to this rule. You won't always be in a position to delegate lower-rate tasks. But simply considering an appropriate rate for each of your tasks helps you identify which of these makes sense to seek help with. Or which you should work toward delegating in the near future.

DEVELOP YOUR TEAM

Investing in your team is a great way to both help them and expand the pool of people you can seek help from. The more time you spend training others, the more skilled they become, which means there will be increasing possibilities to delegate tasks to them. I encourage you to commit to sharing regular feedback. The most effective feedback you can give is acknowledgement for doing things right. This both rewards and promotes the ideal actions. The most effective teams recognize this and embrace approximately a 6:1 ratio — six positive feedback comments for every negative comment.[3] Conversely, low-performance teams tend to have a 1:2 ratio — one positive comment for every two negative comments.

Another effective feedback strategy is to prompt a conversation. At key milestones, ask your colleagues what they think they did well and what would be even more effective. In many cases, they'll offer up the suggestions you wanted to share. And people are more open to their own ideas. But even if they don't suggest improvement opportunities, this conversation allows you to both reinforce strengths and offer your own suggestions for "even more effective."

As you accumulate experience, it's so tempting to share your wisdom with others. But you will do a better job of developing your team if you adopt an ask versus tell approach. Ask them for their recommendations before you suggest a solution. And when they ask for your advice, encourage them to think through key factors with questions such as, "What do you think the client would want us to do?" or "When else have we experienced a similar situation and what can we learn from that time?" The more they problem-solve, the more ownership they assume and the more delegating options you have. Just because they aren't ready now doesn't mean they won't be ready soon — especially if you invest in their development.

EXPAND YOUR TEAM

If you and your colleagues have been running flat out for as long as you can remember, it might be time to add a new salaried team member. But before you do so, I encourage you to truly reflect on whether you've embraced all the other concepts outlined in this book. You might want to ask a mentor whether they can suggest any opportunities for you to simplify. You don't want to jump into adding a new team member without careful consideration. After all, paying an extra salary is a significant commitment.

If you're convinced you need a new team member, you could consider hiring a consultant, contractor, or co-op student. This helps to match the added cost to your needs. If a key project wraps up and you have less need for support, you can put their contract on hold.

I am a big proponent of growth, and the truth is that we can only do so much with a fixed number of team members. Of course, it is easier to absorb the cost of a new team member if this new person steps into a revenue-generating role. But once again, it is worth seeking a second opinion before you absorb this long-term cost.

⧗

Are you wondering how the hockey bag saga turned out? Well, I can't decide if I'm proud or appalled about what I did next: I called an Uber. Yes — for the hockey bag. I paid to have someone else deliver the hockey bag to our son.

As I stood there wondering what to do, a stranger made the mistake of pausing beside me. I turned to her and asked for help. *"I'm in a bit of a jam. Would you mind helping me carry these things across this giant lobby and out to the curb?"* The kind stranger, who was understandably wary at first, quickly came to understand my predicament. *"I'm a hockey mom, too,"* she said. Then she picked up the box while I managed to carry/drag/will everything else to the curb. I popped the hockey bag into the Uber and headed off to my client meeting.

A few days later, after the first hockey game, the hockey coach approached me and couldn't contain her laughter. She said, *"I thought I had seen it all with hockey — but this one tops it all — an Uber for a hockey bag!"* I could only muster a meek headshake.

Was it worth it? Son Christopher felt it was. And I must say, I felt an extra bolt of parenting joy when he scored a goal in the semi-finals later that season and looked up to the stands to give me a fist pump. But ultimately, I learned a valuable lesson (besides always checking my trunk): there are always people to help when we look hard enough.

YOUR SIMPLIFY FILTER CHECKLIST

We have covered multiple Workday Warrior strategies in part 3. Admittedly, it is tough to keep all of these in mind for each of our daily tasks. So I created the following checklist for you (see figure 14). Keep this handy so you can apply the Simplify Filter to every one of your tasks. You can find a digital version of this checklist at clearconceptinc.ca /WorkdayWarrior.

Scale back
- ☐ Fill up on your core priorities
- ☐ Maintain a time buffer
- ☐ Manage up
- ☐ Say no
- ☐ Say yes to some, not all
- ☐ Renegotiate timelines
- ☐ Drop the right ball
- ☐ Avoid tangents
- ☐ Scale back on meetings
- ☐ Eliminate time wasters
- ☐ Reconsider what is on your list
- ☐ Invite suggestions
- ☐ Reframe your assumptions

Streamline
- ☐ Use a timer
- ☐ Track your time
- ☐ Let go of perfectionism
- ☐ Plan for interim steps
- ☐ Automate
- ☐ Standardize
- ☐ Use checklists and templates
- ☐ Streamline meetings
- ☐ Simplify decisions
- ☐ Do it now
- ☐ Be brief
- ☐ Be organized
- ☐ Go digital
- ☐ Lean into flexible work
- ☐ Commute smarter

Seek help
- ☐ Delegate — and ask for help before you need it
- ☐ Be creative about who can help you — mentors, partners, colleagues, leaders, etc.
- ☐ Don't reclaim work
- ☐ Accept help
- ☐ Ask others to cover you
- ☐ Consider the rate: Would you pay someone your rate to do this task?
- ☐ Develop your team with stretch assignments
- ☐ Expand your team
- ☐ Outsource

Figure 14. The Simplify Filter checklist

This wraps up part 3. In parts 1 and 2, I encouraged you to build new tools: your MAP and Proactive Routine. In part 3, I'm encouraging you to build a new habit by consistently applying the Simplify Filter. With everything you do, I encourage you to think about where you can scale back, streamline, and seek help. The more often you consider your options, the more opportunities you will find.

We have discussed many ways to simplify your work, but I'm sure you could identify several others. Ultimately, the Simplify Filter helps you think like a "multiplier" (as referenced in chapter 15) so you can create more leverage with your time. These consistent small steps can result in radically different days — *simplified* days with amplified results.

Action Plan:
Be a Workday Warrior

> If it has to happen, it has to happen first.
> — Laura Vanderkam

LAURA VANDERKAM, TIME-MANAGEMENT EXPERT AND AUTHOR of several bestsellers, including *I Know How She Does It*,[1] led a comprehensive study examining 1,001 days of time diaries of busy working mothers earning more than $100,000 a year. In the midst of this time-tracking study, one of the women came home to find her water heater had broken. This unfortunate homeowner had no choice but to take the time to address the water that was all over her basement floor, which included coordinating support from plumbers, cleaners, and more. Since she was tracking her time, she was able to precisely see that she spent a total of seven hours dealing with all the ensuing fallout from this issue.

If you had asked this woman a few days earlier whether she could free up seven hours over the next week, or one hour a day, she probably would have said a firm no. But when forced to do so, she made it happen. This example demonstrates that we often do have more flexibility in our day than we may think we do. As Vanderkam points out, if we treat our priorities like that broken water heater, we *can* find the time, and she wisely says, "If it has to happen, then it has to happen first."

I love this story as it truly captures the essence of this book. Ultimately, as a Workday Warrior, you prioritize what is most important, just like this woman did with her can't-ignore-it broken water heater. You focus on your three core priorities. You protect your time for your most important goals, before your time becomes consumed by any number of other pursuits. And you simplify your work — after all, work (and life) can be far too complicated.

Obviously, we can't save up time. Time marches on, regardless of what we do. But we can *invest* our time in what we value most. The three Workday Warrior tools allow us to make better choices about how we spend our time.

YOUR ACTION PLAN

In this final chapter, I encourage you to consider what comes next. I am sharing the highlights of the three Workday Warrior strategies: clarify, fortify, and simplify. I am also sharing an action plan to help you fully embrace the three Workday Warrior tools.

You have invested time in reading this book. Now it's time to turn theory into action so you can get the biggest return on your investment. Resist simply closing this book and walking away. Time excellence only comes when you put these ideas into action. Your results hinge on what you do next.

Part 1: Clarify

We began by discussing one of the most common time challenges: too many priorities. As you know, when we try to do too much at once, we dilute our efforts and delay our progress. So as a Workday Warrior, you want to identify and commit to your three most important goals — your core priorities.

Once you have your three core priorities clearly identified, you want to define a specific goal for each one. What do you want to do by when? And why is this important to you? These clear goal statements will help you be even more focused and operate in true warrior fashion.

Your Main Action Plan — your MAP — is the key tool to support your core priorities, along with all of your tasks, deadlines, commitments, and goals. Your MAP is your sophisticated priority management system — one that will help you thrive at elite levels. This is your most important Workday Warrior tool. It prompts you to plan your day, stay relentlessly focused on your core priorities, and resist spending time on any future priorities or distractions. Once you establish your MAP, you'll wonder how you ever worked without it.

Part 1: Clarify

Key lesson: Clearly identify your three core priorities.

Workday Warrior Tool: Your Main Action Plan (MAP)

Workday Warrior Action Steps:

- ☐ Identify your three core priorities and define a specific goal (what/when/why) for each one (~15 minutes).
- ☐ Build your MAP (~30 minutes).
- ☐ Consult your MAP every day when planning for tomorrow. Update your MAP in real time as new tasks arise, as deadlines shift, and as you complete tasks (~2 minutes/day).
- ☐ Consider sharing your MAP with your leader to ensure you are aligned on your priorities (~10 minutes).
- ☐ Teach someone else how to build their MAP. This will help reinforce your learnings and will help them become a Workday Warrior as well (~30 minutes).

Part 2: Fortify

With your core priorities clearly established, we moved on to protecting your time. Your attention is your most valuable resource — and it is constantly under attack. We are bombarded with interruptions. So, like true warriors, we need to fortify our boundaries and protect time for our most important goals *first*.

Your Proactive Routine is built around your ideal time budget and the activities you value most — in both your professional and personal life. This is a tool that elite performers embrace to make the most of their precious time. Flexibility is nice in select instances. But structure is the secret to protecting time for your core priorities.

Part 2: Fortify

Key lesson: Protect time for your core priorities first.

Workday Warrior Tool: Your Proactive Routine

Workday Warrior Action Steps:

☐ Define your realistic ideal time budget (~15 minutes).

☐ Build your Proactive Routine (~30 minutes).

☐ Implement your Proactive Routine (~2 weeks to roll out schedule adjustments).

☐ Consider sharing your Proactive Routine with your inner circle at both work and home. This helps them to support your routines, and they may have some advice to help you make your routines even stronger. Plus, you may inspire them to create their own Proactive Routines. We all benefit by committing to become a Workday Warrior (~15 minutes/conversation).

Part 3: Simplify

In part 1 and part 2, you learned the core Workday Warrior strategies. In part 3, you learned how to take these lessons even further. But ironically, the more effective you become at work, the more opportunities you are granted. Workday Warriors are often rewarded with more work. But this doesn't mean your work should become increasingly more complicated. Instead, you want to simplify so you can amplify. You cannot continue to grow by working the way you always have.

As you know, the third and final Workday Warrior tool is the Simplify Filter. This is a set of questions you integrate into your daily work. With each step along your journey, ask yourself, *How can I scale back? How can I streamline? How can I seek help?* And these are the questions I encourage you to ask yourself every single day.

Part 3: Simplify

Key lesson: When we simplify our work, we amplify our results.

Workday Warrior Tool: The Simplify Filter

Workday Warrior Action Steps:

☐ For every task, deadline, commitment, and goal, consider how you can scale back, streamline, and seek help (~5 minutes per day).

☐ Invite suggestions from your leader, mentor, and other trusted advisers. Encourage them to help you identify opportunities to simplify (discuss during existing meetings).

☐ Prompt conversations with your colleagues. How can you all simplify to amplify? (Discuss during existing meetings.)

☐ Remember that you don't need to apply this tool perfectly every time. We often learn most from when we stumble.

This may be a tough message to hear, but busy is a choice. We *choose* to say yes to that extra project. We *choose* to add those extra details. We *choose* not to delegate. We *choose* to change a system that is already good enough. But there are no medals for complicating our work. Thankfully, we can choose differently. We can choose to simplify.

We often have multiple opportunities to simplify our work. When we shift our mindset, we see how many choices we have. Simplifying isn't about playing small. Rather, it is about extending our reach and growing our impact. When we simplify our work, we amplify our results.

HELP IS ONLY ONE CLICK AWAY

As you are about to close this book, I want to remind you that help is only one click away. I mentioned many book bonuses throughout this book, tools to help you implement these Workday Warrior strategies, plus so much more. You can find these and many other complimentary resources at clearconceptinc.ca/WorkdayWarrior.

As well, if you or your colleagues are interested in connecting with me or my team, please use our Contact Us page or find us on social media. We would love to hear how these principles are working for you! And we would love to help you empower other Workday Warriors.

Finally, I'd like to remind you that you don't need to apply these principles perfectly all the time. If you stumble on this path, know that you are not alone. No one is immune to setbacks and challenges, and that definitely includes me! But the Japanese proverb *Nana korobi ya oki*, (roughly translated: Fall down seven times, get up eight) reminds us of the importance of investing in our resiliency. What I know for sure is that these Workday Warrior strategies allow us to get up faster and stronger.

⧗

With that, we have come to the end of your Workday Warrior training, but your journey will continue. Thank you for allowing me to accompany you to this point. Please know that I will be cheering you on from afar as you continue to make the most of your time. I am confident you are now ready to take over the reins as a Workday Warrior, throughout the rest of your incredible career. You will always be a Workday Warrior. This isn't the end. This is the beginning.

Acknowledgements

THERE IS NO DOUBT ABOUT IT — BOOKS ARE A LABOUR OF love. Like a child, a book requires a village to raise. Despite applying the best of my Workday Warrior strategies, I never could have brought this book to life without this network of generous supporters.

First and most importantly, I'd like to acknowledge all the clients who have invited my team and I to help them over the past two decades. We have learned so much from everyone we have worked with. This productivity program is strong *because* of their willingness to experiment and share their feedback with us. And after all these years, I still find so much joy in helping people take control of busy days.

Next, of course, I want to acknowledge my incredible publication team, starting with my literary and speaking agent, Rob Firing, and the Transatlantic Agency team who saw the vision for this book and connected me to the Dundurn Press all-star team. To associate publisher Kathryn Lane, thank you for being as excited about this book as I am. To my editor, Dominic Farrell, thank you for tirelessly and patiently guiding me through many helpful iterations. Thank you to Laura Boyle for your many creative designs, ultimately leading to this cover, which I love. To the managing editor, Elena Radic, for championing every component of this book. To publicist Alyssa Boyden and the sales and marketing team for helping to tell all busy people about this book. And, finally, to Kwame Scott Fraser and the entire Dundurn Press team for believing in *Workday Warrior*.

I would also like to thank the many experts who allowed me to pick their brains, cite their research, and quote their wisdom. I love learning from content gurus like all of you! This book is richer because of your abundant contributions.

It is also imperative to acknowledge my team at Clear Concept Inc. First and foremost, my business partner, Susan Pons — thank you for sharing a common passion to help high-performance teams and individuals do their best work. Thank you to Marlo Leunissen for partnering with me in book editing, strategizing, and dreaming. Thank you to my other dedicated colleagues, who each played an important role in this book while doing so much more to support our team. This includes Gaya Astvatsatryan, Pamela Burwash, Sarah Morgenstern, and Geraldine Santos-Lee. Thank you as well to our many facilitators and coaches who are always an honour to collaborate with, including Ruth Alexandor, Shilpa Barchha, Frances Biernacki, Deborah Glatter, Precy Kearns, Miriam Kotsopoulos, Teresa Krupa, Ron Monteiro, Jennifer Salter, Maxine Skerrett, Natalie Stuart, Charlotte Verbiest, and Marla Warner. Thank you to our other key experts and collaborators, including Diane Andonovski, Suzanne Doyle, and Rebecca Hessels. And thank you to our friends and collaborators at Waterston Human Capital, Nicole Bendaly, Bruce Bowser, and Marty Parker. I am humbled to work with such an incredible group. You are truly a high-performance team.

Over the years, I've been fortunate to adopt some incredible mentors. I am so fortunate to have had their willingness to coach and challenge me. Thank you, Lenora Ausbon-Odom, Mike Cloutier, Marg Hachey, Reggie Humphrey, Tony Pampena, Silvia Pencak, and Laura Williams. I know I will continue to learn so much from all of you.

I'd also love to thank my extended team. This includes my long-standing writing coach, Daphne Gray-Grant, who has helped to groom me as a writer. Next, I'd like to thank Samra Zafar, a bestselling author, human rights activist, and dear friend, who was instrumental in helping me launch this book journey. As well, I'd like to thank all of my CEO mastermind colleagues, who are consistently amazing sources of inspiration, encouragement, and friendship. This includes Shelli Baltman, Tania Desa, Christie Henderson,

Kristi Herold, Robbin McManne, Julie Mitchell, Marisa Murray, Paula Rizzo, Jane Southren, Alyson Schafer, Lisa Stam, and Christine Thomlinson.

I'd also love to acknowledge many of my dear friends who have shown such support and interest in this book. Nicole Bynoe — I still remember your enthusiasm when I shared the vision for this book over fifteen years ago. As well, I am incredibly grateful for the love, support (and breaks from editing) offered so freely by Moya Bordone, Roberta Capuano, Anne Goodfellow, Samantha Heiydt, Kareena Rego, and many others.

Finally, I would like to acknowledge my family. To my dad, Charlie Goldsmith, who has filled me with confidence; my mom, Lorraine Goldsmith, who is beaming down on me from heaven; my favourite (and only) sister, Laurie Goldsmith; incredible in-laws Carole and Enrique Gomez Sr.; "practically a sister" sister-in-law Milagro Wassef; and Maricel Fiesta, who checks all the boxes as both a friend and sister.

To close, I'd love to acknowledge my ultimate supporters, including my always-encouraging husband, Enrique, who makes everything possible and fun at the same time. As well, to our four amazing children, Christopher, Taylor, Michael, and Daniel. Together, you provide me with daily inspiration to make the most of our precious time. I couldn't think of a better reason to be a Workday Warrior.

Notes

Introduction

1   Oliver Burkeman, *Four Thousand Weeks: Time Management for Mortals* (New York: Farrar, Straus and Giroux, 2021).

1   Time Barrier #1: Too Many Priorities

1   Karen Martin, *The Outstanding Organization: Generate Business Results by Eliminating Chaos and Building the Foundation for Everyday Excellence* (New York: McGraw-Hill Education, 2012).

2   The American Institute of Stress, "Workplace Stress," stress.org /workplace-stress.

3   William J. Becker, Liuba Y. Belkin, Samantha A. Conroy, and Sarah Tuskey, "Killing Me Softly: Organizational E-mail Monitoring Expectations' Impact on Employee and Significant Other Well-Being," *Journal of Management* 47, no. 4 (December 2019): 1024–52.

4   Gary Keller and Jay Papasan, *The One Thing: The Surprisingly Simple Truth About Extraordinary Results* (Portland: Bard Press, 2013).

5   Kevin Kruse, "Proper Priorities," February 18, 2016, kevinkruse .com/proper-priorities/.

6   Teresa Amabile and Stephen Kramer, *The Progress Principle: Using Small Wins to Ignite Joy, Engagement, and Creativity at Work* (Boston: Harvard Business Review Press, 2011).

7   Chris McChesney, Sean Covey, and Jim Huling, *The 4 Disciplines of*

Execution: Achieving Your Wildly Important Goals (New York: Simon & Schuster, 2012).

2 The Power of Three

1 For more insight into how Steve Jobs led Apple, I recommend reading Walter Isaacson, *Steve Jobs* (New York: Simon & Schuster, 2011).

2 Tim Cook said this during the Goldman Sachs Tech Conference 2009. Dan Frommer, "Apple COO Tim Cook: 'We Have No Interest in Being in the TV Market,'" *Business Insider*, February 23, 2010, businessinsider.com/live-apple-coo-tim-cook-at-the-goldman -tech-conference-2010-2#:~:text=We%20are%20the,was%20%2440%20 billion.

3 Paul Leinwand and Cesare Mainardi, "Stop Chasing Too Many Priorities," *Harvard Business Review*, April 14, 2011, hbr.org/2011/04 /stop-chasing-too-many-prioriti.

4 Tricia Gregg and Boris Groysberg, "Amazon's Priorities Over the Years, Based on Jeff Bezos's Letters to Shareholders," *Harvard Business Review*, May 17, 2019, hbr.org/2019/05/amazons-priorities-over-the-years -based-on-jeff-bezoss-letters-to-shareholders.

5 Mark Gottfredson, "The Focused Company," Bain & Company, June 28, 2012, bain.com/insights/the-focused-company/.

6 McChesney, Covey, and Huling, *The 4 Disciplines of Execution*.

7 Yes, he said, "man" and "him." I changed it.

8 *Key Results* is a term Google uses to assign clear outcomes to their objectives. Objectives are Google's equivalent of core priorities. Collectively, Google calls these "OKRs." Luis Gonçalves, "Objective and Key Results: A Tool to Engage Your Employees," Adapt Methodology, April 3, 2021, adaptmethodology.com/objective-and-key-results/.

9 This quote is widely attributed to American author, Napoleon Hill (1883–1970). As well, many business leaders have shared variations of this quote such as Gina Raimondo, BrainyQuote.com, accessed July 22, 2022, brainyquote.com/quotes/gina_raimondo_781741.

3 How to Deal with Your Other Work

1   "Daily Time Spent on Social Networking by Internet Users Worldwide," Statista, June 21, 2022, statista.com/statistics/433871/daily-social-media-usage-worldwide/#:~:text=How%20much%20time%20do%20people,minutes%20in%20the%20previous%20year.

4 Your Most Essential Productivity Tool

1   Mayo Oshin, "The Ivy Lee Method: A 100-year-old, 15-Minute Routine for Stress-Free Productivity," May 21, 2018, mayooshin.com/the-ivy-lee-method/.

2   George A. Miller, "The Magical Number Seven, Plus or Minus Two: Some Limits on Our Capacity for Processing Information." *Psychological Review* 101, no. 2 (1994): 343–352. doi.org/10.1037/0033-295X.101.2.343.

3   Jeff Atwood, "The Magical Number Seven Plus or Minus Two," Coding Horror, August 14, 2006, codinghorror.com/blog/2006/08/the-magical-number-seven-plus-or-minus-two.html.

4   Nelson Cowan, "The Magical Number 4 in Short-Term Memory: A Reconsideration of Mental Storage Capacity," *Behavioral and Brain Sciences* 24, no. 1 (2001): 87–114.

5   Touro University Worldwide, "The Mind and Mental Health: How Stress Affects the Brain," Health and Human Services, July 26, 2016, accessed July 21, 2022, tuw.edu/health/how-stress-affects-the-brain/.

6   Yale University, "How Stress and Depression Can Shrink the Brain," ScienceDaily, August 12, 2012, accessed July 21, 2022, sciencedaily.com/releases/2012/08/120812151659.htm.

7   David Allen, *Getting Things Done: The Art of Stress-Free Productivity* (New York: Penguin, 2001).

8   This quote is widely attributed to Albert Einstein. Albert Einstein, "On the Method of Theoretical Physics," (Herbert Spencer lecture, Oxford University, Oxford, UK, June 10, 1933).

5 How to Build Your Main Action Plan

1   Some schools award the student with the highest marks the honour of being the valedictorian. In Canada, it is also common for many schools

choose to have the valedictorians elected by their student peers. The elected valedictorian then delivers a speech at the convocation/commencement ceremony. We eventually did get the university to approve the valedictorians and I snuck into the back of all six convocation ceremonies that year to hear the speeches. I still remember the joy I felt listening to these articulate, inspiring, and funny student representatives. To this day, I still believe that valedictorian speeches are the best part of any graduation ceremony.

2　This is a shout out to everyone who spent their childhood honing their negotiation skills over ruthless games of Monopoly.

3　Nicholas G. Carr, "Curbing the Procrastination Instinct," *Harvard Business Review*, October 2001, hbr.org/2001/10/curbing-the-procrastination -instinct.

6　How to Plan Your Day

1　Einstein, "On the Method of Theoretical Physics."

2　Michael K. Scullin et al. "The Effects of Bedtime Writing on Difficulty Falling Asleep: A Polysomnographic Study Comparing To-Do Lists and Completed Activity Lists," *Journal of Experimental Psychology* 147, no. 1 (2018): 139–46. ncbi.nlm.nih.gov/pmc/articles/PMC5758411/.

3　Francisco Sáez, "Micro-Tasks. The Pleasure of Checking Off," FacileThings (blog), facilethings.com/blog/en/micro-tasks.

7　Time Barrier #2: Too Much Flexibility

1　Anders Ericsson and Robert Pool, *Peak: Secrets from the New Science of Expertise* (Boston: Houghton Mifflin Harcourt, 2016).

2　Angela Duckworth, *Grit: The Power of Passion and Perseverance* (New York: Scribner, 2016).

3　Daphne Gray-Grant shared the advice to write at the beginning of our day during a coaching session for her Get it Done program, publicationcoach .com/get-it-done/.

8 Introducing Your Proactive Routine

1 These extremely successful people also embrace a thrive mindset (bold goals, work with purpose, confidence) and build a robust team around themselves, but this is a discussion for another day. This book is dedicated to helping you adopt the superior work habits of elite performers.

2 Stephen R. Covey, *The 7 Habits of Highly Effective People* (New York: Simon & Schuster, 1989).

3 Faizan Imtiaz, "Why Your Brain Hates Uncertainty and How to Overcome It," Smith Business Insight (Smith School of Business, Queen's University), April 1, 2021, smith.queensu.ca/insight/content/why-your-brain-hates -uncertainty-and-how-to-overcome-it.php.

9 Habits Drive Results

1 James Clear, *Atomic Habits: An Easy & Proven Way to Build Good Habits & Break Bad Ones* (New York: Avery, 2018).

2 Regina Conti, "Delay of Gratification," *Encyclopedia Britannica*, March 19, 2019, britannica.com/science/delay-of-gratification.

3 Andrew Matthews Creative, "How Habits Are Formed," *Science Connected*, September 20, 2018, magazine.scienceconnected.org/2018/09/how -habits-are-formed/#:~:text=Our%20brains%20form%20neural%20 pathways,when%20it%20becomes%20a%20habit.

4 Society for Personality and Social Psychology, "How We Form Habits, Change Existing Ones," ScienceDaily, sciencedaily.com/releases /2014/08/140808111931.htm.

5 Tony Schwartz, "Six Keys to Changing Almost Anything," *Harvard Business Review*, January 17, 2011, hbr.org/2011/01/six-keys-to-changing -almost-an.html.

6 Robin Sharma, *The World-Changer's Manifesto* (Luzern: The Titan Academy Global AG, 2019).

7 Barbara J. Sahakian and Jamie Nicole LaBuzetta, *Bad Moves: How Decision Making Goes Wrong, and the Ethics of Smart Drugs* (Oxford: Oxford University Press, 2013).

8 Brian Wansink and Jeffery Sobal, "Mindless Eating: The 200 Daily Food Decisions We Overlook," *Environment and Behavior* 39, no. 1 (January

2007), researchgate.net/publication/227344004_Mindless_Eating
_The_200_Daily_Food_Decisions_We_Overlook.

9   Shai Danziger, Jonathan Levav, and Liora Avnaim-Pesso, "Extraneous
     Factors in Judicial Decisions," *PNAS* 108, no. 17 (2011): 6889.

10   Roy F. Baumeister and John Tierney, *Willpower: Rediscovering the Greatest
     Human Strength* (New York: Penguin, 2011).

11   Roy F. Baumeister, Ellen Bratslavsky, Mark Muraven, and Dianne M.
     Tice, "Ego Depletion: Is the Active Self a Limited Resource?," *Journal of
     Personality and Social Psychology* 74, no. 5 (1998): 1252–65,
     faculty.washington.edu/jdb/345/345%20Articles/Baumeister%20et%20
     al.%20%281998%29.pdf.

12   Barry Schwartz. *The Paradox of Choice: Why More is Less* (New York: Ecco,
     2004, 2016).

13   Michael Lewis, "Obama's Way," *Vanity Fair*, September 11, 2012, 210.

14   Verne Harnish and the Editors of *Fortune*, *The Greatest Business Decisions of
     All Time: How Apple, Ford, IBM, Zappos, and Others Made Radical Choices
     That Changed the Course of Business* (Time Home Entertainment, 2012).

15   Clear, *Atomic Habits*.

10 Energy Oscillates

1   Daniel H. Pink, *When: The Scientific Secrets of Perfect Timing* (New York:
     Riverhead Books, 2018).

2   Steven Kotler, "Create a Work Environment that Fosters Flow," *Harvard
     Business Review*, updated October 11, 2019, hbr.org/2014/05
     /create-a-work-environment-that-fosters-flow.

3   Hans Henrik Sievertsen, Francesca Gino, and Marco Piovesan, "Cognitive
     Fatigue Influences Students' Performance on Standardized Tests," *PNAS*
     113, no. 10 (2016): 2621–24. pnas.org/content/pnas/early/2016/02/09
     /1516947113.full.pdf.

4   Sarah Shoen, "Siestas," Sleep Foundation: A OneCare Media Company,
     updated April 25, 2022, sleepfoundation.org/circadian-rhythm/siestas.

5   Elizabeth Scott, "The Overwhelming Benefits of Power Napping,"
     Verywell Mind, updated January 2, 2020, verywellmind.com/power
     -napping-health-benefits-and-tips-stress-3144702#:~:text=Studies%20

show%20that%2020%20minutes,special%20benefits%20of%20their
%20own.

6   Intrigued? Check this out: The Nappuccino Café is located right in the
     heart of Barcelona, Spain.

7   Tibi Puiu, "Why Music Makes You Feel Less Tired While Exercising,"
     ZME Science (blog), August 27, 2018, zmescience.com/medicine
     /music-less-tired-04323/; Carly Stec, "The 7 Best Music Playlists for
     Productivity, According to Science," Marketing (blog), updated June 10,
     2021, blog.hubspot.com/marketing/productivity-playlists.

11 Focus Beats Multi-tasking

1   Shyamal Parikh, "Is Time Pressure the Key to Increase Productivity at
     Work?" Smart Task (blog) August 6, 2018, smarttask.io/blog
     /time-pressure-the-key-to-increase-productivity.

2   "Ford Factory Workers Get 40-hour Week," History.com, August 2, 2022,
     history.com/this-day-in-history/ford-factory-workers-get-40-hour-week.

3   Lisa Eadicicco, "Companies from Microsoft to Shake Shack Have
     Experimented with a Shorter, 4-Day Workweek — and Most of the Time, It's
     Had Incredible Results," Insider (blog), November 10, 2019, businessinsider
     .com/microsoft-shake-shack-4-day-work-week-productivity-life-balance
     -2019-11#shake-shack-is-one-of-several-companiesexperimenting-with-a
     -four-day-workweek-1.

4   Allison Jones, "Ontario NDP, Liberals Eye Four-Day Work Weeks in
     Proposed Pilot Projects," CBC News, May 13, 2022, cbc.ca/news
     /canada/toronto/ndp-liberals-four-day-work-week-pilot-1.6452885.

5   Karen Tiber Leland, "You Could Be Your Own Biggest Interruption.
     Here's How to Stop and Find Your Focus," Inc., August 12, 2019, inc.com
     /karen-tiber-leland/you-could-be-your-own-biggest-interruption-heres
     -how-to-stop-find-your-focus.html.

6   Dave Crenshaw, The Myth of Multitasking: How "Doing It All" Gets
     Nothing Done, 2nd ed. (Coral Gables, FL: Mango Publishing, 2021).

7   "Study Finds Lure of Entertainment, Work Hard for People to Resist,"
     UChicago News, January 27, 2012, news.uchicago.edu/story
     /study-finds-lure-entertainment-work-hard-people-resist.

8 Julia Gifford, "The Secret of the 10% Most Productive People? Breaking!"
   DeskTime (blog), May 14, 2018, desktime.com/blog/17-52-ratio-most
   -productive-people.

9 Hans Henrik Sievertsen, Francesca Gino, and Marco Piovesan, "Cognitive
   Fatigue Influences Students' Performance on Standardized Tests," *PNAS*
   113, no. 10 (2016): 2621–24, pnas.org/content/pnas/early/2016/02/09
   /1516947113.full.pdf.

10 Danziger, Levav, and Avnaim-Pesso, "Extraneous Factors in Judicial
   Decisions," *PNAS* 108, no. 17 (2011): 6889–92, doi.org/10.1073/pnas
   .1018033108.

12 Define Your Time Budget

1 Brendon Burchard, *High Performance Habits: How Extraordinary People
   Become That Way* (Carlsbad, CA: Hay House, 2017).

2 Mark Ellwood, "So What?" GetMoreDone, Pace Productivity, accessed
   July 18, 2022, getmoredone.com/time-study-benchmarks.

13 Build Your Proactive Routine

1 David Chilton, *The Wealthy Barber: The Common Sense Guide to Successful
   Financial Planning* (North York: Stoddart Publishing, 1995).

2 "Research Proves Your Brain Needs Breaks," Microsoft *WorkLab* (blog),
   April 20, 2021, microsoft.com/en-us/worklab/work-trend-index
   /brain-research.

3 Centers for Disease Control and Prevention, "1 in 3 Adults Don't Get
   Enough Sleep," page last reviewed February 16, 2016, accessed July 18,
   2022, cdc.gov/media/releases/2016/p0215-enough-sleep.html.

4 Rebecca Robillard et al., "Profile of Sleep Changes During the COVID-19
   Pandemic: Demographic, Behavioural and Psychological Factors," *Journal
   of Sleep Research* 30, no. 1 (2020), February 2021, onlinelibrary.wiley.com
   /doi/10.1111/jsr.13231.

5 Liz Mineo, "Good Genes Are Nice, But Joy Is Better," *The Harvard
   Gazette*, April 11, 2017, news.harvard.edu/gazette/story/2017/04/over
   -nearly-80-years-harvard-study-has-been-showing-how-to-live-a-healthy-
   and-happy-life/.

6   Kristen Bateman, "How I Get It Done: Sara Blakely of Spanx," The Cut, June 26, 2018, thecut.com/2018/06/how-i-get-it-done-sara-blakely-of -spanx.html.

7   Shelli Baltman shared her "Block it Big" approach in a personal conversation.

14 Implement Your Proactive Routine

1   Cal Newport, *Deep Work: Rules for Focused Success in a Distracted World* (New York: Grand Central Publishing, 2016).

2   B.J. Fogg, *Tiny Habits: The Small Changes That Change Everything* (Boston: Houghton Mifflin Harcourt, 2020).

3   Gretchen Rubin, "What You Do Every Day Matters More Than What You Do Once In a While," November 7, 2011, gretchenrubin.com/2011/11 /what-you-do-every-day-matters-more-than-what-you-do-once-in-a-while/.

15 Time Barrier #3: Too Much Complication

1   Julian Birkinshaw and Jordan Cohen, "Make Time for the Work That Matters," *Harvard Business Review*, September 2013, hbr.org/2013/09 /make-time-for-the-work-that-matters.

2   Rory Vaden, *Procrastinate on Purpose: 5 Permissions to Multiply Your Time* (New York: TarcherPerigee, 2015).

16 The Simplify Filter: Scale Back

1   Jeff Haden, "Oprah Winfrey Uses the Same 3 Sentences to Get Every Meeting Off to the Perfect Start," *Inc.*, September 19, 2018, inc.com/jeff -haden/oprah-winfrey-uses-same-3-sentences-to-get-every-meeting-off-to -perfect-start.html.

17 The Simplify Filter: Streamline

1   Amrita Mandal, "The Pomodoro Technique: An Effective Time Management Tool," Eunice Kennedy Shriver National Institute of Child Health and Human Development, May 2020, science.nichd.nih.gov /confluence/display/newsletter/2020/05/07/The+Pomodoro +Technique%3A+An+Effective+Time+Management+Tool.

2   Atul Gawande, *The Checklist Manifesto: How to Get Things Right* (New York: Picador, 2011).

3   Christopher Sirk, "The History of Kaizen," Crm.org, August 5, 2020, crm.org/articles/the-history-of-kaizen.

4   Search Engine Land, "Google SEO News: Google Algorithm Updates," searchengineland.com/google-seo-news-google-algorithm-updates.

5   Bob Frisch and Cary Greene, "Make Time for Small Talk in Your Virtual Meetings," *Harvard Business Review*, February 18, 2021, hbr.org/2021/02/make-time-for-small-talk-in-your-virtual-meetings.

6   Barbara Minto, *The Pyramid Principle: Logic in Writing and Thinking* (New Jersey: Financial Times Prentice Hall, 2008).

7   Julie Morgenstern, *Organizing from the Inside Out: The Foolproof System For Organizing Your Home, Your Office and Your Life*, 2nd ed. (New York: Henry Holt and Company, 2004).

8   Marie Kondo, *The Life-Changing Magic of Tidying Up: The Japanese Art of Decluttering and Organizing* (Berkeley: Ten Speed Press, 2014).

9   Julian Birkinshaw, Jordan Cohen, and Pawel Stach, "Research: Knowledge Workers are More Productive from Home," *Harvard Business Review*, August 31, 2020, hbsp.harvard.edu/product/H05T92-PDF-ENG.

18 The Simplify Filter: Seek Help

1   William Oncken Jr. and Donald L. Wass, "Management Time: Who's Got the Monkey?" *Harvard Business Review*, November–December 1999, hbr.org/1999/11/management-time-whos-got-the-monkey.

2   James Surowiecki, *The Wisdom of Crowds* (New York: Anchor Books, 2005).

3   Marcial Losada and Emily Heaphy, "The Role of Positivity and Connectivity in the Performance of Business Teams: A Nonlinear Dynamics Model," *American Behavioral Scientist* 47, no. 6 (2004): 740–65.

Action Plan: Be a Workday Warrior

1   Laura Vanderkam, *I Know How She Does It: How Successful Women Make the Most of Their Time* (New York: Portfolio/Penguin, 2015).

About the Author

Ann Gomez is the founding president of Clear Concept Inc., an international training company. Ann is also an engaging speaker and a USA Today bestselling author. Her first book, *The Email Warrior: How to Clear Your Inbox and Keep It That Way* has been consistently cited as a book that transforms how busy people work.

Ann is passionate about helping people do their best work at all stages of their career and has twenty years of experience delivering compelling and practical talks about productivity, collaboration, mindset, and well-being. Ann and her team help busy people around the world, across industries, and with the world's leading organizations.

Prior to launching Clear Concept Inc., Ann was a management consultant with Kearney and a pharmaceutical representative with Searle. She has an MBA from Queen's University and a BSc from McMaster University.

Ann has been featured in the *Globe and Mail* and has appeared on CBC Radio, Global TV, BNN, and Huffington Thrive Global. Outside of work, Ann and her husband love spending time with their four active kids.

For more information, visit clearconceptinc.ca.